The Proustian Quest

The Proustian Quest

William C. Carter

NEW YORK UNIVERSITY PRESS
NEW YORK AND LONDON

NEW YORK UNIVERSITY PRESS
New York and London

Library of Congress Cataloging-in-Publication Data
Carter, William C., 1941–
     The Proustian quest / by William C. Carter.
          p. cm.
     Includes bibliographical references and index.
     ISBN 0-8147-1470-6
     1. Proust, Marcel, 1871–1922.   A la recherche du temps perdu.
2. Social change in literature. 3. Speed in literature. I. Title.
PQ2631.R63A7827   1992
843'.912–dc20   92-3037
                                                          CIP

To the memory of my mother,

SARAH CAUSEY CARTER,

who first read to me and taught me to love books.

Que voulez-vous, mon cher,
Anaxagore l'a dit, la vie est un voyage.
　　　　—Marcel Proust, *La Prisonnière*

Contents

Illustrations

Acknowledgments

I would like to express my sincere thanks to the University of Alabama at Birmingham for supporting this project through a sabbatical leave and a Graduate School Research Grant which allowed me to undertake the work that resulted in this book.

I am grateful to Tinker B. Dunbar, of the Reference Department of Mervyn H. Sterne Library at the University of Alabama at Birmingham, for her skill in locating and obtaining rare books and other documents; to Richard Bleiler, Humanities Librarian, for his efforts in maintaining and strengthening our Proust holdings, now the third largest in the world. I am also indebted to Florence Callu, head of the manuscript department at the Bibliothèque Nationale and cataloguer of the Proust's manuscripts, who, on many occasions graciously provided important assistance. The illustrations that grace this book are reproduced through the generosity of the Association des Amis de Jacques-Henri Lartigue, the Collège de France, the Philadelphia Museum of Art, Stanford University Archives, and Mme Odile Gévaudan—all of whom I thank.

Friends who have aided and encouraged me along the way include Robert E. Bowden, E. Culpepper Clark, Marie-Colette Lefort, and Clay Nordan. I am especially grateful to my wife, Lynn, for her constant support and invaluable editorial suggestions. To my children, Josephine, Sarah, and Susanna, for their patience and wonderful distractions.

I would also like to thank my editor, Jason Renker, and the editorial staff at New York University Press for their faith in this project, and Henry Krawitz for his excellent copy-editing.

—W.C.C.

CHAPTER 1

The Age of Speed

Le monde a moins changé depuis Jésus-Christ qu'il n'a changé depuis trente ans.
— Charles Péguy, *L'Argent* (1913)

Marcel Proust lived from 1871 until 1922, an epoch that he himself characterized as the age of locomotion and speed because of the conquest of land and air.[1] The end of the nineteenth century and the first quarter of the twentieth may be seen as a great turning point in Western history, when tremendous changes occurred in the way people lived. This era saw rapid developments in transportation, including the invention of the bicycle, automobile, airplane, and the continued expansion of train service. In 1850, Emperor Napoléon III made the trip from Paris to Marseille in an ultralight train that reached an average speed of ninety-six kilometers an hour; only a few years earlier, such voyages took at least several days and sometimes more than a week.[2] It was progress in metallurgy that made possible the invention, development, and mass production of machines for rapid transit: trains, ocean liners, airplanes, automobiles, as well as bicycles. Both the themes of speed and travel associated with the appearance of these new inventions are reflected in the literature and art of the period, and especially in Proust's *A la recherche du temps perdu*.[3]

Electric lighting, plumbing, more leisure time, and new ways of heating significantly enhanced the standard of living. Communication and entertainment industries made extraordinary progress thanks to the invention of movable type, the telegraph, the telephone, the phonograph, and the movie projector. Three key words that define the tenor of this period are machine, modern, and speed.[4] In 1905, Einstein's theory of relativity revolutionized the view of the physical universe by stating that "the geometric nature of our world is fashioned by mass and speed."[5]

The sports daily *l'Auto-Vélo,* which would become the leading newspaper in its field, carried this comment in its first issue on October 16, 1900: "Nous vivons mieux et nous vivons plus vite qu'autrefois."[6] However, such dramatic changes did not extend immediately to all classes of society; many French citizens still lived under conditions that had not changed significantly since medieval times. Proust and his friends belonged to a class that could instantly enjoy the benefits of the new age. One of his acquaintances was duc Armand de Guiche, a pioneer in aerodynamics who stimulated Proust's interest in aviation well before Alfred Agostinelli, the novelist's handsome Italian chauffeur, began to study flying. Machines such as the automobile and the airplane, at first the exclusive domain of wealthy sportsmen, were taken up quickly by the middle class since the practical applications were obvious and mass production soon resulted in lowered prices.

The age of cheap mass transport had arrived, bringing with it easy access to various types of leisure, including sports facilities and vacation spots that had previously been the reserve of the wealthy. Now families of modest means could take a Sunday outing, while those of the middle class could go on extended holidays. In 1900, the first Michelin Guides—those indispensable green-colored travel books whose appearance ushered in the age of tourism—rolled off the presses. The Grand-Hôtel at Cabourg and others like it were built at the turn of the century to meet the needs of the nouveaux riches vacationers who were arriving in large numbers by train. After the disappointing failure of *Les*

Plaisirs et les jours in 1896, Proust resolved to address himself in his next work to this new class, which read inexpensive novels on the train.[7] It would take the novelist more than a decade to find the unique structure of the book he had always wanted to write and to discover his individual voice as a mature artist.

The grand hotels that sprang up to accommodate the new generation of travelers were illuminated by another modern wonder—electric lighting. In fact, the nineteenth century has been called the age of the conquest of darkness.[8] Previously, the rhythms of human life had always followed the cycle of natural light; now a new, clean, artificial light suspended time and made it serve man's convenience. In *la Recherche,* Mme Verdurin, Proust's tyrannical, avant-garde hostess, who is always among the first to try something new, buys a town house that is to be lighted entirely by electricity. Light could now be controlled, standardized, and put to a number of practical and aesthetic uses.[9] Paris became the City of Light.

Photographs and stock footage from films made around 1900 show Paris streets bustling with an incredible variety of pedestrians, ambulatory vendors, drivers and their horses, and a number of the new, self-propelling "automobiles." Automobile production in France increased at an astonishing rate, from two hundred in 1894 to fourteen thousand by 1905. By the year *Du côté de chez Swann* was published (1913), there were ninety-five thousand cars in France. In 1925, three years after Proust's death, the figure was close to three-quarters of a million. As the number of cars increased on Paris streets, one could see a way of life vanishing before one's eyes.[10] The cries of Proust's beloved street vendors would soon be smothered by the roar of traffic. At the end of *Du côté de chez Swann,* the Narrator, trying to recover the ambience of the olden days when he used to go to the Bois de Boulogne to watch Mme Swann passing by, discovers instead how rapidly time is fleeting as Paris enters the twentieth century: "Hélas! il n'y avait plus que des automobiles conduites par des mécaniciens moustachus . . ." (I, 425).

Beneath Paris's ancient cobblestoned streets, a new way of transporting urban masses was being created. The year 1900 saw the inauguration of the Paris Chemin de fer métropolitain, still considered by many to be the best in the world. The métro was extremely successful; in less than a decade, as fares were reduced, the number of subway travelers grew dramatically from 15 million in 1900 to 312 million in 1909. One of the major effects of mass transit was a leveling of social distinctions; people from all social classes were brought together within the physical confines of a public conveyance. The Vicomte d'Avenel, a contemporary observer of the rapidly changing social scene, rejoiced in 1905, "Today duchesses and millionaires rub shoulders with cooks and clerks."[11]

In *la Recherche*, this leveling effect, "the new democracy of public transport,"[12] is resisted vehemently by Dr. Cottard. The worthy doctor, in his capacity as medical officer for the railway company, has a farm laborer he considers to be riffraff ejected from the little train at Balbec because the man dared enter the car "reserved" for the members of the little clan en route to the Verdurins' summer villa at la Raspelière (II, 875). The physician, awed by anyone with a title, fears that the man's presence might contaminate the atmosphere for the putative Russian princess Sherbatoff. On the other hand, the baron Charlus, the haughtiest of aristocrats and the most sexually driven character in the novel, uses public transportation for a leveling effect of a different kind: he pursues drunken coach drivers and handsome young conductors in hopes of seducing them.

The modern safety bicycle—with wheels of approximately equal size, pneumatic tires, and the free wheel—dates from the mid-1880s. Despite a fairly high price tag, there were over four hundred thousand bicycles in France by 1897. The speed at which cyclists moved increased phenomenally in a short period of time: in 1900 a cyclist named Taylor reached the speed of one kilometer a minute; in 1903 a new record was set at ninety kilometers an hour. The Tour de France, still the country's premier sporting event, was established in 1903.[13]

The popularity of biking and other sports, coupled with the establishment of vacation resorts, also hastened the liberation of the human body.[14] Cycling played an important part in the advancement of womens' rights, freeing the female body by developing shoulder and leg muscles, as well as giving women a greater sense of independence. Machines and sports created new fashions, as the Narrator notes when he first sees Albertine pushing a bicycle along the beach at Balbec.[15] Freed from the imprisoning corset, women now required lighter and less restrictive clothing. They were acutely aware that the bicycle played an important role in the liberation of their sex; at the banquet following the feminist congress of 1896, the president, Maria Pognon, raised her glass in a toast to the "equalitarian and leveling bicycle."[16]

Proust's father, Dr. Adrien Proust (1834–1903), was a physician and public health official who distinguished himself as a teacher, practicing physician, epidemiologist, and writer on medicine. His successful efforts in stopping the cholera epidemics that had periodically ravaged Europe for centuries were recognized in 1870 when he was awarded the Legion of Honor by the Empress-Regent Eugénie. During his career he wrote twenty-five books and numerous articles and reports on international hygiene, tuberculosis, rabies, paralysis, nerve-related and cerebral maladies, aphasia, and occupational disorders.[17] He also coauthored the first book on neurasthenia with Georges Ballet in 1897. Neurasthenia, characterized by nervous exhaustion[18] and lack of will, was a disorder that afflicted Dr. Proust's elder son, Marcel, and one of the latter's most famous literary creations, the hypochondriacal Aunt Léonie.

As a noted hygienist, Dr. Proust encouraged the wearing of clothing that allowed a person freedom of movement, exposure to fresh air, and the ability to exercise. These changes in life-style are worthy of the Narrator's grandmother, who hates confinement and stultification in any form and likes to walk on the beach and in the garden—even during a thunderstorm. She is the opposite of the hypercautious, self-imprisoned Aunt Léonie.

One of the questions that plagues the protagonist during his quest is which of these two relatives he will resemble as he grows older. Proust's parents worried (as did the writer himself) that he would never be sufficiently strong to succeed at anything.

In *la Recherche,* Proust takes note of the new vogue for sports and the decline of romantic ennui:

> depuis la faveur dont jouissent les exercices physiques, l'oisiveté a pris une forme sportive, même en dehors des heures de sport, et qui se traduit non plus par de la nonchalance, mais par une vivacité fébrile qui croit ne pas laisser à l'ennui le temps ni la place de se développer. (III, 699)

At the end of the nineteenth century, sports caught on rapidly in France as a result of the British influence.[19] The popularity of sports in Britain received great impetus when they were added to the educational program. In 1892, on the initiative of two Frenchmen, Pierre de Coubertin and Georges de Saint-Clair, a French rugby team went to England and inaugurated the first international sports events, which eventually led to the creation (in 1896) of the modern Olympic Games. Coubertin, like many of his confrères following the humiliating defeat in the Franco-Prussian War, feared that the youth of France had degenerated morally and physically. In 1887, he announced that a national sports program would save the young by hardening "a flabby, listless confined youth, [both] its body and its character. . . ."[20] The contests between the British and French were a great success and French enthusiasm for sports spread rapidly to all classes.

By the late 1890s, there was a proliferation of sporting clubs and magazines. At least ten newspapers about "automobilism" appeared, all eager to publish new speed records as quickly as they were broken.[21] The breaking of speed records was yet another aspect of the increased consciousness of time, and instruments were developed to measure split seconds. Toulouse-

Lautrec's posters of bicycle races in the 1890s show officials and coaches holding chronometers.[22]

Sports, the new machines of mass transportation, and moving pictures made people aware of motion as never before. Chroniclers of the new century constantly referred to the cult of speed and the religion of velocity, welcoming the new machines as abolishers of time and space. Proust notes the way new inventions change our perception of the world by altering time-space relationships. Trains, he tells us in *la Recherche,* made everyone aware of the minute divisions of time and the necessity for punctuality:

> Depuis qu'il existe des chemins de fer, la nécessité de ne pas manquer le train nous a appris à tenir compte des minutes, alors que chez les anciens Romains, dont l'astronomie n'était pas seulement plus sommaire mais aussi la vie moins pressée, la notion, non pas de minutes, mais même d'heures fixes, existait à peine. (II, 825)

Proust also observes how works of architecture that once seemed far apart geographically now inhabit the same temporal zone, making it possible to visit them on the same outing.[23]

Conquering the land and air now became a real possibility as man freed himself from limitations that had held him back for centuries. Gravity was a force from which men longed to be liberated, as can be seen in this remark by Paul Souriau, made in 1889 in anticipation of the first manned flight: "le vol semble la plus belle victoire remportée contre l'inertie et la pesanteur, une véritable émancipation de la matière."[24] Free, sustained flight— one of man's oldest and noblest dreams—was about to be realized. There was tremendous excitement among Proust's contemporaries, who were the first to believe that they might actually conquer time and space. As Jacques Nathan has pointed out, whereas trains and ocean liners turned passengers into passive subjects of speed, the bicycle, automobile, and airplane had a tremendously liberating effect: atop the bicycle the rider is free and is propelled by muscular energy; in the automobile and the airplane the driver and pilot control the machines and cover a vast area of space in a relatively short span of time.[25]

These machines not only changed the way people moved through space but also how they perceived themselves and the world. People had the impression of living not only at a much faster pace but also more intensely than at any previous time in history. The French Cubist painter Fernand Léger observed that a "modern man registers a hundred times more sensory impressions than an eighteenth-century artist."[26] Octave Uzanne, the French journalist and bibliophile, said that in a short period of time man had replaced twenty centuries of horse-drawn movement with three new inventions: trains, automobiles, and airplanes. These innovations accelerated the pace at which people lived to such a degree that Proust's contemporaries believed the human physiognomy might be altered by the new kinetic experiences. Some feared that the speed of riding a bicycle was beyond human endurance and could cause disfigurement: "The bicycle was about four times faster than walking and warnings were issued about getting 'bicycle face' by moving against the wind at such high speeds. . . ."[27] The face of modern man was marked by velocity: " 'il vizio della velocità' devient un trait caractéristique de l'homme moderne, qui, au dire des plus enthousiastes, sous peu s'élancera à travers le monde à l'instar d'un boulet de canon ou d'un bolide."[28]

The exhilarating feeling of moving through space with the explosive speed of a cannonball is precisely how Proust described the impression he had while riding through the Normandy countryside in a red taxi, with Agostinelli at the wheel.[29] The motorists of Proust's day had the feeling of being rapidly borne away since they were poorly protected from the weather and were constantly jostled and jarred by the many potholes on the roads. An episode from his excursions with Agostinelli that Proust wrote for *Le Figaro* became the basis for the famous passage describing the steeples of Martinville in *la Recherche,* where the Narrator experiences parallax vision while observing the steeples in multiple perspectives from the fast-moving carriage.

In his writings, Proust describes the influence of sports and machines of speed on fashion, being especially struck by the androgynous look of chauffeurs. For example, the novelist compares Agostinelli in his motoring attire, consisting of a long coat with hood and goggles, to a "nun of speed."[30] Some of Proust's contemporaries feared that when women began to wear pants—largely as a result of the popularity and practicality of cycling—the distinctions between the sexes would become somewhat blurred. Historians have pointed out that during periods of transition, the androgyne, which figures significantly in Proust's presentation of human sexuality, appears more frequently in art, painting, and fashion. As we shall see in the chapter on "Speed and Desire," rapid movement through space characterizes those Proustian creatures who are desirable or whose sexuality is ambiguous.

The desire to travel, which the Narrator often confuses with erotic desire, establishes the powerful Proustian dialectic of stasis and kinesis. The protagonist's personality is split, as was Proust's, between that of a sedentary, sickly recluse and a curious, even passionate explorer. In the novel, these two penchants are represented by Aunt Léonie and the grandmother. These conflicting traits may be seen in Proust himself: his desire to travel was complicated by health problems (whether psychosomatic or real is still being debated); his reclusive, sedentary nature contrasts with his modest enthusiasm for sports[31] and his surprising adaptation to military life during a year of voluntary service (1889-90).

Stillness and mobility relate to art and desire in Proust's world. Speed is almost always an incitement of Proustian desire and a major factor in the elaboration of two antithetical Proustian themes: the prisoner and the fugitive.[32] Girls in motion, most often on bicycles, arouse desire in the Narrator. It is speed—motion through space—that more than anything else marks the kinship of Albertine and Saint-Loup. As a young man Proust was attracted to vivacious girls such as Marie de Bénardaky and Jeanne Pouquet, both of whom lent something to the characters of Gilberte and Albertine, as well as to young men like Bertrand de Fénelon and Alfred Agostinelli. According to Proust's housekeeper, Céleste Albaret, the latter had the reputation of a daredevil among his friends.[33] Agostinelli belonged to the group who frequented *aérodromes*,[34] as airports were called at the time; he also went to bicycle and car races and was generally fascinated by speed. He entered Proust's life on two crucial occasions. His flight from Proust and tragic death in an airplane accident in 1914 plunged Proust into a period of intense grief and inspired the novelist to add new dimensions to the character of Albertine. The allure of athletic young men was an important aspect of Proust's fictional characterizations as early as 1896-99 when he was working on the novel *Jean Santeuil*, which he later abandoned, but which was published posthumously.

Girls on bicycles are a dominant motif in Proust's exploration of erotic desire. When the Narrator first spots Albertine on the beach at Balbec, she is pushing a bicycle in the company of other girls belonging to the little band. Because of their attire and outlandish behavior, he thinks these strange, attractive creatures must all be the mistresses of cyclists. The girls on bicycles to whom he is attracted become winged creatures[35] and possess a charm unknown to ordinary girls. To seize and to possess desirable creatures who are fugitive becomes one of the Narrator's enduring obsessions. In an attempt to understand, to see these girls as they really are, the Narrator often decomposes the figures in motion by using photographic analogies. The problem of speed, desire, and fugacity must be solved before he can discover his vocation as a writer.

While Proust was still in his formative period, photographers, painters, sculptors, physiologists, sportsmen, and the curious were studying motion as never before. Some were drawn to the beauty of the human figure in motion, while others were more interested in the practical applications for science, medicine, aviation, and sports. Etienne-Jules Marey's (1830-1904) chrono-photographs ("pictures of time") were innovations that resulted from the study of motion. Marey, a physiologist, was ingenious when it came to inventing instruments to record living phenomena. In 1881, while studying the flight of birds as part of his research into the development of flying machines, he discovered the work of Eadweard Muybridge (1830-1904), whose zooprax-iscope projected animated pictures on a screen and was a forerunner of the moving picture. Marey asked the American to try and photograph birds in flight, but he was disappointed with the results. The French physiologist went to work and by 1882 had developed a photographic gun that exposed film at a rapid "firing" rate. Dissatisfied because the images it obtained were not sharp enough, Marey shortly thereafter invented chronophotography, which allowed him to capture perfectly a figure in motion in its consecutive phases. Placing his subjects against a black background and using a rotary shutter with an incredibly fast exposure, Marey was able to obtain a series of pictures of a moving figure on the same photographic plate.

Proust was familiar with Muybridge's innovative work in this field and must have also known about Marey's invention. This pioneer in the study of animal and human locomotion was, like Adrien Proust, a doctor, a specialist on cholera, and a member of the Académie de Médecine. Although Proust does not mention Muybridge's name, the first photographic analogy in la Recherche is a reference to the earliest motion picture sequence ever made, that of Muybridge's 1879 photographs of a running horse, known as "Occident Trotting." With the arrival of Thomas A. Edison's kinetoscope and Emile Reynaud's Optical Theater, which opened in Paris in 1888, the movies were about to be born. The first projection of moving pictures by the cinematograph, an invention of the Lumière brothers, took place in Paris on December 15, 1895, at the Café de la Paix.

The novelist Octave Mirbeau described the sensation of motion experienced during a car ride by using a cinematographic analogy: "Everywhere life is rushing insanely like a cavalry charge, and it vanishes cinematographically like trees and silhouettes along a road. Everything around man jumps, dances, gallops in a movement out of phase with his own."[36] Proust was also struck by the changing pace of life and the movement of figures through space, which would become a recurring motif in *la Recherche*. There is a passage in his novel, similar to the one by Mirbeau, where the prince de Sagan and other equestrian riders greet Odette:

> le prince, faisant comme dans une apothéose de théâtre, de cirque, ou dans un tableau ancien, faire front à son cheval, adressait à Odette un grand salut théâtral. . . . Mme Swann était saluée par les derniers cavaliers attardés, comme cinématographiés au galop sur l'ensoleillement blanc de l'avenue. . . . (I, 640)

In depicting as moving pictures the parade of men on horseback who greet Mme Swann, Proust is thinking of the motion pictures produced by Thomas A. Edison's kinetoscope and the early cinema. By comparing the scene to an apotheosis in the theater, a circus, and an old painting, with the sun as the fixed white agent through which the riders move, the novelist presents us with a recurrent image that weds stillness and mobility. Odette remains the fixed, central point of this activity; the moving panorama of the returning cavaliers who greet her serves as a spectacular backdrop for the beautiful woman.

The cinema was seen to be the natural companion of the airplane and the automobile, as can be seen in this remark by Fernand Léger: "le cinéma et l'aviation vont bras-dessus bras-dessous dans la vie, ils sont nés le même jour. . . ."[37] The early cinema captured perfectly the rapid tempo at which people believed they had begun to live by reproducing "the mechanization, jerkiness, and rush of modern times."[38] Léger, who was keenly attuned to this aspect of social change, observed in 1913 that life was "more fragmented and faster moving than in previous periods," and that people sought a dynamic art to depict it.[39] Robert Delaunay, who painted the Eiffel Tower an incredible seventy-seven times, believed that the modern world was characterized by movement.[40]

Guillaume Apollinaire, one of the earliest supporters of and most astute commentators on the work of the Cubists, wrote in 1908 of the Cubists' ambition to create an art of mobility and a vision of unity: "Il faut . . . embrasser d'un coup d'œil: le passé, le présent et l'avenir. La toile doit présenter cette unité essentielle qui seule provoque l'extase."[41] Proust's Narrator experiences a similar ecstatic unity of time and space at the end of *Le Temps retrouvé* upon discovering the key to his vocation as an artist.[42]

Jacques Rivière, a writer and editor at the *Nouvelle Revue Française*, was among the first to understand the true nature, themes, and structure of *la Recherche*. He saw a direct relationship between Proust and the Cubists. Rivière was aware of the contemporaneity of Proust's work and used painterly analogies to describe the novelist's technique and style:

> une chose . . . qui m'est apparue pour la première fois, c'est votre relation avec le mouvement cubiste, et plus profondément votre profonde immersion dans la réalité esthétique contemporaine. . . . d'autre part sur un tel livre il n'y a rien à dire, *tant il est proche de ce qu'il peint*. Jamais encore on n'était arrivé à une pareille identification avec l'objet.[43]

Cubism was influenced by motion pictures and other contemporary developments. Stephen Kern surmises that "chronophotography and cinema no doubt had some effect, however indirect, on the way Cubists rendered space and sought to give a sense of the development of an object in time as a construction of successive points of view."[44] In 1911, the Cubist painter Jean Metzinger explained how the Cubists' multiple perspectives had added temporality to painting: "They have allowed themselves to move round the object, in order to give a concrete representation of it, made up of several successive aspects. Formerly a picture took possession of space, now it reigns also in time."[45] Like the Cubists, Proust depicts various aspects of an object seen in rapid succession, such as the steeples of Martinville or Albertine's face when the Narrator bends over her to bestow a kiss, but unlike the Cubists he presents such perspectives as a spontaneous and successive vision rather than an intellectualized and recomposed vision.

For these French artists, as well as for many others at the time, the new hero was a man of action at the center of events and at the wheel of an automobile or airplane. Pär Bergman gives us a portrait of the new ideal:

> [L'homme moderne] se trouve toujours au centre des événements et enregistre directement, à l'instar d'un appareil Morse, toute la vie ambiante, explosive et tourbillonnante dans sa modernité. Il préfère l'aéro-drome et le cinéma à l'église, il a du goût pour les vols et les voyages en automobile plus qu'il n'en a pour les musées, et il chante le dieu des temps nouveaux— l'Homme—en célébrant le héros du siècle, l'aviateur sans peur.[46]

For Proust and his contemporaries the chauffeur and the aviator were linked in an evolutionary way. To them the progression from cyclist to chauffeur to pilot was an observable and logical one. The immediate mechanical progression from car to airplane was self-evident since the airplane was in many respects an automobile with wings. Proust's frequent analogies describing a desirable cyclist who becomes airborne may owe something to the cycling competitions that the athletic Agostinelli—certainly an "homme moderne" in his zeal to become a pilot—must have frequented. Jacques-Henri Lartigue's photographs and diaries are an important source of documentation for the development of machines of speed in France during Proust's lifetime. The photographer took many pictures of the first automobiles, actual winged bicycles known as *aviettes,* airplanes, gliders, and so forth, as he documented the history of speed in early twentieth-century France. In his notes we find Lartigue, like Proust, describing cars as horizontal vehicles that gather speed and ascend to the skies.[47] At the *vélodrome,* as the bicycle-racing track was known in the Parc des Princes, Lartigue took a series of photographs of these winged bicycles, whose drivers pedaled furiously in an attempt to achieve elevation. The dream of a human-propelled flying machine would not be realized until many years later, certainly long after Proust's death.

The new heroes—the cyclist, the chauffeur, and the aviator[48]—all appear in Proust's writings. The cyclist and the aviator are important figures: the former is a mysterious, erotic creature, while the latter is the primary symbol of the creative person. The horizontal and vertical axes respectively represent those things that are earthbound and those that permit ascension. The earthbound, horizontal explorer who discovers how to become an airborne visionary is a key Proustian metaphor. In *la Recherche,* it is above all the aviator who symbolizes the freedom, vision, and individuality of the artist.

Although Proust wrote many pages that are in keeping with the Futurists' dictum that an artist should "chanter l'homme moderne . . . l'homme actif et 'dynamique' de son propre temps, tels le chauffeur et l'aviateur,"[49] he was primarily interested in modern inventions because they allow us to attain new perspectives. In this regard he is unlike the Futurists, who were obsessed by the machine itself and found in it a new god: "Le moteur devient presque un dieu, la machine une déesse. Au 'regno animale' succède 'il regno meccanico.'. . . [Marinetti] proclame aussi 'la prochaine découverte des lois d'une véritable sensibilité des machines.' "[50] Proust is indifferent to the concept of "sensibilità motrice," employing machines as analogies to explain or illustrate human perception and to depict reactions to new kinetic experiences. The Narrator's first ride in an elevator, for example, owes part of its description to Proust's automobile excursions with Agostinelli.

Proust's frequent analogies and examples drawn from optical devices, machines of transportation, and inventions relating to communication describe new kinetic experiences. Although other writers of the period depicted early automobile and airplane rides, Proust for the most part made original use of the material in his similes and metaphors. His comparison of an automobile to an organ in the passage describing Albertine at the pianola, of Bergotte to an automobile that becomes an airplane, or of Giotto's angels in the Arena Chapel to the loopings of Roland Garros's aviation students are bold analogies that would not have occurred to most novelists.

The Futurists glorified the modern world, machines, speed, and violence in an effort to free Italy from its oppressive past. They sought to render motion by the simultaneous presentation of successive aspects of forms in motion. Proust often creates the literary equivalent of this technique by presenting stop-action views of moving figures, the most remarkable being the successive "snapshots" of Saint-Loup running across benches in a restaurant. But the similarity between Proust and the Futurists is limited to his interest in machines and speed; he does not downplay the human figure but instead prizes individuality. Nor does Proust engage in polemics or write manifestoes.

In an early version of a text for *Le Temps retrouvé*, Proust describes the changes in society that have come about thanks to modern inventions. (Much of this material was later dispersed throughout the novel.) What interests him above all is the impact of these inventions on fashion, habits, social mores, perception, and our understanding of the laws of nature: "à un petit changement entre 2 aiguilles correspond dans une machine le déplacement d'énormes masses." He points out that such changes have taken place not by violating known laws but through the discovery of previously unknown laws: "Qui m'eût dit à Combray qu'on pourrait causer de Paris à Balbec j'aurais cru qu'il me disait un conte de fées. Le téléphone existait partout." Proust finds yet another example:

[On nous avait assuré] que le problème de la navigation
aérienne était insoluble, et maintenant de lourdes automobiles démarraient, couraient quelques pas sur l'herbe
et brusquement s'enlevaient, conduisant les dieux
pareils à celui qui avait effrayé mon cheval sur la route
solitaire de Doville. . . .51

In his novel, Proust chronicles the impact of technology
on Françoise, the venerable but stubborn family servant and
touchstone of Old France, who has her own complex social and
ethical code. Conservative in her political views and resistant to
any change in her habits, she refuses to speak over the telephone.
Her stubbornness amuses the family but also creates an inconve-
nience. Proust sums up her attitude in a statement about progress
and human adaptability to change:

Les progrès de la civilisation permettent à chacun de
manifester des qualités insoupçonnées ou de nouveaux
vices qui les rendent plus chers ou plus insupportables à
leurs amis. C'est ainsi que la découverte d'Edison avait
permis à Françoise d'acquérir un défaut de plus, qui
était de se refuser, quelque utilité, quelque urgence
qu'il y eût, à se servir du téléphone. (II, 730)52

Later in life, it was Proust who inconvenienced his servant,
Céleste. In order not to be disturbed, the writer had his telephone
disconnected and required her to make his calls from a nearby café
or tobacco shop.

The effect that time and the discovery of new laws have
on individuals and society is the main theme of Proust's *Recherche*.
His elaboration of the theme of time shows that he is not only
aware of the constantly changing nature of things but is haunted
by it. Change and the reaction to change set the tone of the
period.53 According to Proust, it was primarily the repercussions
of the Dreyfus affair and those of modern technology that altered
French society prior to World War I.54 The Great War, the first
in which airplanes were used to launch bombs, accelerated the

process of transformation and provided the coup de grace to an aristocracy soon to be replaced by such new society queens as Proust's dreadful Mme Verdurin, who, following the death of her husband and after subsequent remarriages, becomes the princesse de Guermantes. Implacable and ingenious in her campaign to ruin Charlus socially, Mme Verdurin succeeds in labeling him "avant guerre" and thus hopelessly out of fashion. After the war the Guermantes salon, once the epitome of Parisian aristocratic elegance and snobbery, is a broken-down machine that is no longer "functioning" properly and lets in the riffraff (III, 957). Mme Swann, a former cocotte, and Mme Bontemps, a middle-class hostess with social ambitions, are among those who rise to levels previously thought unattainable. The world of society is made neither better nor worse by such kaleidoscopic changes; it remains just as vain, vicious, and sterile as ever. The glamorous faubourg Saint-Germain is equally subject to the laws of time. As the Narrator observes in a grand period near the end of the novel:

> Ainsi change la figure des choses de ce monde; ainsi le centre des empires, et le cadastre des fortunes, et la charte des situations, tout ce qui semblait définitif est-il perpétuellement remanié, et les yeux d'un homme qui a vécu peuvent-ils contempler le changement le plus complet là où justement il lui paraissait le plus impossible. (III, 1019)[55]

Perpetual change and evolution is the great law of life. One of the most powerful scenes in the novel is the masked ball episode in which Proust brings back all the surviving members of his cast of characters in order to illustrate graphically the effects of time on them. They have become, he says, puppets of time: "Des poupées baignant dans les couleurs immatérielles des années, des poupées extériorisant le Temps . . ." (III, 924).

Proust's novel, said by Vladimir Nabokov and other eminent writers and critics to be the greatest in recent memory, explores many aspects of the human experience and contains a wealth of description and discourse enveloped in a panorama of history. But, as in Homer's *Odyssey*, the distinguished ancestor of the modern novel, the major theme is one of loss, quest, and rediscovery. *A la recherche du temps perdu* is, as its title implies, the story of a quest, of a young man's search for self-identity—and especially for his own voice as a writer. This quest involves the exploration of inner space, what Proust calls the "moi profond" (the deep or real self) wherein lies the mysterious fountainhead of creativity, yet it also involves an investigation of the exterior world, an attempt to gain knowledge of others, ultimately culminating in the search for order out of chaos. The purpose of the Narrator's quest is to sound the depths of his being in order to find a vision that matches his idealism, while at the same time acquiring the craft and drive to become a writer.

At the beginning of *la Recherche*, all is chaos. The Narrator does not know where he is, who he is, and—since he is subject to suggestion—not even what he is. In his contemplations he becomes whatever he has been reading: a church, a quartet, or a historical quarrel between rival monarchs of the Renaissance. All the elements that define and orient a personality are absent: time, place, and the nature of one's being. The extreme suggestibility of the hero is but the first indication of his protean nature.

In *la Recherche*, there are two moments of separation that are crucial to the Narrator's entire experience: the withholding of his mother's good-night kiss in Combray as a child and the disappearance and death of Albertine. As a mature adult in love, the Narrator comes to identify his passion for Albertine with his infantile dependency on his mother. Terry Eagleton links the Freudian depiction of this basic experience of loss and recovery to the birth of narration. One day Freud was watching his grandson playing in his stroller. The child would throw a toy out of the carriage and exclaim "fort!" (gone). Then, hauling it in on a string, the boy would scream "da!" (here). In *Beyond the Pleasure Principle*, Freud interpreted the "fort-da" game as "the infant's symbolic mastery of its mother's absence. *Fort-da* is perhaps the shortest story we can imagine: an object is lost, and then recovered. But even the most complex narratives can be read as variants on this model. . . ." Eagleton goes on to say that narrative is a source of consolation. Since lost objects cause anxiety and symbolize deeper unconscious losses, it is always pleasurable when we are able to find them and put them securely back in place: "In Lacanian theory, it is an original lost object—the mother's body—which drives forward the narrative of our lives, impelling us to pursue substitutes for this lost paradise in the endless metonymic movement of desire."[56] In Proust's case his biographers have viewed the death of his mother as a release and a powerful incentive to begin work in earnest. Some see *la Recherche* as a monumental apology to his parents, especially his mother. In any case, she was never—even in death—far from his thoughts. The source of *la Recherche,* the acorn from which grew the mighty oak of one of the most successfully sustained narrations in Western literature, is an imaginary conversation with his mother about Charles-Augustin Sainte-Beuve's critical method.

In the course of his quest, the Narrator seeks both a reality that matches his inner vision and the craft, stamina, and willpower necessary to become a writer. It is only after many false starts that he finds the key and realizes that he must create a work of art in which the two aspects of life—the ideal and the real—are contrasted and wed. In elaborating his entire experience, he thus makes accessible to others the totality of his vision.

Proust's quest fits perfectly the definition of a monomyth, a term coined by James Joyce in *Finnegans Wake* and borrowed by Joseph Campbell, according to whom

> the standard path of the mythological adventure of the hero is a magnification of the formula represented in the rites of passage: *separation—initiation—return:* which might be named the nuclear unit of the monomyth.
>
> A hero ventures forth from the world of common day into a region of supernatural wonder: fabulous forces are there encountered and a decisive victory is

won: the hero comes back from this mysterious adventure with the power to bestow boons on his fellow
man.[57]

At the end of *la Recherche*, Proust's unlikely hero triumphs
over vanity, becomes an altruistic creator, and offers the fruits of
his labors to his fellow man. As is usually the case in myths, the
Proustian voyage is a trial. What is new in Proust is the nature of
the hero undergoing the trial. He is apparently a weakling,
doomed to hypochondria and failure and plagued by self-doubts:
Can he become a writer? Does he have what it takes? Will he
begin in time? Seeking one thing, he always finds something else
that is unexpected and initially misunderstood and disappointing.
Berma's acting, the seaside resort of Balbec, the salon of the
duchesse de Guermantes, and the experience of erotic love are
nothing like his anticipations of them. Only at the end of the
quest does he see how his entire past forms the subject of his
book.

Many of the Futurists embraced materialistic goals and
eventually adopted Fascist ideologies, going to extremes in their
worship of machines and endorsing indiscriminate iconoclasm
and violence to the detriment of humanistic values. The narrow-
ness of their belligerent ideology doomed the movement. In his
vision of life as a time-space continuum of human experience,
Proust professes a timeless, universal, and cosmic view. He delights
in combining the ancient and the modern, the arts and the sciences, the mythological and the mechanical in images that reveal
their similarities *sub specie aeternitatis*. Although Proust continues
the grand tradition of Western literature that began with Homer's
quests, he is very much a man of his time and follows his own
aesthetic dictum as to what an original artist should do, namely,
create the world anew.

Proust's compass is large. His view of human experience
does not deprive us of our cultural heritage; rather it establishes its
endurance while rejoicing in its fecundity as new laws about the
human condition and the nature of the universe are discovered.

The past inhabits the present through human memory and monu-
ments such as Gothic cathedrals, which Proust compares to ships
sailing through time. Rather than being iconoclastic, Proust is
encyclopedic[58] and shows how easily and naturally the new takes
its place alongside the old, how the model for *la Recherche* is the
universe, an ever-expanding cosmos, a circle of constellations,
kaleidoscopic images constantly undergoing permutations yet
moving in harmony with basic laws whose discovery remains the
goal of the Proustian quest.

CHAPTER 2

Women as Landscapes

Aimer et mourir
Au pays qui te ressemble!
　　　—Charles Baudelaire

Votre âme est un paysage choisi . . .
　　　—Paul Verlaine

en étant amoureux d'une femme nous projetons simplement en elle un état de notre âme; que par conséquent l'important n'est pas la valeur de la femme, mais la profondeur de l'état. . . . (I, 833)

All the women desired by Proust's narrator have two elements in common: their fugacity and their identification with a precise geographic location. And all of them are seen for the first time out-of-doors and in motion.[1] Indeed, for Proust the constant identification of girl and landscape—as though the experience of sighting a girl moving along the beach or in a forest was total and unique—seems to indicate that the girl has no being and no life distinct from that of the locale in which she is seen; yet, for reasons that I will examine, the girl herself and her past remain deeply mysterious.

　　　The young Narrator first desired a peasant girl of Combray when he was strolling near Roussainville, just prior to witnessing the lesbian love scene between Mlle Vinteuil and her friend. In his mature years, he comments on his early belief that each person and each site was unique, the one a product of the other:

> nous croyons d'une foi profonde à l'originalité, à la vie individuelle du lieu où nous nous trouvons—la passante qu'appelait mon désir me semblait être non un exemplaire quelconque de ce type général: la femme, mais un produit nécessaire et naturel de ce sol. (I, 156-57)

In the same passage he remarks, "elle était . . . pour moi comme une plante locale. . . ."[2] For the concept of each girl as a "plante locale" Proust may have been influenced by Darwinism.[3] The Narrator's way of discovering these women resembles that of a naturalist or botanist exploring the animal or floral kingdoms in that each woman is a part of the flora and fauna of her native region, the place in which the Narrator first sees her: "Entre cette province et le tempérament de la jeune fille . . . je percevais un beau dialogue. Dialogue, non pas discorde. Aucune ne saurait diviser la jeune fille et son pays natal. Elle, c'est lui encore" (I, 910).[4]

In depicting the *passantes*, Proust combines naturalism for the origin of the species, wherein each girl embodies a unique species and is the product of a particular habitat, with impressionism, wherein each girl is seen outdoors in the light of a specific time and place. Just as the Impressionists depicted an entire series of railway stations, bridges, cathedrals, poplar trees, water lilies, and so forth, with each painting in the series reflecting the light of a particular moment, Proust gives us many versions of the major female characters as they appear at different times and in different surroundings. Proust's manner of representation is that of an Impressionist in that his descriptions of these *passantes* always take into account the location and the "couleur du temps" in which each of them is seen.

Une femme-paysage

Proust's conception of *femme-paysage* may have been inspired in part by the "Carte du Tendre," an allegorical map on which the joys and dangers of love were represented by such geographic features as Petits Soins, Empressement, Le Lac d'Indifférence, and La Mer d'Inimitié. This topological representation of eros was created in the seventeenth century by Madeleine de Scudéry and those who frequented her salon, and was introduced to the public in her novel *Clélie* (1656). In *la Recherche*, when Odette is visiting the château of Pierrefonds with the Verdurins—who have banished the possessive, jealous Swann—Proust compares the map of Compiègne, near Pierrefonds, to the "Carte du Tendre" (I, 295), which Swann supplements with photographs of the castle to create the illusion of following Odette's movements.

The idea of possession or imprisonment through cartography is a variation on the theme of capturing the beloved's essence through a framing device or visual image.[5] A notable example of this is Swann's ritualistic use of the photograph of Botticelli's painting of *Zephora,* which he comes to regard as a photograph of Odette (I, 223-25). When the Narrator is infatuated with the duchesse de Guermantes, he pleads with Saint-Loup to give him a photograph of the duchesse, who is the latter's aunt; once obtained, he studies the photograph in order to gain a perspective into the character and life of the duchesse (II, 79-80).[6]

Swann and the Narrator both envisage abandoning and then forgetting their mistresses as a train trip back through the "countries" that each associates with the woman he loves: "[Swann] aurait voulu apercevoir, comme un paysage qui allait disparaître, cet amour [Odette] qu'il venait de quitter . . ." (I, 378). The smooth gliding of the train on the rails as it moves away from the "country of Odette" makes the break with her seem painless, since there is no abrupt moment of separation.[7] In Swann's dream, the dreamer plays a double role: he is both the traveler departing the "country of Odette" and the young man standing on the platform, undecided about whether or not to leave the woman-landscape. It is as if wisdom and folly are equally divided between the two halves of Swann's character: the Swann on the train tries to convince the Swann on the platform to give up Odette by taking a voyage away from the locale of their love.

The protagonist and his mentor both use maps and train schedules to track down the elusive and presumably unfaithful Odette and Albertine during periods of intense jealousy: "[Swann] se plongeait dans le plus enivrant des romans d'amour, l'indicateur des chemins de fer, qui lui apprenait les moyens de la rejoindre . . . ce matin même!" (I, 293). In the case of the Narrator, it is his aesthetic desires that he seeks to satisfy when he thinks of taking the train to Venice: "bien que mon exaltation eût pour motif un désir de jouissances artistiques, les guides l'entretenaient encore plus que les livres d'esthétique et, plus que les guides, l'indicateur des chemins de fer" (I, 391).[8]

After Albertine's death, when the Narrator imagines forgetting the fugitive girl, he, like Swann, envisions the process of growing indifferent to her memory as a train trip back through the "country of Albertine," but he adds that the topography will not necessarily be in the same order on the "return trip."[9] Proust uses this analogy to make the point that since the process of memory is subjective and fortuitous, the images of memory seldom represent experiences in chronological order: "ces moments du passé ne sont pas immobiles" (III, 558). Proust describes a cruel illusion caused by memory in this retrograde process. Since the Narrator is making a sentimental journey back through the "country of Albertine," as he leaves and forgets her a space-time confusion occurs, making him think that he is going forward in time and into the "geography of Albertine," toward rather than away from the object of his passion: "on a un instant l'illusion qu'on repart, mais dans la direction du lieu d'où l'on vient, comme l'on avait fait la première fois. . . . telle est la cruauté du souvenir" (III, 558).

Not only are all our immediate perceptions fugitive and fragmented, but so perforce is our memory of them. The perceptions of memory are not like the individual frames of a film held together in the order of exposure; our mind always cuts, edits, and splices together scenes from our past in a free-associative way over which we often have no control.

Travel and Desire

It was his older schoolmate Bloch who first gave the Narrator the idea that he might easily possess the girls he desires (I, 711). But the physical possession that Bloch is talking about is not the kind sought by the youthful Narrator, who says that as soon as he knew the girls in motion could be possessed physically, he became curious about their souls: "Pour les belles filles qui passaient, du jour où j'avais su que leurs joues pouvaient être embrassées, j'étais devenu curieux de leur âme" (I, 712). He identifies each desired girl's "soul" with a particular essence of a city or landscape that he yearns to explore. He imagines sexual contentment as a voyage, but, like Baudelaire's voyager, the protagonist never finds what he seeks: "Il ne peut pas y en avoir [de calme] dans l'amour, puisque ce qu'on a obtenu n'est jamais qu'un nouveau point de départ pour désirer davantage" (I, 581).[10]

The first identification between eros and travel occurs early in Proust's text when the young Narrator masturbates while gazing at the tower of Roussainville, a view that embraces the geographic and architectural elements he associates with desire: the landscape from which spring the phallic tower and the *passantes* of Méséglise. He is both stimulated and afraid, comparing his activity to a dangerous voyage: "avec les hésitations héroïques du voyageur qui entreprend une exploration ou du désespéré qui se suicide, défaillant, je me frayais en moi-même une route inconnue et que je croyais mortelle" (I, 158). Later he expends his frustrated sexual energy by beating the trees at Roussainville with a stick (I, 558), accompanied by repeated outbursts such as "Zut, zut, zut," which also express his exasperation at not being able to find the words to describe the impression made on him by the countryside around Combray (I, 555). In his old age, the Narrator learns from Gilberte herself that while he was caressing his penis and gazing at the tower of Roussainville, she—the girl he thought unattainable—was in the tower engaging in acts of debauchery with Théodore, the grocery boy, while wishing she were making love with the Narrator.

Years later, when the jealous hero makes Albertine a "prisoner," he comes to resent her presence since it deprives him of the opportunity to pursue any of the working-class girls whom he associates with his long-postponed and now abandoned dreams of visiting Venice and other Italian cities: "La vie de ces jolies filles . . . me paraissait . . . quelque chose . . . d'aussi désirable que les villes les plus merveilleuses que promet le voyage" (III, 171). How, he asks himself, can he continue to believe in the geographic reality of Italy and the desired girls without going there? He then resolves to leave Albertine in order to investigate the source and nature of the force that endows unknown girls and cities with such mystery: "ces similitudes mêmes du désir et du voyage firent que je me promis de serrer un jour d'un peu plus près la nature de cette force . . . qui portait si haut les cités, les femmes, tant que je ne les connaissais pas . . ." (III, 172).

These elevated thoughts are based on false expectations. What he seeks in his dreams of the desired cities and the trips to Balbec and Venice are "des vérités appartenant à un monde plus réel que celui où je vivais . . ." (I, 441). In possessing the girls, he seeks intimate knowledge of their entire beings and past history. Such flights of fancy are doomed because life seldom matches the expectations of our imagination and desires: "on ne trouve jamais aussi hauts qu'on avait espéré une cathédrale, une vague dans la tempête, le bond d'un danseur . . ." (I, 528). These vertical aspirations will not be realized until he sinks into despair and discovers the true nature of his vocation as an artist.

Albertine and the Sea

The appearance of Albertine and her friends on the beach is reminiscent of the birth of Venus. Eros in the form of Albertine first appears to the Narrator in profile against a seascape. Before

the girls develop distinct characteristics and individual facial features, the Narrator desires them in the conglomerate. Albertine
is the source of many Proustian metaphors, but by far the most
constant representation of her is as an embodiment of the sea.
The primary memory the Narrator has of Albertine is her first
appearance on the beach at Balbec, pushing a bicycle while surrounded by other members of the little band. It is this vision of
her that the Narrator always pursues. The gesture she makes the
first time he sees her on the beach creates a visual memory
capable of evoking the marine setting whenever she repeats the
motion in a different locale. The initial imprint on his mind of
Albertine on the beach remains so strong that it resurfaces or
echoes throughout the later metamorphoses of Albertine, even
during her captivity in the Narrator's Paris apartment. André
Ferré has observed that it is the Narrator's desire that fixes a girl
in a particular locale: "une femme aimée est liée à une région
moins parce qu'elle en est originaire que parce qu'elle y a excité,
de façon peut-être fortuite, la curiosité du narrateur. . . ."[11]
Thus, no matter what Albertine's life may be like later on, she
remains the girl of Balbec, the beach, and the sea.[12] This is the
image he preserves in his mind years after her death:

> C'est ainsi, faisant halte, les yeux brillants sous son
> 'polo', que je la revois encore maintenant, silhouettée
> sur l'écran que lui fait, au fond, la mer, et séparée de
> moi par un espace transparent et azuré, le temps écoulé
> depuis lors, première image, toute mince dans mon
> souvenir, désirée, poursuivie, puis oubliée, puis retrou-
> vée. . . . (I, 829)

Throughout most of the novel the Narrator believes that
Albertine is an idealized embodiment of the essence of Balbec and
the sea that he cannot possess; yet there is a passage in the concluding pages of *Sodome et Gomorrhe* that indicates the sort of
happy lovemaking one would expect of a young couple at a seaside resort. Albertine, marinelike and athletic, is here presented

with her essential qualities of speed and lubricity. During their lovemaking in the dunes under the stars, even the sea suspends its mobility:

> nous nous étendions en contrebas des dunes; ce même corps dans la souplesse duquel vivait toute la grâce féminine, marine et sportive, des jeunes filles que j'avais vues passer la première fois devant l'horizon du flot, je le tenais serré contre le mien, sous une même couverture, tout au bord de la mer immobile divisée par un rayon tremblant. . . . (II, 1020)

But there is no useful information, no consequential revelation to be found in such moments. Proust is not a writer who praises the ordinary pleasures of lovemaking. In keeping with the cosmic nature of his quest, the Proustian narrator is ever wanting, ever restless. He must suffer and be purged by the fire of obsessive sexual jealousy before he can attain the final self-illumination.

The similarities between travel and desire will culminate in the Albertine-Fortuny-Venice passages, where Proust combines the themes of eroticism, painting, and geography when the Narrator dresses Albertine in Fortuny gowns. Mariano Fortuny y Madrazo (1871-1949) revived the design motifs on fabrics worn by figures depicted in the Venetian paintings of Carpaccio and Titian. The Narrator—one of whose great, unfulfilled dreams is to travel to Venice—finds in Albertine, clothed in a Fortuny gown, the living embodiment of the Italian city and the paintings of these old masters: "La robe de Fortuny que portait ce soir-là Albertine me semblait comme l'ombre tentatrice de cette invisible Venise" (III, 394). In spite of these rich, aesthetic trappings, he rejects the temptation to consider Albertine a work of art, as Swann did for Odette during her Botticelli phase.

But when the Narrator embraces her in a Fortuny dress, he holds Albertine-Venice in his arms, "serrant contre mon cœur l'azur miroitant et doré du Grand Canal et les oiseaux accouplés, symboles de mort et de résurrection" (III, 399).[13] The lovebirds and the death-resurrection theme echo the Agostinelli-Albertine episode, where the Narrator finally travels to Venice after Albertine's death and the initial stages of bereavement. For this section, Proust borrows elements of his own experience of grief after the accidental death of Agostinelli. Shortly after his arrival in Venice, the Narrator receives a telegram that he at first thinks is from Albertine. This event marks the third and final stage of the hero's indifference to Albertine's death (III, 641). After reading the wire and feeling no joy at her return from the dead, he realizes that Albertine has died within him and he has recovered from his grief and his love. The fact that he is incapable of mourning for an extended period the deaths of his grandmother and Albertine, that he cannot be faithful to their memory, is in itself a source of bitter disappointment. Remembering that when Albertine disappeared, she carried away with her a "Venetian" dress, that is, one designed by Fortuny, the Narrator quotes the phrase from Agostinelli's letter that Proust received the day of the aviator's death, "ce triste jour . . . 'deux fois crépusculaire puisque la nuit tombait et que nous allions nous quitter'" (III, 647).[14] The letter, quoted earlier in the passage when Albertine wrote to the Narrator after fleeing his apartment (III, 468, 506), is reprised here because this is the final adieu to Albertine as the object of his passion. Ultimately, the vision of Albertine as an embodiment of the sea is all that remains and the circle is closed. Her prediction that the sea would be her tomb is true in the sense that in the Narrator's memory she is reabsorbed by the marine landscape from which she sprang (III, 848).[15]

The Geometry of Love

In la Recherche Proust gives us a physics and a geometry of love. The mobility of space-time and its arousal of sexual desire is a constant of Proustian eroticism. During their first encounter, the

young cyclist looks at the Narrator with eyes that are those of a
creature from another universe. Thus, from the beginning the distance that separates him and Albertine is cosmic: "Du sein de quel
univers me distinguait-elle? . . . Je savais que je ne posséderais pas
cette jeune cycliste, si je ne possédais pas ce qu'il y avait dans ses
yeux.[16] Et c'était par conséquent toute sa vie qui m'inspirait du
désir . . ." (I, 794).

Although Proust usually presents a woman as a landscape
the Narrator yearns to possess, occasionally the exploration of the
terrain itself is presented as an erotic experience. Here, as the Narrator approaches a town in an automobile, the cityscape becomes
the mobile prey:

> ces cercles, de plus en plus rapprochés, que décrit
> l'automobile autour d'une ville fascinée qui fuyait dans
> tous les sens pour échapper, et sur laquelle finalement il
> fonce tout droit, à pic, au fond de la vallée où elle reste
> gisante à terre [la voiture nous donne l'impression] de
> découvrir [ce point unique], de le déterminer nous-
> même . . . de nous aider à sentir d'une main plus
> amoureusement exploratrice . . . la véritable géométrie,
> la belle "mesure de la terre" (II, 1006).[17]

Proust's erotic response to travel is expressed in a letter to
Georges de Lauris concerning a train trip from Paris to Evian-les-
Bains. Speaking of sleeping cities observed from the train at dawn,
Proust says that he had an insane urge to rape them: "Au matin
un désir fou de violer des petites villes endormies (lisez bien ville
et non des petites filles endormies!). . ."[18] The urge to rape
"sleeping" cities reminds us of the Narrator's possession of the
sleeping Albertine, a possession that is geographic, marine, and
floral (III, 67-75).

In passages that use such analogies, Proust presents the
possession of women in terms of a mathematical or geometric
chart, as though desire and possession were a rational, quantifiable process. The examination of the duchesse de Guermantes's
photograph is compared to a geometric study in which the

Narrator sees details impossible to observe during her normally rapid trajectories: "Ces lignes [de son visage] qu'il me semblait presque défendu de regarder, je pourrais les étudier là comme dans un traité de la seule géométrie qui eût de la valeur pour moi" (II, 80). Proust employs such analogies to draw a sharp contrast between the Narrator's naïve expectations and reality, between human capacity and cosmic desire, which proffers the false hope of being assuaged through the possession of a corporeal body.

The Narrator believes that he can solve the problem of desire and visual perception by possessing a highly coveted object of beauty, a *femme-paysage*, and through this act of comprehension thereby recreate the aesthetic equivalent of the mysteries of such beauty. By using imagery evoking space-time, speed, logarithms, and geometry, Proust creates a mobile frieze that allows the girls to maintain their motion while at the same time slowing them down enough for the hero to observe them and perhaps make them accessible if he can discover a way to join them. The concept of the Narrator as the excluded, weak, nervous, untalented, inept traveler—often depicted by Proust as the "petit personnage" in the corner of a landscape painting or photograph of a major architectural monument—is one of Proust's most successful narrative ruses, allowing the reader to delight in the Narrator's assumption of vast, creative powers at the conclusion of the novel, where the protagonist will triumph over time in anticipation of finally being able to write his book if he can hold death at bay long enough. A prime source of the novel's narrative drive comes from the Narrator's fluctuations between, on the one hand, anxiety and jealous self-torture over Albertine's presumed infidelities and, on the other, those periods of calm when he believes he has "captured" her.

In the Narrator's case, mere sexual desire is attenuated or held in check by the much greater desire to penetrate a life. He is driven by his own naïveté and by the longing that Baudelaire identified as the taste for the infinite. Sexual appetite is provoked by the desire to capture and possess those who are beautiful, other, and mysterious. The naïve Narrator envisages the beloved as terrain to be conquered by the metaphorical planting of a flagpole or the actual insertion of a penis. But it is the nature of desire to remain unabated, and only a fool would think of such conquests as definitive. Time and time again Proust demonstrates for us that it is the elusive individual who is most desirable—indeed, who is *alone* desirable. He reminds us that we are always more intrigued by a fish in water than by one that has been caught and laid on the table, underscoring again the importance of witnessing the creature—girl or fish—in its native surroundings, where it is endowed with movement, freedom, and potentiality. The qualities that are important to the Narrator as he seeks to solve the mystery of his desire for the elusive prey—kinesis and change—are those of life itself: "Il faut qu'entre nous et le poisson . . . s'interpose . . . le remous à la surface duquel viennent affleurer . . . le poli d'une chair, l'indécision d'une forme, dans la fluidité d'un transparent et mobile azur" (I, 796).

Given the absolute nature of Proustian desire, disappointment is inevitable. We are confronted with creatures who are cosmic, while we are handicapped by deficiencies in our apparatus for possessing them, as is demonstrated in the passage on kissing Albertine (III, 365). The Narrator realizes that Albertine is like any desired being, like the sea itself—a creature of infinite variety. The vastness and ever-changing nature of the sea is recognized by the Narrator just before he spots Albertine strolling down the beach: "je ne vis jamais deux fois la même [mer]" (I, 705). Then Albertine appears and becomes the incarnation of the sea's everchanging nature. Later he recognizes how unrealistic his expectations have been with regard to the fugitive being, seeing the impossible, cosmic nature of his desire:

> pour Albertine . . . je sentais que je n'étais rien. Et je comprenais l'impossibilité où se heurte l'amour. Nous nous imaginons qu'il a pour objet un être qui peut être

couché devant nous, enfermé dans un corps. Hélas! Il est l'extension de cet être à *tous les points de l'espace et du temps* que cet être a occupés et occupera. Si nous ne possédons pas son contact avec tel lieu, avec telle heure, nous ne le possédons pas. Or nous ne pouvons toucher tous ces points. (III, 100; emphasis added)

Depending on one's point of view, the lover's predicament is tragic or risible because he projects onto a mere creature of flesh and blood desire that is cosmic. The person he desires is not, as he thought, clear and immobile before him (II, 67) but, on the contrary, fugitive, always fleeing, *insaisissable*, moving away from him at a rate that increases in direct proportion to his desire. The conception of woman as the geometric embodiment of space-time is expressed in a maxim: "L'amour, c'est l'espace et le temps rendus sensibles au cœur" (III, 385). The Narrator's suspicion that each person is a planet, part of a separate universe, is confirmed by his experience in love. Sexual possession is a complete disappointment, "la possession physique—où d'ailleurs l'on ne possède rien," as in Swann's possession of Odette (I, 234). This discovery, which Proust spends many pages demonstrating, was forecast early in the novel: "j'étais pour longtemps encore à l'âge où l'on n'a pas encore abstrait ce plaisir de la possession des femmes différentes avec lesquelles on l'a goûté, où l'on ne l'a pas réduit à une notion générale qui les fait considérer dès lors comme les instruments interchangeables d'un plaisir toujours identique" (I, 157). As for Proust's hero, he is not a mere seducer, as, apparently, is the disappointed Swann; the latter's yearnings and curiosity are sincere, but he is condemned to remain a creature of the surface. The Narrator seeks nothing more nor less than absolute, total possession of the woman desired:

nous ne regardons pas les yeux d'une fille que nous ne connaissons pas comme nous ferions d'une petite plaque d'opale ou d'agate. Nous savons que le petit rayon qui les irise . . . [est] tout ce que nous pouvons voir d'une pensée, d'une volonté, d'une mémoire où résident la maison familiale que nous ne connaissons pas. . . ." (III, 171)

Here we see again the motif of a ray of light coming from an unknown source in the universe. The protagonist mistakenly incorporates in Albertine his cosmic desire for space-time; such desire becomes monstrous as he seeks to attain the essence of a place and recapture the past through possession of the girl. This is impossible, of course, since no girl of flesh and blood can work such wonders, even in the most privileged moments. This is a variation on the Swann-Odette-Botticelli theme, but Swann, handicapped in his ability to concentrate and analyze a situation, actually believes that he can gain an intimate knowledge of Botticelli's art by making love to Odette. Although the Narrator cannot know this yet, his frustrated sexual expectations advance his quest by moving him farther along the path that leads to art and the assumption of his vocation.

At the point in the novel where he is afraid to let Albertine go alone to the Bon Marché or Trois-Quartiers department stores, he realizes the impossibility of his desire. Comparing Albertine to the vastness of the sea, over which he has no control, he sees that his desire for total knowledge and power over her thoughts and actions is insane and recalls Xerxes' ridiculous attempt to punish the sea for having swallowed up his ships:

> un être [comme Albertine], *disséminé dans l'espace et dans le temps,* n'est plus pour nous une femme, mais une suite d'événements sur lesquels nous ne pouvons faire la lumière, *une suite de problèmes insolubles,* une mer que nous essayons ridiculement, comme Xerxès, de battre pour la punir de ce qu'elle a englouti. Une fois cette période commencée, on est forcément vaincu. (III, 104; emphasis added)

The Narrator again equates erotic possession and mathematics by seeking to make love rational, quantifiable, and hence understandable; such an ambition is always frustrated, and the mystery of desire and possession remains unsolvable.

Proustian characters are not conceived absolutely or ideally; the latest version is always a "correction" of an earlier impression. According to Proust's theory of the multiple self perceiving the multiple other, there can be no end to the series; indeed, one person can only see the part of another's trajectory through space that happens to pass before him, with the desired other remaining totally unknowable and unpossessable, since we can never get beyond ourselves. "L'homme est l'être qui ne peut sortir de soi, qui ne connaît les autres qu'en soi, et, en disant le contraire, ment" (III, 450). The loneliness of the Proustian lover is limitless and without end. This presentation of his characters as multiple and unknowable is one of the most forward-looking aspects of Proust's novel.

CHAPTER 3

Girls in Motion

Chaque être est détruit quand nous cessons de le voir; puis son apparition suivante est une création nouvelle. . . . (I, 917)

Proust was as fascinated by the influence of speed on the way we perceive figures in motion as was the photographer Jacques-Henri Lartigue (1894-1986). Both moved easily among the well-to-do upper bourgeoisie and aristocracy, being roughly contemporary as far as their early creative years are concerned. Lartigue's father gave him his first camera at the age of eight, and the youth began assembling his extraordinary photographic record of the new age in transportation and sports in 1902—well before Proust began writing *la Recherche* in 1907 or 1908.[1]

The enthusiasm of the Lartigues for the new machines of speed was boundless. The father owned a succession of early-model automobiles and the young Lartigue kept up with the rapidly evolving technology by taking many pictures of the first days of automobiles and airplanes in France. Among his favorite subjects were automobile races, boats, trains, glider launchings, the first propeller-driven airplanes, the horse races at Auteuil, and the first public bathing forays at Biarritz and Etretat.[2] He also photographed the more traditional parade of beautiful and fashionable women along the avenue du Bois (now the avenue Foch) and especially in the prime Proustian location, the allée des Acacias in the Bois de Boulogne. Here the precocious photographer set up his camera day after day and waited for the "professional beauties" to pass by, just as the Narrator does for Mme Swann. There are a number of striking similarities between these photographs and Proust's descriptions of girls in motion; both the photographer and the writer caught scenes that are notable for their dynamism, freshness, and spontaneity. Lartigue has left us a record of the period fashion in sporting attire and of the design of ace cars and airplanes, as well as assorted objects of luxury, not to mention beautiful women photographed in startling positions or angles. (While on their honeymoon, he photographed his first wife, Bibi, sitting on the toilet!)

The religion of speed noted by Octave Mirbeau, Guillaume Apollinaire, and others of the period—especially the Futurists—can be seen in many of Lartigue's photographs of speeding machines and human figures flying through space. Among Lartigue's well-known photographs of the early years are the following Proustian *instantanés:* young ladies, boys, and men leaping on the beach,[3] diving into swimming pools, or riding bicycles; speeding motorcars arrested in motion; airplanes soaring and sometimes crashing; and tennis players, golfers, and cyclists. Lartigue's photographs have an air of innocent, youthful exuberance and do not contain the strong and troubling erotic tones with which Proust endows his figures in motion.

Lartigue's pictures captured the antics and insouciance of the belle epoque as it truly was for those of the middle and upper classes, a splendid period of energy and progress that lasted until the outbreak of World War I. In his photographs of the period, there is no hint of trouble or impending danger; only young, dynamic, radiant people ready to conquer the domains of land and air. One of his most famous photographs shows a fashionable woman walking her dogs in the Bois de Boulogne. On the right side of the avenue, a horse-drawn carriage is about to disappear from the frame, while on the left advances one of the first motorcars. (See p. 41.) Lartigue and Proust are both sensitive to such moments of transition, intent on capturing them in their respective medias.

Jacques–Henri Lartigue, Avenue du Bois de Boulogne,
Paris, January 15, 1911 (© Association des Amis
de Jacques–Henri Lartigue).

The young Lartigue went to the Bois not only because he was eager to try out his new photographic equipment but in order to preserve his memories of the beauties who daily walked along the allée des Acacias. Lartigue tells us in his memoirs that there were three parallel paths:

> Piétons, cavaliers, automobiles (cinq ou six), beaux équipages mélangés aux fiacres descendent aussi l'avenue du Bois . . . pour se retrouver tous ensemble aux Acacias et commencer une promenade en va-et-vient qui leur permettra de se croiser, de se voir, de se saluer, de se re-croiser, se re-voir, se re-saluer . . . les uns restant dans leur voiture ou à cheval, les autres, surtout s'il y a une jolie robe à montrer, descendant pour marcher dans le "Sentier de la Vertu". Car, aux Acacias, il y a trois allées: celle des voitures, celle des cavaliers, et le petit chemin des piétons, sous les arbres, appelé "Sentier de la Vertu".[4]

Lartigue, who never doubted the validity of his craft, made photographs of *passantes* that Proust's narrator mistakenly believes must always remain fleeting (*fugitives*). Although Proust seems to reject photography as being too realistic, too banal, the documentary aspect is one that he approved of, as his character Charlus confirms: "La photographie acquiert un peu de la dignité qui lui manque, quand elle cesse d'être une reproduction du réel et nous montre des choses qui n'existent plus" (I, 764). Although the Narrator rejects photography as an art form—perhaps because it is a convenient way to denigrate realism—Proust himself was fascinated by the medium that transformed the concept of perceiving an object. The novelist kept in a box a collection of photographs of writers, actresses, and demimondaines that he often contemplated. Lucien Daudet recalls that he was shown these pictures on his first visit to Proust's apartment.[5] But the author of *la Recherche* maintains that a snapshot cannot contain all the rich complexity of color and line that one can find in a painting, where a number of moments are fused in the same light of day and in the same vision, namely, that of the artist who created the picture.

In the novel, one of the primary functions of the photographic analogies is to demonstrate the elusiveness of a desired being; a mere snapshot cannot capture the many facets of a girl in motion. Not only is Albertine a creature who loves speed, but because the Narrator desires her, she becomes the essence of elusiveness. The inadequate photographs only serve to heighten the Narrator's frustration over his thwarted attempts to seize this volatile girl whom he yearns to possess:

> ce n'est qu'après voir [*sic*] reconnu . . . les erreurs d'optique du début qu'on pourrait arriver à la connaissance exacte d'un être si cette connaissance était possible. Mais elle ne l'est pas; car tandis que se rectifie la vision que nous avons de lui, lui-même, qui n'est pas un objectif inerte, change pour son compte, nous pensons le rattraper, il se déplace, et, croyant le voir enfin plus clairement, ce n'est que les images anciennes que nous en avions prises que nous avons réussi à éclaircir, mais qui ne le représentent plus. (I, 874)

Proust later generalizes this observation that a fixed image is insufficient to represent such creatures by applying it to all individuals as well as to the kaleidoscopic changes occurring in society: "un caractère . . . ne change pas moins qu'elles [les sociétés et les passions] et si on veut clicher ce qu'il a de relativement immuable, on le voit présenter successivement des aspects différents (impliquant qu'il ne sait pas garder l'immobilité, mais bouge) à l'objectif déconcerté" (III, 327). The "disconcerted lens" is the sedentary, static, centric Narrator who yearns to arrest and fix permanently the great whirling motions of existence.

His first experience in trying to "photograph" a girl had been with Gilberte. As he tries to seize this seaside band of creatures of flight and fix them in his memory, he borrows analogies from the plastic arts: statues, friezes, frescoes, and photographs. In addition to the Impressionists, who also sought to capture fleeting moments of light and color, Proust was influenced by ancient friezes and, as we shall see, by the modern development of chronophotography, both of which freeze motion. But the analogical results of his mental camera are always disappointing because "ainsi figés ces êtres ne livrent pas de secrets." Hope, despair, anticipation, "tout cela rend notre attention en face de l'être aimé trop tremblante pour qu'elle puisse obtenir de lui une image bien nette. . . . Le modèle chéri . . . bouge; on n'en a jamais que des photographies manquées" (I, 489-90).[6]

The couple Narrator-Albertine is representative of the very nature of Proustian art—perhaps of all art—where the ephemeral, the mobile, and the fugitive (kinesis) is wedded to the sedentary, the fixed, and the passive (stasis). We see such a relationship explicitly described in a passage on Elstir's paintings—a passage that may serve as a statement of Proust's novel[7] in miniature:

> Or [Elstir] avait su immortellement arrêter le mouvement des heures à cet instant lumineux où la dame avait eu chaud et avait cessé de danser où l'arbre était cerné d'un pourtour d'ombre, où les voiles semblaient glisser sur un vernis d'or.

After stasis, there is a return to kinesis:

> Mais justement parce que l'instant pesait sur nous avec tant de force, cette toile si fixée donnait l'impression la plus fugitive, on sentait que la dame allait bientôt s'en retourner, les bateaux disparaître, l'ombre changer de place, la nuit venir, que le plaisir finit, que la vie passe et que *les instants, montrés à la fois par tant de lumières qui y voisinent ensemble,* ne se retrouvent pas. (II, 421; emphasis added)

Stress is placed on the composite nature of the instants we experience; they are multiple, separate, fugitive, and ephemeral segments. Elstir is the artist who belongs to the Albertine cycle—just as Vinteuil is associated with the Swann-Odette story[8] and Bergotte with the Narrator's infatuation for Gilberte—and the subjects that Elstir proposes as meriting depiction by contemporary painters are those connected with the new fascination for speed: yachts, motorcars, and the fashionable sporting attire that the boats and cars inspired. During his first stay at Balbec, the protagonist is still in a heroic, classical frame of mind; at Balbec he expects to find a primeval, rugged, stormy seacoast.[9] Until he meets Elstir, the young man has been under the influence of his grandmother and Swann, both of whom think of painting in terms of the old masters. The awareness that beauty may be found in the contemporary attire of sporting events such as motoring and yachting is a lesson he has yet to learn from Albertine and Elstir. This modern vision, linking Elstir's pictures to those of such painters as Manet and Degas, will be one of the most important consequences of his first trip to Balbec, for Elstir will radically alter his way of looking at things—"un peintre que j'allais rencontrer à Balbec et qui eut une influence si profonde sur ma vision des choses, Elstir" (I, 653).

Prior to meeting Elstir, the Narrator had conceived of artistic beauty in terms of the old masters and classical landscapes. Once he has seen Elstir's watercolors, he looks for beauty in the ordinary objects of daily life: "j'essayais de trouver la beauté là où je ne m'étais jamais figuré qu'elle fût, dans les choses les plus usuelles, dans la vie profonde des 'natures mortes'" (I, 869). Proust provides a list of ordinary things in which the Narrator now finds such beauty: "maintenant, tout ce que j'avais dédaigné, écarté de ma vue, non seulement les effets de soleil, mais même les régates, les courses de chevaux, je l'eusse recherché avec passion . . ." (I, 897). Now, when the vacationer rides along the seacoast, he no longer tries to block out views of steamers and "tous ces fastidieux perfectionnements de l'industrie" in order to see the primeval sea as it must have been before the appearance of man; instead, he seeks the blue shadows of Elstir's paintings (I, 902-3).[10]

A girl in motion is often described by Proust in a way that is similar to Impressionist and Cubist paintings, which present the viewer with a figure seen in a particular landscape or in multiple perspectives and unusual juxtapositions.[11] The theory that an object is as multiple and complex as are the possible views of it is similar to the perception that inspired the Impressionists to paint in series, the Cubists to juxtapose objects, and the Futurists to create paintings and sculptures vibrant with motion and containing speeding persons and objects. The great frustration the Narrator experiences in his attempts to arrest the flight of desired women and coveted objects arises from the multiplicity of points of view, of varying perspectives. With respect to the women he wants to possess and know intimately, there is a succession of *moi successifs* pursuing *toi successifs*.

> Ce n'était pas Albertine seule qui n'était qu'une succession de moments, c'était aussi moi-même. . . . Je n'étais pas un seul homme, mais le défilé d'une armée composite où il y avait des passionnés, des indifférents, des jaloux—des jaloux dont pas un n'était jaloux de la même femme. (III, 489)

Never is there a moment of coincidence with the desired creature because the Narrator wants to accomplish the impossible: to arrest what is mobile through his own perception. He cannot do this yet because he has not discovered how to convert these impressions to their artistic equivalent. In life things move and evolve, and this is the impression he wants to create in art: arrested motion; that it be the same and yet changing; that it be frozen and yet endowed with the potentiality of movement.

The Narrator desires only those girls who are in motion or those whom he sees while he is moving, which also endows them with fugacity. Proust describes this aspect of desire in a lapidary phrase: "les charmes de la passante sont généralement en relation directe avec la rapidité du passage" (I, 713). When a desired woman is immobilized, the spell is broken at once because the reduction in speed allows the Narrator to observe a flaw in her appearance, usually a facial blemish.[12] Even before he imprisons Albertine, she is no exception to this rule: "immobile auprès de moi, elle me semblait souvent une bien pauvre rose devant laquelle j'aurais bien voulu fermer les yeux pour ne pas voir tel défaut des pétales . . ." (II, 352). There is never a moment in his experience with the girls when what he learns through observation or possession matches his great expectations.

He especially desires those whom he calls the *passantes*; the name itself, designating girls who pass by, implies speed and movement through space. It is this quality of being the same and yet different that attracts him upon noticing the rapidity with which the young girls[13] at Balbec move through space: "Et même le plaisir que me donnait la petite bande, noble comme si elle était composée de vierges helléniques, venait de ce qu'elle avait quelque chose de la fuite des passantes sur la route" (I, 796).

Thus, the girls who attract the Narrator are walking or leaping on the beach or speeding past him on bicycles. The velocity of desirable beings is especially remarkable among very young girls. When he spots the little band of girls at Balbec, he is struck by their "beauté fluide, collective et mobile" (I, 790) and by "la beauté mobile de la jeunesse" (I, 905). This mobility has a triple source: (1) the rapid movements that are natural to the young; (2) the accelerated changes youths undergo as they mature; and (3) his urgent desire to possess them.

Through biological regeneration, the forms of men and women that inspired the paintings and sculptures of the past continue to live among us.[14] Unfortunately, each of the girls in motion contains within her the seeds of old age: "Hélas! dans la fleur la plus fraîche on peut distinguer les points imperceptibles qui pour l'esprit averti dessinent déjà ce qui sera, par la dessiccation ou la fructification des chairs aujourd'hui en fleur, la forme immuable et déjà prédestinée de la graine." Proust goes on to say that often we inherit not only our physical characteristics from our parents but our political beliefs as well: "tel dreyfusisme, tel cléricalisme, tel héroïsme national et féodal. . . . peut-être . . . tenons-nous de notre famille, comme les papillonacées la forme de leur graine, aussi bien les idées dont nous vivons que la maladie dont nous mourrons" (I, 891-92).

The great pendant to the scenes of girls in motion occurs many years later at the famous "Matinée de la princesse de Guermantes," where the Narrator, who has been absent from society for a long time, returns only to discover that all his former friends have been "greatly slowed down" by time and now are incredibly old, a mass of wrinkles, white hair, and vacillating limbs. He then discovers that the universe is in motion, carried away by time (III, 936). There is a precise reference to this phenomenon of immobility/decrepitude as he watches the young girls on the beach. This passage can be taken as Proust's *carpe diem:* "Il vient si vite, le moment où l'on n'a plus rien à attendre, où le corps est figé dans une immobilité qui ne promet plus de surprises, où l'on perd toute espérance en voyant . . . des cheveux qui tombent ou blanchissent, il est si court, ce matin radieux, qu'on en vient à n'aimer que les très jeunes filles . . ." (I, 905). In the same passage, he makes clear again the kinship between the girls and the sea:

> l'adolescence est antérieure à la solidification complète et de là vient qu'on éprouve auprès des jeunes filles ce rafraîchissement que donne le spectacle des formes sans cesse en train de changer, de jouer en une instable opposition qui fait penser à cette perpétuelle recréation des éléments primordiaux de la nature qu'on contemple devant la mer. (I, 906)

There is a variation on this theme with respect to Gilberte. She may be said to have a "mobile" face in that at times the Narrator notices traits she inherited from her father, while at others features belonging to her mother are apparent. Proust's concluding sentence describing the changing nature of Gilberte's face contains verbs that indicate a powerful liquid force at work: "on voyait ces deux natures de M. et de Mme Swann onduler, refluer, empiéter tour à tour l'une sur l'autre, dans le corps de cette Mélusine" (I, 565).

The mobility and fluidity of the girls in motion are often compared to the progression of musical phrases. At the first sighting of the little band, the theme of music is linked to their appearance on the beach: "toutes les gammes de couleurs . . . [l'ordre] confus comme une musique, un flottement harmonieux . . . la translation continue d'une beauté fluide, collective et mobile . . ." (I, 791).[15] The confusion between the hero's longings to possess both girls and music and the lessons he derives from them arises from Proust's elaboration of music and love as sacred and profane. Throughout *la Recherche,* the theme of music functions on two levels, linking Swann's pursuit of Odette to Vinteuil's compositions and, in a more complex way, linking Albertine to Mlle Vinteuil and the Narrator's search for his vocation as a writer. In the concluding chapter, "The Cosmos Builder," we will see how Proust resolves the theme of profane love and music, especially his desire to possess an unknown girl in motion.

In Proust's novel, there are always subtle connections among the themes of desired women, music, art, and other objects of beauty. There is a remarkable Proustian metaphor where the rich details in the stitchery of Odette's jacket—details not normally visible to observers but which the Narrator sees because Odette asks him to carry the garment—are likened to the infinitely complex, inaudible parts of a musical composition and the normally invisible statues high on the towers of a Gothic cathedral.[16] Thus, Odette's taste in clothing becomes music, architecture, and the landscape embracing the towers, sky, and an entire city. In Proust's universe beautiful things, often commonplace[17] and even unnoticeable, take on vast proportions and the "infiniment petit" suddenly becomes the "infiniment grand."

The frequent identifications by Swann and the Narrator of people as works of art may give the appearance of a dilettantish game, but it is also meant to establish the enduring link between the art of the past and the living descendants of its models. For example, watching the girls strolling down the beach in their sporting attire reminds the Narrator of classical friezes and paintings by

Giotto: "l'harmonie qui régnait entre les jeunes corps que j'avais vus se déployer sur la plage en une procession sportive digne de l'antique et de Giotto" (I, 807). In a later passage, where he rides in an elevator for the first time at the Grand-Hôtel, this new experience provokes a metaphor involving women in motion and classical art.[18] Proust is writing about kinetic impressions that had not been possible previously, or at least not with the intensity and frequency that were now being felt.[19] The chambermaids glimpsed on different floors of the hotel as the elevator rises are compared to a classical frieze: "Les couloirs des étages dérobaient une fuite de cámeristes et de courrières, belles sur la mer comme la frise[20] des Panathénées . . ." (II, 774).

The Narrator finds the members of the little band so extraordinary that he cannot imagine that someone like himself could ever become part of the picture (in this case a frieze or fresco) by joining the procession and being loved by such divinities: "cette supposition me paraissait enfermer en elle une contradiction aussi insoluble que si, devant quelque frise attique ou quelque fresque figurant un cortège, j'avais cru possible, moi spectateur, de prendre place, aimé d'elles, entre les divines processionnaires" (I, 795). In this case, as in many other instances, the Narrator sees himself in the guise of "le petit personnage," someone who is not worthy, who can only play a minor role. Throughout the novel, he is portrayed as a failure, which increases the dramatic interest and makes possible the spectacular reversal at the conclusion, when he discovers the secrets of his vocation. The only exceptions to this treatment of himself as unworthy occur during the moments of his social triumphs—triumphs that he later realizes are empty when he comprehends the vain, sterile nature of society.

Nowhere is the fugitive nature of time and all our impressions, memories, and desires better summed up than at the end of *Du côté de chez Swann*, where the Narrator—who does not yet understand how to use art to arrest time's fleeting nature—returns to the locales of his youth, hoping to find Mme Swann promenading along the allée des Acacias:

La réalité que j'avais connue n'existait plus. Il
suffisait que Mme Swann n'arrivât pas toute pareille
au même moment, pour que l'Avenue fût autre. Les
lieux que nous avons connus n'appartiennent qu'au
monde de l'espace où nous les situons pour plus de
facilité. Ils n'étaient qu'une mince tranche au milieu
d'impressions contiguës qui formaient notre vie
d'alors; le souvenir d'une certaine image n'est que
le regret d'un certain instant; et les maisons, les
routes, les avenues, sont fugitives, hélas! comme les
années. (I, 427)

Thus, the impressionistic, subjective nature of vision and
memory is confirmed by experience. Something as solid and stationary as a road or a house is constantly changing in relation to
the perceiver; a place cannot, in spite of its concreteness, retain
the scene he yearns to recapture. Girls and landscapes are all fugitive. Space, through desire, becomes time, and—at this point in
his experience—the latter is maddeningly elusive. What interests
Proust are the changes, the multiplicity, the constant evolution of
a person or object. This explains his acceptance and enlargement
of the aesthetics of the Impressionists, why in the Proustian universe there can never be a static, ultimate view but always a series
of new configurations of the cosmos.

Albertine

It is Albertine, above all, who represents the group that Proust
calls "les êtres de fuite" (creatures of flight), beings who are fugitive. She always exhibits an enthusiasm for sports and machines of
speed, including bicycles, automobiles, airplanes, and yachts. Fast
by nature, Albertine becomes, through the Narrator's obsessive
jealousy, a truly volatile figure:

Des yeux, par mensonge toujours immobiles et passifs,
mais dynamiques, mesurables par les mètres ou kilo-
mètres à franchir pour se trouver au rendez-vous voulu,
implacablement voulu. . . . Entre vos mains mêmes, ces

> êtres-là sont des êtres de fuite. Pour comprendre les
> émotions qu'ils donnent et que d'autres êtres même
> plus beaux, ne donnent pas, il faut calculer qu'ils sont
> non pas immobiles, mais en mouvement, et ajouter à
> leur personne un signe correspondant à ce qu'en
> physique est le signe qui signifie vitesse. (III, 91–92)

The sign in physics that stands for speed is V, shorthand for velocity, a V whose shape resembles that of wings, a motif that is often
used in connection with Albertine. The importance that Proust
attaches to the erotic themes of capture and flight can be seen in
the titles he gave to the two volumes of the novel where these
notions dominate: *La Prisonnière* and *La Fugitive*.[21]

From the very first mention of Albertine, Proust establishes the fact that she is mobile and that speed is one of her
essential traits. He does this through an ingenious use of the
English word "fast." It is Gilberte who first speaks to the Narrator of Albertine, a friend of hers from school, long before her
appearance on the beach at Balbec: "la fameuse 'Albertine'. Elle
sera sûrement très 'fast', mais en attendant elle a une drôle de
touche" (I, 512). We do not know what signs lead Gilberte to
make the prediction that Albertine will be "fast," but it is evident that Proust chose the English word because of its double
meaning: rapid movement through space and sexual promiscu-
ity. When the Narrator sees Albertine and the little band of girls
for the first time—unaware that he is seeing "the famous Albertine"—he wonders about their sexual mores because of their
sporting attire, the golf clubs, and the bicycle, accoutrements
and equipment that indicate agility, speed, and, for the Narrator, undefined social categories. Because of Albertine's appearance—especially the bicycle and golf clubs—and her insolent
manner, he makes the following assumption about the girls' sexual conduct:

> une fille aux yeux brillants, rieurs . . . sous un "polo"
> noir, enfoncé sur sa tête, qui poussait une bicyclette
> avec un dandinement de hanches si dégingandé, en

employant des termes d'argot si voyous[22] et criés si fort
. . . je conclus . . . que toutes ces filles appartenaient à
la population qui fréquente les vélodromes, et devaient
être les très jeunes maîtresses de coureurs cyclistes. . . .
dans aucune de mes suppositions, ne figurait celle
qu'elles eussent pu être vertueuses.[23] (I, 793)

Albertine and her friends appear so different in their
sporting attire from anyone he has known that he describes them
at one point as looking as though they had come from another
planet (I, 794). The Narrator is witnessing the rise of the less conservative elements of the middle class, who are the first to deck
themselves out in the recommended attire for sports activities:
"leur accoutrement tranchait sur celui des autres jeunes filles de
Balbec, parmi lesquelles quelques-unes . . . se livraient aux sports,
mais sans adopter pour cela une tenue spéciale" (I, 788).[24]

Both epithets he chooses for Albertine mention the sporting aspect of her appearance and have strong erotic connotations:
"la bacchante à bicyclette, la muse orgiaque du golf" (I, 873).
When he encounters one member of the little band, he reacts
with a strong physical attraction and an awareness of danger manifested by their diabolical motion: "c'était comme si j'avais vu pro-
jeté en face de moi dans une hallucination mobile et diabolique
un peu du rêve ennemi et pourtant passionnément convoité . . ."
(I, 832).

Eugen Weber points out that by the 1890s so many
women had taken to wearing trousers because of the popularity of
biking that the Minister of the Interior issued a circular advising
all prefectures that "the wearing of masculine clothes by women
is only tolerated for the purposes of velocipedic sport." Weber
goes on to say that biking thus provided a sanction for female
transvestism, giving women cyclists an ambiguous nature. The
adoption of men's clothing by the fair sex was seen by many
Frenchmen as signaling the disappearance of the last vestiges of
feminine modesty.[25] This attitude explains the Narrator's reaction
when he sees the members of the little band in sporting attire,

with Albertine bearing golf clubs and pushing a bicycle. We should thus realize that at the moment the hero first sights Albertine, she is—although he does not mention this aspect—an androgynous figure.[26] (See p. 55.)

Albertine seems almost overburdened with athletic equipment, as though Proust wants to make certain that we do not overlook this aspect of her personality and the sharp contrast between the sedentary Narrator and the athletic girl. Proust reminds us constantly about her love of sports. As we have seen, when the Narrator later holds Albertine in his arms, he finds in her body "toute la grâce féminine, marine et sportive, des jeunes filles que j'avais vues passer la première fois devant l'horizon du flot . . ." (II, 1020). The girl is aware that he does not share her tastes and calls him a lizard for being so sedentary: "Ah! vous aimez à faire le lézard? . . . Je vois que vous n'êtes pas comme moi, j'adore tous les sports!"[27] (I, 877).

Later, when the Narrator becomes a recluse, he regrets no longer being able to watch girls going by:

> Pour évaluer la perte que me faisait éprouver la réclusion . . . il eût fallu intercepter dans le long déroulement de la frise animée quelque fillette portant son linge ou son lait, la faire passer un moment, comme la silhouette d'un décor mobile entre les portants, dans le cadre de ma porte, et la retenir sous mes yeux. . . . (III, 138-39)

Framing is often used by Swann and the Narrator as a device that arrests motion and permits a temporary but illusory and incomplete form of possession. The comparison ends with analogies indicating the space covered by a desired figure in motion, the fugitive nature of the girls, and the tagging of birds and fish by naturalists in order to track the animals' migratory routes.

A Proustian formula for the phenomenon of the desirability of girls in motion might be expressed as follows: "Vélocité donne volupté." This is his variation on the romantic topos of

Jacques-Henri Lartigue, On the Road to Paris at
Rouzat, November 2, 1919 (© Association des Amis
de Jacques-Henri Lartigue).

"ennui" or spleen and the desire to travel in order to escape the present and the known. What we cannot have or seize is always a greater prize than something we already possess. On one occasion, the Narrator, lying in bed, now a sedentary hypochondriac like Aunt Léonie, smells gasoline from an automobile passing in the street; the association of this smell—not at all offensive or noxious to the reclining young man—and the speed of the car arouse in him the desire to take risks, explore new countries, and seduce an unknown woman, "faire l'amour dans des lieux nouveaux avec une femme inconnue" (III, 412).

We have already seen the importance of the bicycle in the erotic themes associated with Albertine and other *passantes*. The elusive, unobtainable, and ideal *femme-paysage* presents herself to his mind as a creature capable of great speed and altitude, an airborne goddess who soars above ordinary beings. In a passage that recalls the Narrator's first sighting of an airplane at Balbec, a girl mounting a bicycle becomes a winged being: "Pendant un instant la bicyclette tangua, et le jeune corps semblait s'être accru d'une voile, d'une aile immense; et bientôt nous vîmes s'éloigner à toute vitesse la jeune créature mi-humaine, mi-ailée, ange ou péri, poursuivant son voyage" (III, 172).

Bicycles were all the rage during the fin de siècle and belle epoque periods, appearing in many books, illustrations, posters, and photographs. Jacques-Henri Lartigue described winged bicycles (*aviettes*) of all kinds that were commonly seen at the turn of the century on such bicycle-racing tracks as the Buffalo in Paris. Given his love of speed and his determination to become a pilot, Agostinelli must have frequented such establishments. One will recall that when the Narrator meets Albertine and the little band of girls on the beach, it is the bicycle, their sporting attire, and vulgar language that make him assume they are the mistresses of bicycle racers. Though none of the "winged" cyclists at the Buffalo ever succeeded in rising above the ground, the intent was to gain enough speed so that the bicycle would become airborne. (See p. 57.) It is worth pointing out that the first men who did

Jacques–Henri Lartigue, Second race of the aviettes at the
Vélodrome in the Parc des Princes, Paris, November 24, 1912
(© Association des Amis de Jacques-Henri Lartigue).

succeed in flying, the brothers Orville and Wilbur Wright, were by profession bicycle mechanics. Here is Lartigue's description of the *aviettes*:

> Dimanche, à Paris. Je suis à Buffalo, où se trouve la piste de course de bicyclettes, pour voir les courses d'aviettes. . . . Une aviette est une bicyclette ailée. Les coureurs espèrent voler, voler comme des oiseaux sans moteur, sans vent, sans être tirés par une automobile. . . . Même si elles échouent toujours, elles sont bien amusantes à regarder, ces aviettes. Il y en a de toutes les formes et certaines sont étrangement belles.[28]

Another contemporary of Proust's, Apollinaire, also envisaged bicycles as winged creatures, in this case as angels. Here he is writing about the Futurists' "religion of speed":

> la nouvelle religion[29] de la vélocité—"Véloce" c'est-à-dire "ce vélo! . . ." cette exclamation quasi pantagruélique éveilla en vous je ne sais quel sentiment religieux qui transfigura la bécane en en faisant tourner les roues avec cette vitesse fulgurante qui était jusqu'ici l'apanage de cette classe d'anges appelée ofaninim qui dans l'angéologie hébraïque sont les roues du char céleste.[30]

Proust seems to have been the only writer of his time to use the bicycle and speed as a means of erotic arousal. In Maurice Leblanc's novel *Voici des ailes!*, in which bicycles play a major role, the two-wheeled machine is merely a vehicle for the narrative line. (See p. 59.) The bicycles do become liberating forces in that the two married couples who set out on a biking journey through Brittany and Normandy shed some of their traditional clothing and mores along the way as they adapt their life-style to the exhilarating freedom and unfettered movement afforded them by the bicycles. But motion itself, the sight of figures moving, is not presented as sexually stimulating, as it is in Proust. In Leblanc's novel, the erotic scene occurs when the women remove their blouses in

MAURICE LEBLANC

VOICI DES AILES!

DESSINS

DE

LUCIEN MÉTIVET

PARIS

PAUL OLLENDORFF, ÉDITEUR

28 *bis*, RUE DE RICHELIEU, 28 *bis*

1898

Maurice Leblanc's *Voici des ailes!*

the privacy of the open road and the couples end up falling in love with each others' spouses, with the new couples going their separate ways at the end. The Brittany and Normandy landscapes through which the foursome pedal are undistinguished and serve no purpose other than the routine one of providing a frame for the story. Proust's use of the bicycle is more complex than Leblanc's in that when the Narrator sights a girl in motion, his desire for the girl is aroused because of the multiple perspectives of a figure moving rapidly, causing him to assume that she is a rare, fugitive being.

It is through Albertine's love of speed that Proust pays homage to Agostinelli and not—in spite of what many commentators have said—in the scene where the Narrator sees his first airplane.[31] The airplane belongs to the vertical creative axis and not to the cycle of Albertine. Albertine is not Agostinelli; she is, above all, a great literary creation. But, at the same time, it cannot be denied that Agostinelli contributed to her portrait, the most obvious element they share being their love of speed, a passion born with the turn of the century and still alive today. It was to his passion for speed that Agostinelli eventually sacrificed his life. By emphasizing Albertine's love of speed, Proust underlines her fugitive nature and that of his chauffeur-secretary Agostinelli, who shared the same passion and fled Proust's apartment in order to take flying lessons. The following quote, describing Albertine's love of speed, might have been inspired by Agostinelli: "Je l'avais même laissée alors . . . s'absenter pendant trois jours, seule avec le chauffeur, et aller jusqu'auprès de Balbec, tant elle avait envie de faire de la route sur simple châssis, en grande vitesse" (III, 136).

When, in *La Fugitive*, the Narrator attempts to persuade Albertine to come back to him, he tempts her with presents that are also to be placed under the sign of speed: horses, a yacht, and a Rolls-Royce. The symbol of the Rolls-Royce, represented by its hood ornament, is a Winged Victory named Ecstasy. But the winged creature that he seeks to possess in

Albertine always eludes him and he will know ecstasy not in love but in art.

At about this time the Futurists were proclaiming—in a strident comparison that became a rallying cry of their movement—that an automobile was more beautiful than the *Winged Victory of Samothrace*:

> Nous déclarons que la splendeur du monde s'est enrichie d'une beauté nouvelle: la beauté de la vitesse. Une automobile de course avec son coffre orné de gros tuyaux tels des serpents à l'haleine explosive . . . une automobile rugissante, qui a l'air de courir sur de la mitraille, est plus belle que la *Victoire de Samothrace*.[32]

Proust, with an eye to the past as well as to the present and future, combines speed and the Winged Victory by having the Narrator offer a Rolls-Royce to Albertine. Given Proust's use of winged figures in combination with airplanes, automobiles, and bicycles, the Futurists' choice of the *Winged Victory of Samothrace* as an example of worthless ancient art seems particularly ill-advised.

The Narrator's entire existence with Albertine will be remembered as having taken place under the sign of speed. Indeed, in the concluding passages describing their relationship, Proust insists on the elusive nature of the fleeting girl:

> Tout cela qui n'était pour moi que souvenir avait été pour elle action, action précipitée, comme celle d'une tragédie, vers une mort rapide. . . . Comme l'engrenage[33] avait été serré, comme l'évolution de notre amour avait été rapide, et, malgré quelques retardements . . . le dénouement rapide!" (III, 499-500).[34]

CHAPTER 4

Speed and Desire

The association of agitation and motion with unrequited desire appears often in literature. Wallace Fowlie points out that such motifs occur in Dante: "in the second circle [of hell] . . . the sins of carnality are punished and . . . a continuous wind storm buffets the spirits. This is agitation, ceaseless movement designating the insistence of sexual demands."[1] Jean Milly reminds us of Proust's depiction of the rocking motion of sleep in passages from *Jean Santeuil* and the opening pages of *la Recherche*. Milly also finds French literary antecedents in Flaubert's erotic oscillations in *Madame Bovary* and *L'Education sentimentale*, pointing out similar passages in Proust's pastiche of Flaubert as well as in the passage in *la Recherche* on Albertine asleep: "Ce bercement est aussi lié à un rythme sexuel, comme le montre assez la suite du passage."[2] In one of the most unusual erotic scenes in literature, the sleeping Albertine becomes the incarnation of the sea as the Narrator embarks upon the tide of her sleep and makes love to his unconscious prisoner (III, 72).

The use of such motifs by Flaubert is quite different from those in *la Recherche*. Flaubert's method is more traditional in that movement, such as the carriage in *Madame Bovary*, is a natural enticement and accompaniment for the thrusting and undulating action of lovemaking. Riding (*chevaucher*) has often been used in French as slang for copulating. In Proust, however, there is a significant departure from the traditional association of motion and desire: it is the motion both real and metaphorical that provokes desire and makes possession impossible. The greater the prize, the greater the speed acquired by the desired person to escape. As we have seen, even physical contact is not sufficient to slow down the speed and may even accelerate it. Once a woman has been possessed or is no longer desired, she loses her speed and becomes worthless, as does Albertine, "une pesante esclave," a Winged Victory whose wings have been clipped.[3]

The other major character whose speed takes on important thematic dimensions is Robert de Saint-Loup. There are significant parallels between him and Albertine, the most obvious of these being their marine origins (both are seen for the first time on the beach at Balbec) and their sexual ambiguity. It is especially characters suspected of being homosexual who are endowed with exceptional speed: Albertine, Saint-Loup, and Legrandin. The speed of these three is due in large part to the ambiguity of their sexual orientation. The confusion that such ambiguity causes the Narrator is expressed in an observation concerning the nature of Albertine's sexuality: "l'incertitude morale est une cause plus grande de difficulté à une exacte perception visuelle que ne serait un défaut matériel de l'œil . . ." (III, 140). Since he cannot determine the exact nature of her sexuality, he does not know who she is nor how to define her because he does not know how to look at her. With such hindered vision, he cannot see her as she really is and is therefore unable to seize and possess her.

Proust demonstrates this point in the case of Charlus. Once the nobleman's sexual orientation is revealed to the Narrator in the opening scene of *Sodome et Gomorrhe*, his bizarre behavior is no longer a mystery and the result is "une révolution, pour mes yeux. . . . Jusque-là, parce que je n'avais pas compris, je n'avais pas vu. . . . C'est la raison qui ouvre les yeux; une erreur dissipée nous donne un sens de plus" (II, 613).

We never do know for a fact that Albertine engaged in lesbian relationships, but there is no doubt that Saint-Loup and Legrandin were homosexuals in their later years. Saint-Loup is a good example of the complexity of Proustian characters: he is duplicitous and cruel in his relations with his wife yet courageous in battle and loving to his men, ultimately sacrificing his life for them. The disappearance and death in battle of Proust's friend Bertrand de Fénelon may have determined the evolution of Saint-Loup's character in terms of his behavior in battle, his heroic death, and the eventual revelation of his homosexuality.[4] When World War I began, Fénelon was serving in the diplomatic corps and was therefore exempt from mobilization, yet he volunteered for duty at the front.[5] Reactions to the shift in Saint-Loup's character have varied considerably among critics and writers. According to those who study sexuality, there is nothing unusual about such changes in sexual orientation.[6] After giving a number of pertinent examples, Proust expresses the following maxim about such dramatic changes in a person's nature: "la nature que nous faisons paraître dans la seconde partie de notre vie n'est pas toujours . . . notre nature première développée ou flétrie . . . elle est quelquefois une nature inverse, un véritable vêtement retourné" (I, 434).

The speed with which Legrandin and Saint-Loup are endowed in *Le Temps retrouvé* results primarily from their desire to shield their homosexuality. Legrandin, after years of extremely cautious behavior, has become a more sexually active homosexual and is afraid of being found out. Thus, he has become "plus élancé et rapide. . . . Cette vélocité avait d'ailleurs des raisons psychologiques. Il avait l'habitude d'aller dans certains mauvais lieux où il aimait qu'on ne le vît ni entrer, ni sortir, il s'y engouffrait." Charlus, on the other hand, now complacent in his "vice" and no longer bothering to hide it, has become heavy and slow ("alourdi et alenti") (III, 665).

The passage describing Legrandin fleeing places of ill repute is practically identical to one on Saint-Loup; had Proust lived to revise the final sections of the novel, he may well have eliminated the Legrandin passage or varied it somewhat. The close similarity of the two passages is not pointed out by the editors of the Pléiade edition. "[Saint-Loup] était devenu plus élancé,

plus rapide, effet contraire d'un même vice. . . . Il avait l'habitude
d'aller dans certains mauvais lieux où, comme il aimait qu'on ne
le vît ni enter ni sortir, il s'engouffrait. . . . Et cette allure de coup
de vent lui était restée" (III, 698-99). This change in speed does
not seem appropriate for Saint-Loup since he has always naturally
moved rapidly through space, as we can see from the following
passage describing him prior to his homosexual phase:

> Saint-Loup salua [un officier] et immobilisa la per-
> pétuelle instabilité de son corps le temps de tenir la
> main à la hauteur du képi. Mais il l'y avait précipitée
> avec tant de force, se redressant d'un mouvement si sec,
> et, aussitôt le salut fini, la fit retomber par un
> déclenchement si brusque en changeant toutes les posi-
> tions de l'épaule, de la jambe et du monocle, que ce
> moment fut moins d'immobilité que d'*une vibrante ten-*
> *sion où se neutralisaient les mouvements excessifs* qui
> venaient de se produire et ceux qui allaient com-
> mencer. (II, 73; emphasis added)

It is clear from the italicized phrase that Proust is sensitive to and
fascinated by the precise moment of transition between stasis and
kinesis.

The best explanation for Proust's presentation of an even
more accelerated Saint-Loup is that his rapidity now has a different motivation. Perhaps more than any other author before him,
Proust renders consciously and convincingly the attitudes and
motions of his characters. Saint-Loup moves so rapidly through
space that even his monocle flies before him: "partant au pas de
charge, précédé de son monocle qui volait en tous sens . . ." (II,
74).[7] Saint-Loup's act of slapping the homosexual who approaches
him in the streets of Paris is a very modern description of an
object moving through space: "tout d'un coup, comme apparaît
au ciel un phénomène astral, je vis des corps ovoïdes prendre avec
une rapidité vertigineuse toutes les positions qui leur permettaient
de composer, devant Saint-Loup, une instable constellation.
[C'étaient] les deux poings de Saint-Loup, multipliés par leur

vitesse à changer de place . . ." (II, 182). This passage is just one among many examples of Proust's fascination with speed and his attempt to describe objects moving through space.

Saint-Loup's rapid movements here may seem free of homosexual associations until we look more closely at the text and consider the biographical origins of the scene. Saint-Loup's beauty is made clear any number of times by the Narrator, who also points out his extraordinary resemblance to his aunt, the duchesse de Guermantes (II, 80). It is his beauty that attracts the shabby homosexual who accosts him on the street in Paris. Saint-Loup beats the man in a scene that convinces the Narrator and the reader of Saint-Loup's heterosexuality—which we had not, in any case, had any reason to doubt, especially given his arduous, desperate pursuit of Rachel.

Once Saint-Loup's latent homosexuality is given full expression, he has psychological reasons to move rapidly and furtively through space. His speed is depicted as a sign of shame when he tries to leave Jupien's brothel (referred to as the Temple of Dishonor) without being seen, and where, without his realizing it, he has also left behind his military medal, the Croix de guerre. In the dark, the Narrator does not recognize his friend:

> je vis sortir rapidement . . . un officier. . . . [ce qui me frappa était] la disproportion extraordinaire entre le nombre de points différents par où passa son corps et le petit nombre de secondes pendant lesquelles cette sortie, qui avait l'air de la sortie tentée par un assiégé, s'exécuta. . . . *Le militaire capable d'occuper en si peu de temps tant de positions différentes dans l'espace* avait disparu. . . . (III, 810; emphasis added)

Saint-Loup's mobility is such an important feature of his characterization that it is possible to trace in statuary the evolution of the young aristocratic friend, from a cavalier on friezes and anonymous sculptures of the romanesque and Gothic periods to a noble *gisant* after his death in battle.

> Je regardais Saint-Loup, et je me disais que c'est une
> jolie chose quand il n'y a pas de disgrâce physique pour
> servir de vestibule aux grâces intérieures, et que les ailes
> du nez sont délicates et d'un dessin parfait . . . que le
> véritable *opus francigenum*, dont le secret n'a pas été
> perdu depuis le XIIIe siècle . . . ce ne sont pas tant les
> anges de pierre de Saint-André-des-Champs que les
> petits Français, nobles, bourgeois ou paysans, au visage
> sculpté avec cette délicatesse et cette franchise restées
> aussi traditionnelles qu'au porche fameux, mais encore
> créatrices. (II, 409)

It is just after the comparison to the statues of Saint-André-des-Champs that a scene occurs in a restaurant where Saint-Loup, running to bring the Narrator a coat, is described as a figure on a frieze, with each successive position of the young cavalier's body as he moves through space clearly depicted. This outing with Saint-Loup is called "le soir de l'amitié" (II, 413). On a very cold evening, the two friends are dining in a restaurant where a number of Saint-Loup's friends are also present, among them the prince de Foix. Saint-Loup wants his noble companions to meet his brilliant, literary friend but leaves it up to the Narrator to say whether or not he would like to meet them. The would-be author says that he prefers to dine alone with Saint-Loup. Suddenly Saint-Loup disappears and goes into the adjoining room, where the prince de Foix is having his meal, and returns with the Prince's vicuna coat, which he has borrowed to warm his cold friend. Since the latter is blocked in at his table, Saint-Loup leaps up on the cushioned seat that rings the walls of the restaurant and runs toward his shivering friend. Electrical wires jut out of the wall and extend to the lamps on the tables, requiring Saint-Loup to leap over the wires as he runs. Where patrons are seated along the bench, he must surmount the back of it. At this point applause breaks out among those in the restaurant who admire the cavalier's agility. Proust compares Saint-Loup's body to that of a horse on an obstacle course and a rider on a frieze.

Proust sees with the eye of a painter or sculptor who, after having studied Etienne-Jules Marey's chronophotographs (as did Marcel Duchamp before creating his stop-action paintings), wants to represent the human body in each of its successive positions as it moves through space. Proust is not interested in depicting a static figure as seen in a painting or statue, but the multiple, dashing figures that a handsome individual embodies as he moves forward in space and time:

> je sentais que ce plaisir tenait à ce que chacun des mouvements développés le long du mur, sur la banquette, avait sa signification, sa cause, dans la nature individuelle de Saint-Loup peut-être, mais plus encore dans celle que par la naissance et par l'éducation il avait héritée de sa race. (II, 413)

This frieze, containing proof of Saint-Loup's noble heritage and training, is not unlike a historical, genealogical chart, the mature version of the various stages of embryonic development that repeat the evolution of the species. Here it is the racial history of one individual who is representative of his genus. Saint-Loup, who wants to inspire true friendship based on the value of the individual, would not be pleased to know that the Narrator sees him, in spite of his liberal ideas, as a product of race and breeding. If Saint-Loup's velocity in moving through space is later a result of shame and fear, in this passage it is a sign of nobility:

> une noble libéralité qui, ne tenant aucun compte de tant d'avantages matériels . . . les lui faisait fouler aux pieds, comme ces banquettes de pourpre effectivement et symboliquement trépignées, pareilles à un chemin somptueux qui ne plaisait à mon ami qu'en lui permettant de venir vers moi avec plus de grâce et de rapidité; telles étaient les qualités, toutes essentielles à l'aristocratie, qui, derrière ce corps non pas opaque et obscur comme eût été le mien, mais significatif et limpide, transparaissaient, comme à travers une œuvre d'art la puissance industrieuse, efficiente qui l'a créée, et

> rendaient les mouvements de cette course légère que
> Robert avait déroulée le long du mur, aussi intelligibles
> et charmants que ceux de cavaliers sculptés sur une
> frise. (II, 413-14)

The Narrator is even tempted to find an aesthetic pleasure in the sight of his friend in motion, but he realizes that this is only the result of his delight in seeing "ce jeune cavalier déroulant le long du mur la frise de sa course." He now recognizes the intelligence and the sovereign freedom of Saint-Loup's movements that together form the image of "la parfaite amitié" (II, 415).

The most important of the original models for Saint-Loup was, as I have suggested, Proust's aristocratic friend Bertrand de Fénelon. The scene in the restaurant was based on an incident with Fénelon that took place around 1902 at Larue's restaurant in the place de la Madeleine, a favorite haunt of Proust's and his friends.[8] The original event was described in *Jean Santeuil* (IV, 447-55) in a section dealing with Jean's closest friend, Bertrand de Réveillon, whose name echoes that of his real-life counterpart. Although George Painter considers this episode to be "one of the most ill-written (which is saying a great deal) in the whole novel," the passage remains an extremely interesting one because of the light it sheds on Proust's concept of desire and possession; moreover, it allows us to judge the great distance Proust traveled as a writer between *Jean Santeuil* and *la Recherche*. The latter fully orchestrates themes and develops characters that were only sketched in the abandoned novel. *Jean Santeuil,* like most early works and drafts, is closer to autobiography than is *la Recherche*.

Overall, the presentation of the scene is the same: Bertrand has received the perfect heritage, both genetically and culturally, and yet he is totally indifferent to the prestige of his family. He possesses as second nature all the grace, tact, and noblesse oblige that come from such a background. This nobility is manifested in knowing when and how to execute the perfect movement required by a given circumstance, "faire en n'importe quelle circonstance de la vie . . . le mouvement qu'il faut" (451).

Bertrand's attractiveness is the result of breeding, education, and demeanor. Saint-Loup will retain his élan and beauty, but Proust will reveal considerable flaws in his character. As we know, the Narrator is at first dazzled by the apparent brilliance of the aristocratic world, later becoming more contemptuous of the nobility than of any other class.

There are major stylistic differences between the earlier and later versions of the scene in the restaurant, which is not surprising when one recalls that *Jean Santeuil* is in no way a finished work, existing partly in fragments. Often, as is the case here, Proust experiments with different narrative voices within the same passage. For example, it is Bertrand who speaks when he explains to Jean why he ran along the bench to bring Jean the coat; Jean is his preferred friend, and Bertrand, who places the coat at Jean's feet as he would a trophy, is not afraid of making himself ridiculous by rendering this service. But what makes the passage especially interesting is the light it sheds on Proust's concept of desire and possession, for here Jean *does* manage—as the Narrator never does with the girls in motion—to possess the intended gift of Bertrand's entire past through the latter's movement in space. For a page and a half Proust shows Bertrand making a present of his past to Jean through the power of his leg muscles, which had been developed during the years of his youth when they did not know each other.[9] It is Bertrand who speaks:

> "Années passées, Education différente, tout ce qui est impossible à ressaisir . . . tenez tout entières dans la souplesse de mon jarret pour qu'en courant vers lui [Jean] je les lui apporte et qu'il n'y ait plus rien entre nous!" . . . tous ces exercices brillants qu'il [Jean] n'avait jamais pratiqués, toute cette force si éloignée de sa faiblesse étaient autant d'amis de Bertrand dont il était inconsciemment jaloux . . . (IV, 453-54).

Unlike *la Recherche,* where only the Narrator's thoughts are known, in *Jean Santeuil* we read Bertrand's thoughts as he brings the gift of his past to Jean. Thanks to this gift, the jealous desire to possess a beloved's mysterious past—which haunts the Narrator in the case of Albertine, causing him to spend years (even after her death) reconstructing that past—is abolished for Santeuil ("dissipant toute jalousie"). Jean possesses Bertrand's entire past and present being. We again read Bertrand's thoughts: "ce passé insaisissable . . . Ces années lointaines te rendaient triste. . . . Hé bien! les voici toutes . . . je te les amène avec moi dans ma course . . . elles sont à toi et pour toi." Then we read Jean's thoughts: "son être tout entier avec tout son passé rassemblé. . . . toute sa vie dans le présent qu'il nous fait [de son] affection . . ." (IV, 454).

The traces of homosexual desire evident in Jean's infatuation with Bertrand are given over entirely in la Recherche to the Narrator's desire for girls in motion. In the case of the Narrator's relationship with Saint-Loup, all elements of jealousy and possession are removed and resolved in a rare moment of "parfaite amitié." We know that in the mature novel the desire described in Jean Santeuil becomes monstrous and unattainable by ordinary and even extraordinary means: physical possession and imprisonment of the desired girl do not reveal to him the mystery of her past and the secrets of her being.

Proust's awareness of the speed with which a desired person appears to move through space predates by years his encounter with Agostinelli. It seems safe to say that Albertine and Saint-Loup are both modeled on Bertrand de Fénelon as far as their quality of speed is concerned. Both are androgynous figures based on male and female versions of the same type. Proust had a predilection for finding the male in the female, and vice versa, as is evident from the questionnaires he filled out as well as in numerous passages from his letters and other writings.[10] Agostinelli's fascination with speed confirmed a tendency that was already present in the characters in the novel and probably caused Proust to associate Albertine more closely with machines of motion, such as the bicycle, car, and train, but not the airplane. (This will be explained in a later chapter.)

Albertine and Saint-Loup are joined by death and the sea. While thinking about Saint-Loup's death, the Narrator remembers the first time he saw Saint-Loup on the beach at Balbec. His eyes were green and mobile like the sea, "ses yeux verts bougeants comme la mer" (III, 847). The young soldier gave his life without considering the cost, just as in bringing his friend the coat he had run across the bench "pour ne pas me déranger" (III, 847). The Narrator then reviews all the tableaux stored up in his memories of Saint-Loup. It is this same rapidity that, to a large degree, marks the kinship between Saint-Loup and Albertine, a kinship pointed out to us by Proust himself: "[leurs vies] si vite terminées . . . leurs deux vies avaient chacune un secret parallèle et que je n'avais pas soupçonné" (III, 848).

The multiple images of speed associated with both characters are often remarkably similar. When Saint-Loup is killed in action during World War I, the rapid cavalier is compared to the sculpted figures on Proust's imaginary church, Saint-André-des-Champs, whose faces, as we have seen, are said to be the true French œuvres, "le véritable *opus francigenum.*" Although Saint-Loup is presented as an ideal type and is compared, along with Albertine and Françoise, to the statues at Saint-André-des-Champs, Proust is careful to deny a living person the status of art (III, 415). Proust's comparison between the permanence that resides in the timeless stone and the living, biological models who continue to perpetuate the nobility of the sculpted faces in living statues representing all the classes is another variation of the novelist's conception of artistic expression and the force of time: the marriage of kinesis (the living descendants of those who were the models for the statues) and stasis (the permanent works of art).[11] According to Proust's representation of life, the fields of biology, history, and art are parallel bands on the frieze of human existence.

Proust's depiction of figures in motion may have been influenced by Eadweard Muybridge's stop-action photographs and Etienne-Jules Marey's chronophotography. The latter was an innovative technique that took "pictures of time" by capturing a figure or an animal at different stages of a trajectory, making possible the exact representation of figures in motion, which artists had attempted to do for centuries in their statues, friezes, and paintings. This major photographic innovation led directly to the birth of moving pictures. Proust does not mention chronophotography by name, but it is highly likely that he knew of Marey's accomplishments. In addition to being an expert on cholera,[12] he is credited with the invention of the sphygmograph, which recorded the pulse rate and led to the invention of the blood-pressure monitor, the sphygmomanometer.

Eadweard Muybridge's photographs, which represented a pioneering effort in the scientific study of motion in 1879, were the result of a wager made by horse fancier Leland Stanford. Stanford was convinced that all four hooves of a trotting horse left the ground at the same time. He thus set out, as *Pacific Life* stated on June 22, 1878, "to reproduce the action of a horse at every point in his stride" and hired Muybridge to figure out a way to meet the technological challenge. Proust seems to have known the famous twenty-four-frame sequence of a horse, "Occident Trotting," which had been filmed by Muybridge using twenty-four cameras and magnetic shutter trippers. (See p. 75.) A sequel with another horse, "Sallie Gardner Galloping," produced photographs that contradicted the way galloping horses had been depicted since primitive times. The photographs showed that Sallie's legs were bunched or akimbo rather than extended in pairs.[13]

The first photographic analogy used in *la Recherche* refers to the pictures of a running horse seen in a kinetoscope, a hand-cranked device for viewing a sequence of pictures of a changing scene on an endless band of film, thereby creating the illusion of motion. This is mentioned in the opening pages of Combray, when the Narrator is lying in bed and dreaming about his past, which he experiences as a chaos filled with kinetic energy, establishing the fugitive nature of memory and being. In his slumbering uncertainty as to which of the rooms from his past he is really occupying, he says that his mind cannot distinguish among the

Eadweard Muybridge's "Occident Trotting" (Department of Special Collections, Stanford University Libraries).

various suppositions any more than we isolate "en voyant un cheval courir, les positions successives que nous montre le kinéto-scope" (I, 7).

Proust's texts, like chronophotographs and Marcel Duchamp's paintings, break up motion into immobile segments. What Muybridge and Marey sought to document in their photographic series was motion frozen in succeeding frames, the precise fragmentation of time. Louis Bolle has pointed out that Proust often decomposes movement into immobile segments.[14] Such a technique is the literary equivalent of Duchamp's *Nude Descending a Staircase No. 2* (1912), a work produced directly under the influence of Marey's chronophotographs, as the painter stated in an interview. (See p. 77.) What caught Duchamp's attention was the way Marey dressed his subjects in black costumes, with white lines and dots on their limbs and joints, so that as the subjects ran, the position of their arms and legs could be photographed at a speed of one hundred times a second. (See p. 79.) When developed, each photograph revealed the successive positions of a figure in motion:

> J'avais vu dans l'illustration d'un livre de Marey comment il indiquait les gens qui font de l'escrime, ou les chevaux au galop, avec un système de pointillé délimitant les différents mouvements. . . . C'est ce qui m'a donné l'idée de l'exécution du "nu descendant un escalier."[15]

Proust has developed the literary equivalent of Marey's various points of frozen animation to depict the successive positions of Saint-Loup's body in motion. This keen observer brings to the reader's attention the quantity of positions relative to a very brief span of time occupied by a body moving through space: "je vis sortir rapidement . . . un officier. . . . [ce qui me frappa était] *la disproportion extraordinaire entre le nombre de points différents par où passa son corps et le petit nombre de secondes pendant lesquelles cette sortie. . . s'exécuta . . .*" (III, 810; emphasis added).

Marcel Duchamp, *Nude Descending a Staircase, no. 2,*
1912 (Philadelphia Museum of Art: The Louise and
Walter Arensberg Collection).

In passages such as these, Proust produces literary chronophotographs by creating word pictures that are multiple exposures of a person in motion. There are also examples of chronophotographic descriptions of characters who are glimpsed only once in the story. Here is Proust's multiple portrait of a waiter who rushes about serving tables in the dining room and in the adjacent garden. The successive living statues created by the waiter's motion among the tables are tinged with classical sculptural elements:

> Le garçon à la figure rose, *aux cheveux noirs tordus comme une flamme,* s'élançait dans toute cette vaste étendue . . . parfois au loin, dans la salle à manger, parfois plus près, mais au dehors, servant des clients qui avaient préféré déjeuner dans le jardin, on l'apercevait tantôt ici, tantôt là, comme des statues successives d'*un jeune dieu courant.* . . . (II, 1016; emphasis added)

The Lubricious Train

In *la Recherche,* the train is a source of erotic experience in that, like other machines of motion—bicycle and automobile but not the airplane—it is sexually stimulating. Such a belief was not merely the product of a literary mind but was held by many in the medical and scientific community of Proust's day. Freud and other contemporary psychiatrists were convinced that the shaking motion of modern machines incited sexual stimulation:

> Shaking sensations experienced in wagons and railroad trains exert such a fascinating influence on older children that all boys . . . wish to become conductors and drivers. They are wont to ascribe to railroad activities an extraordinary and mysterious interest and during the age of phantastic activity (shortly before puberty) they utilize these as a nucleus for exquisite sexual symbolisms. The desire to connect railroad traveling with sexuality apparently originates from the pleasurable character of the sensation of motion.[16]

Etienne-Jules Marey, Runner on an Inclined Plane,
Geometric Chronophotograph (Collège de France, Paris).

It was commonly believed that the new machines were sexually stimulating to women, even to the point of causing sensual madness. Eugen Weber quotes from a newspaper article in which women are warned against sewing machines and bicycles— two machines with very different purposes but both requiring women to pedal.[17] Another contemporary of Proust's, Dr. Ludovic O'Followell, expressed his belief in *Bicyclette et organes génitaux* that the sewing machine was an even more dangerous source of sexual stimulation than the bicycle, although the latter could " 'procure genital satisfactions, voluptuous sensations' and a kind of 'sportive masturbation.' "[18]

Milton Miller, in his psychoanalytical study of Proust, noticed a number of scenes where Proust sets erotic encounters in trains:

> The orgy of patrons of Jupien's Temple of Dishonor in the underground tunnel during air raids links Proust's images of trains and sexuality in a way that is close to consciousness. Trains bring new arrivals and also take people away: they are a combined symbol of love and death. . . . Charlus first meets Morel at a railroad station. Marcel's envy of Albertine regarding Saint-Loup is on a train, as is Bloch's affair with Odette.[19] And the separation and reunion of Marcel and his mother are at trains. Trains are related to time, death, birth, and sexuality.[20]

Miller might have mentioned a number of other scenes. The revelation by Albertine concerning her close friendship with Mlle Vinteuil—certainly the pivotal scene as far as the action in the second half of the novel is concerned—takes place in a train; Albertine and the Narrator often engage in amorous embraces on the train en route to Mme Verdurin's rented summer villa: "[le] trajet en chemin de fer . . . dans une voiture noire . . . cramponnés l'un à l'autre" (II, 1096). It is during one such session that he and Albertine see the princesse Sherbatoff for the first time and mistake her for a procuress, "une maquerelle en voyage."

Sherbatoff is another of Proust's androgynous creatures, "[une femme] à l'expression masculine" (II, 858).

Alain Robbe-Grillet finds eroticism in the very structure and *movement* of literature and cinema. The specific example he gives is that of a train in an early film by the Lumière brothers, *L'Arrivée du train en gare de La Ciotat*: "all films are erotic films, ever since the famous film by Lumière, where all you see is a train coming into the station at La Ciotat, near Nice—a typically erotic image. . . . all the railway images and things like that which occur in numerous films . . . are erotic images. . . ."[21]

As we have seen, Swann first makes love to Odette in a moving carriage. Indeed, it is the sudden, unexpected movement of the carriage that initiates the lovemaking; Swann, a notorious womanizer who is unnaturally timid toward Odette, seizes upon the pretext of straightening the orchids she is wearing in her bosom in order to begin his amorous caresses. In a famous scene from *Madame Bovary*, Léon makes love to Emma for the first time in a carriage, with drawn curtains, hired to meander all over Rouen.[22]

Charlus makes a specialty of pursuing train conductors and coach drivers, preferably those who are drunk late in the evening and therefore more easily seduced. He is persistent enough to change cars two or three times if necessary, and once he even travels as far as Orléans in pursuit of a young conductor. This is a trait that Charlus shared with the American poet Walt Whitman: "[Whitman] pursued those who were teasingly accessible but equivocal. Motion was important. Young men who worked on streetcars, railways, ferries, whose very work suggested undefined potentiality, lured him particularly."[23] It is precisely the unknown, mysterious, yet apparently extremely desirable qualities of the fugitive girls that attract the Narrator, just as the same qualities in young men appeal to Charlus.

As Miller has observed, trains are used at crucial points in the plot to signal moments of transition in the Narrator's development as he becomes a mature, independent being. When dreaming of a trip to Florence, he had thought of a train station as a magical locale in which the voyager moved almost imperceptibly from the point of destination to the longed-for city (I, 644). When the time comes for him to depart for Balbec and be separated from his mother, the Saint-Lazare station, with its great glass roof, becomes a sinister place, "un de ces grands ateliers vitrés . . . qui déployait au-dessus de la ville éventrée un de ces immenses ciels crus et gros de menaces. . . ." So dreaded is the moment of separation from his mother that he compares the scene to a crucifixion by Mantegna or Veronese, "acte terrible et solennel comme un départ en chemin de fer ou l'érection de la Croix" (I, 645).

As we saw earlier, during periods when Odette is absent, Swann, in a jealous frenzy to track her down, spends hours poring over maps and the train schedule, which he calls "le plus enivrant des romans d'amour" (I, 293). We recall that Swann and the Narrator both imagine the breakup with their mistresses as a train journey away from the countries identified with the women. This leads us to conclude that while Proust presents real trains as sources of erotic stimulation and sexual encounters, in dream-like states the train is seen as a means of escape from erotic obsession. As we shall see in the concluding chapter, the train is also a transition point in the Narrator's journey from horizontal searcher to vertical visionary.

Stasis and Kinesis

The nature of the desirable other is elusive and ultimately unknowable because it is unattainable, as is demonstrated in the passages where Proust depicts successive selves and multiple perspectives. The Narrator, in the center of such a vortex of impressions, is frustrated by the ambiguity, both sexual and aesthetic, that is engendered by this centrifugal system. Throughout his quest, he attempts to seize impressions of girls, objects, and landscapes in order to examine them and penetrate their mystery. In these attempts to arrest what is fleeting, the Narrator uses analogies from photography, painting, sculpture, and architecture. Once Albertine is dead, he remains in the horizontal realm of physical explorations, entering a phase of degradation when he is questioned about corrupting a minor (III, 443). He even resorts to voyeurism when he hires lesbians to perform what he assumes to have been Albertine's amorous practices (III, 550-51).

The velocity of time is a direct challenge to the artist who wants to save his world from destruction. Henri Bergson stated in *Matière et mémoire* that "to perceive means to immobilize."[24] In *la Recherche,* the protagonist attempts to achieve this immobilization of desired objects and women on a number of occasions, but what the Proustian narrator realizes is that everything is constantly in motion; even those things that appear immobile are not permanently fixed but undergo mutation. Not only are they evolving—as is the person perceiving them—but they cannot be perceived fully by a single or even multiple perspectives. The task of the Proustian artist, then, is to immobilize yet *at the same time* create the impression of movement, life, and evolution in order to combine stasis and kinesis. The impression of movement and change will be rendered vertically through a layering technique (*épaisseur*)[25] and elevation imagery; it will be rendered horizontally through images of statues, friezes, photographs, and descriptions that are the literary equivalents of chronophotographs.

For Proust, the only enduring and enriching perception is made possible by art. The work of art represents the ultimate act of slowing down, but for the Proustian artist it must also contain, without stifling it, the potentiality of motion. This long process of search, exposure, development, contemplation, and, ultimately, expression must come from the artist's deepest and truest self as he strives to create his vision of the world. This vision, which will contain layers of experience and memory dating back to different epochs, will take into account the permanent, creative self (*le moi profond*) as well as what Proust calls the "successive selves":

> On dit, et c'est ce qui explique l'affaiblissement pro-
> gressif de certaines affections nerveuses, que notre sys-
> tème nerveux vieillit. Cela n'est pas vrai seulement
> pour notre moi permanent, qui se prolonge pendant

> toute la durée de notre vie, mais pour tous nos moi suc-
> cessifs qui, en somme, le composent en partie. (III, 696)

What Proust strives for in his art is the combination of both the
static and the kinetic in order to create an epic tableau of his era,
while at the same time giving the impression that his work is a
living, moving, organic entity and not just a pale reproduction of
everyday reality. Proust combines the ephemeral and the eternal;
false starts, errors, and wrong paths later prove to be the right
ones as the Narrator describes for us the twists and turns of his
search for the truth.

The importance of rendering the impression of motion
can be seen in various passages that Proust wrote for the final,
grand recognition scene in *la Recherche* where various stimuli of
touch and sound, such as the noise of a spoon hitting a plate
or the texture of a napkin, resurrect the living memory of the
dining room at Balbec and visions of the sea. In the following
notes for the concluding section of the novel, one can feel
Proust's excitement as he sets for himself the goal of making his
work lifelike:

> Comme les ailes de chérubins qui *font mille tours* en un
> moment toutes les sensations que j'éprouvais en même
> temps que celle-là, l'odeur de la chambre, le désir du
> déjeuner, l'incertitude de la promenade, la présence du
> plafond pyramidal au-dessus de moi, tout cela attaché
> ensemble et *tournant comme les mille ailes* des chérubins
> qui *font [mille] tours à la minute*, caresse mon âme du
> souvenir d'un monde évanoui, mais d'*un monde qui non
> pas tableau plat comme les tableaux de la mémoire* à toutes
> les dimensions, toutes les qualités sensibles, est accom-
> pagné de mon être d'alors, de ma pensée d'alors, *tourne
> complet, plein, existant réellement total.*[26]

In the plenitude of lucid, creative contemplation he realizes that his goal is not to reproduce flat, "realistic" pictures
through conscious recall but to create the full, total, and vibrant

textures of real life—the spinning globe as opposed to the flat painting. It is the nature of Proust's imagination to be expansive and all-embracing, to think cosmically, to connect his hero's experience to that of the universe, to find in the eternal flux of experience rapid, successive tableaux that allow us to perceive the evolution of space and the flow of time. Proust combines stasis, kinesis, and ubiquity in a passage from *Jean Santeuil* comparing the speed of electricity and the telephone with that of memory. He employs the medieval conception of angels, whose wings have a global expanse, to indicate the cosmic proportions of his emotions:

> L'électricité ne met pas moins de temps à conduire à notre oreille penchée sur un cornet téléphonique une voix pourtant bien éloignée, que la mémoire, cet autre élément puissant de la nature qui, comme la lumière ou l'électricité, *dans un mouvement si vertigineux qu'il nous semble un repos immense*, une sorte d'omniprésence, est à la fois partout autour de la terre, aux quatre coins du monde où palpitent sans cesse ses ailes gigantesques, comme un de ces anges que le Moyen Age imaginait.[27]
> (IV, 243; emphasis added)

Not only does speed imbue the impressions that are regained from the past, but the idea of movement through time and space is one of the major aspects of the Proustian novel. In the concluding sentence, the Narrator tells us that he will not fail to show the effects of time on his characters. For Proust, the evolution of his characters (most notably the Narrator, Albertine, Odette, Charlus, Saint-Loup, and Swann) over a period of time—often in surprising shifts or reversals—is what makes them mobile and therefore lifelike. If a novel is to represent us as we really are, and as we perceive ourselves to be at different stages of our existence, then this mobility must be present in the description of the characters, who, like planets, voyage through space and time. In the analogies Proust draws from mathematics and molecular chemistry, contained in his early notes for *la Recherche*, we see that he wants to create a work that is true to life in all its dynamism:

Encore si l'œuvre est un roman faudrait-il ne pas se contenter d'étudier ces caractères comme s'ils étaient immobiles. Mais pour emprunter le langage de la géométrie, non point une psychologie plane, mais une psychologie dans l'espace et faire subir aux caractères les mouvements en quelque sorte mathématiques qui se passent à l'intérieur d'un caractère étant indirectement soumis à d'autres mouvements qui agissent sur le caractère lui-même et à la fois altèrent ses molécules, et au-dehors [les font] lentement changer de place dans l'ensemble des autres êtres qui réagissent sur lui.[28]

One of the most remarkable set pieces in the novel is Proust's description of Hubert Robert's fountain (II, 656-57), in which stasis and kinesis, form and function, are perfectly fused. Seen from a distance, the fountain—svelte, immobile, rigid—appears to be a work of art rather than rising water; even the cloud of mist that constantly forms above the column of water seems to have a precise eighteenth-century shape. But as the Narrator draws nearer, he sees that while the continuously rising jets of water give the impression of following an architectural design, in fact the fountain consists of "mille bonds épars pouvant seuls donner à distance l'impression d'un unique élan." From closer still he observes that what appears to be a single column of water is composed of a number of jets, each rising higher than the last. Furthermore, this constant upward thrust of the water is often broken by drops of water falling back down upon the rising column. Spray from these collisions creates an oblong cloud "fait de mille gouttelettes, mais en apparence peint en brun doré et immuable, qui montait, infrangible, immobile, élancé et rapide, s'ajouter aux nuages du ciel." Proust presents the paradox of the point of demarcation between stasis and kinesis in the spray of the fountain, which is simultaneously *immobile* and *rapide*. The fountain may undergo violent, rapid change whenever a gust of wind sends the vertical column of water splashing to the ground.

The Hubert Robert fountain, as described by Proust, has obvious erotic connotations; in early versions of the text it was associated with the scenes of childhood masturbation at Combray.[29] The erotic elements become explicit when Madame d'Arpajon, one of the duc de Guermantes's former mistresses, ventures near the fountain just as a blast of warm air hits it and sends the column of water crashing down upon her, "[ce qui] inondait si complètement la belle dame que, l'eau dégoulinant de son décolletage dans l'intérieur de sa robe, elle fut aussi trempée que si on l'avait plongée dans un bain."

Eroticism, in its paradoxical merging of the life force and intimation of death, lies at the heart of such images of Proustian desire. Philippe Lejeune presents a Freudian reading wherein he finds a sexual basis for Proust's creative drive. He links the portrait of the painting that hangs in the Narrator's room at Combray and the description of the fountain in *Sodome et Gomorrhe* with the hero's acknowledgment that Combray is the single source (*source* also means spring, or fountain, in French) of the entire work: "le narrateur compare Combray à un bassin unique d'où sont sortis une série de jets d'eaux parallèles qui se rejoignent finalement dans *le Temps Retrouvé* (III, 968), ce qui suggère que l'œuvre est une architecture de jets jaillis d'une source unique: Combray. . . ." [30]

According to Lejeune's reading, the charm of the memory of Combray derives from the oral attachment to the mother and the voluptuous, narcissistic pleasures of masturbation. This gentle rapture underlies the charm experienced by the reader, who unconsciously delights in the enthrallment of youthful voluptuousness described by Proust, which contains "la puberté dans toute sa fraîcheur et sa vigueur. . . ." Time regained, according to Lejeune, is not mummified time rediscovered through involuntary memory provoked by madeleines and tea but time in the full, visceral expansion of orgasm.[31] Eroticism in its baser, common elements will be transcended, together with all of life's experiences, in an all-encompassing and salutary vision at the end of the Narrator's quest.

In the experience of reading itself, where a fixed, linear text is set in motion by the encounter between the reader and the author's words, whereby the expression of the work becomes the impression for the reader, the fountain seems an appropriate architectural archetype for the genesis of the novel and its dynamic recreation by the reader.[32] Orgasm, the ultimate expression of nature's physical drive to multiply, reminds us of the obvious link between "create" and "procreate." Books are the result of a writer's efforts to cast the physical and spiritual—the dual aspects of man's nature—into a pleasing and durable form.

It is the dynamic quality of Proust's novel that continues to attract readers, just as the Narrator was compelled to examine the fountain as both a work of architecture in its distant, abstract appearance and as a body of (generally) controlled, surging water. The exploration and contemplation of the fountain in its simultaneously static and kinetic states is much like the reading of any work of art: we follow the lines that we are given, yet the reading is not constant and repetitive; our mind, like the wind, may veer; the collision of drops and the resultant cloud of mist formed will vary from page to page and reading to reading; and yet the experience will always remain within certain structural lines laid out by the architect of la Recherche. If the "mist" that collects above the text appears to belong to the fin-de-siècle period, closer inspection reveals that the droplets that form the mist remain youthful and dynamic. Like Impressionist painting, in which the image dissolves in a maze of brushstrokes of paint when the observer draws near, the fountain seen up close reveals the dynamism of its structural elements.

The desired synthesis of motion and stasis is expressed at one point in the form of a maxim: "Les traits de notre visage ne sont guère que des gestes devenus, par l'habitude, définitifs. La nature, comme la catastrophe de Pompéi, comme une métamorphose de nymphe, nous a immobilisés dans le mouvement accoutumé" (I, 909).[33] Desire, however, releases what has been immobilized and renders it pure motion again. Life is a series of energy transferrals from the static to the kinetic, and vice versa, as is the reading of a book. Alone on the shelf, a text is static; placed in the hands of a reader, it becomes active.

Desire is the impetus that sets in motion a person who is immobile and stable for others. Such is the case with the actress Rachel, who for Saint-Loup becomes a figure in motion, a fugitive being, but for the Narrator remains the frozen, flat image of a cheap bawd. This explains the paradox of why the Narrator can see Rachel for what she really is, whereas Saint-Loup never can, although he suspects that the photographs he has taken with his own hand-held Kodak camera do not do her justice (I, 783).[34] Proust makes the same point concerning Albertine in a parallel scene, where the Narrator, about to send Saint-Loup to Touraine to bring back the fugitive Albertine, is reluctant to show him a recent photograph of the girl who has totally disrupted his life because he knows that his friend will only see the effigy of what to an unobsessed person must be a fairly ordinary-looking girl (III, 436-37).

In the case of the grandmother's photograph, the snapshot looks entirely different to the Narrator than to his mother; he sees only his grandmother as she appeared to him that day on the beach, whereas his mother sees the shadow of the grandmother's illness and impending doom. In this case, experience and point of view are the only relative factors, since both the Narrator and his mother study the same frozen image.[35] Proustian characterization, in this regard, is truly modern—Einsteinian through the use of relativity, as Edmund Wilson and others have pointed out. Without the techniques of arrested motion and relative point of view, it would not be possible to present two opposing views of the same object.

Proust's method of characterization, particularly in relation to facial traits, is compared by Gerald Cahen to that of Balzac,

> chez qui le visage est déjà tout entier contenu dans le Nom. La physiognomie, science vénérée par Balzac, donne à l'écrivain la matière absolue d'un dieu-

créateur; quand chez Proust, au contraire, le visage est
le mystère qu'aucune science des Noms ne saurait *a pri-
ori et objectivement* capter.[36]

With Proust, physiognomy—the science of observing a static face
that can be read once and for all[37]—is replaced by the perilous
and troublesome observation of faces seen in multiple perspectives
or in fragmented sections. Balzac's method is static and absolute,
whereas Proust's is kinetic and relative. In the twentieth century,
narrators and readers no longer feel comfortable being prescient
and omniscient.

The speed of characters traveling through space-time in
Proust's universe will result in two dominant images for the
famous "bal de têtes" scene in the concluding pages of the
novel: the loss of speed and the vacillating, vertical motions of
the elderly, who will soon topple into their graves. Age has
slowed the characters down and totally transformed them, as we
see in the case of a formerly nimble waltzer whose physical
agility has diminished considerably, resulting in an enormous
body and even altering her sex ("substituer à la légère blonde ce
vieux maréchal ventripotent") (III, 939). The space-time tra-
versed by the characters is represented vertically by the image of
the old people bestriding the long years they have lived as
though on tall stilts. The vibrant, dynamic, muscular forward
motion of youth has become the tottering, perilous, vertical
movement of old age as the grave yawns for those of the Narrator's generation.

As we shall see in the concluding chapter, Proust achieves
the Herculean task of dramatizing the *infiniment petit* and the
infiniment grand, demonstrating that the same laws operate in
nature on the cosmic and human scales. For Proust, science and
art are perfectly wedded; the glamour of nature derives from the
precision and harmony of its laws, whereas the vision and beauty
of art derives from the revelation of new laws and new worlds
that are cast in permanent form. *La Recherche* presents us with
the transitory experiences of a number of characters who, in

variations on the central Proustian themes, prove both the repetitive and diverse nature of life.

Proust was as intent at representing the dynamics of life as were the Futurists, but his vision was universal and comprehensive, unlike that of the Futurists, who in their iconoclastic zeal rejected the past and traditional art, failing to see how its documentary aspect, its persistent energy and beauty, could be revitalized and made to serve contemporary needs.

Louis Bolle compares Proust with Zeno of Elea, the Greek philosopher, who thought the absolute was to be found in the being, unified and unchanging.[38] But it seems more likely, based on texts from the novel, that Proust wants to have it both ways—to take a snapshot and represent within it the constant flux of time—as in Elstir's paintings, wherein stasis and kinesis are both present, the former in the permanence of the material painting, the latter suggested by the painter's technique. This is why Proust wrote a circular novel—not a simple circular novel but a complex one. Proust's circles are not repetitive and superposable but expanding; not a ring that tilts this way or that while remaining the same ring, but the seemingly endless rings—occurring when a stone is dropped into water or in the kaleidoscopic and varied lozenges of a rose window— that reach out to infinity. In the Proustian scheme of things, all events are cosmic and everything about us and within us is in flux. The greatest effort the Narrator makes to arrest speed by seizing a fugitive being occurs when he imprisons Albertine.

CHAPTER 5

The Prison

J'appelle ici amour une torture récriproque. (III, 109)

Le corps enferme l'esprit dans une forteresse. . . . (III, 1035)

While Proust's novel continues Balzac's depiction of the human comedy, *la Recherche* is also a divine comedy, the spiritual autobiography of a soul. It is the story of paradise lost and regained: a child loses his will at Combray, experiences years of wandering in the arid social desert in pursuit of mirages, and finally is reborn and ascends to a state of time regained. Success, however, comes at the price of a long and difficult struggle. In the prison section of the novel, the main question becomes whether or not the Narrator will free himself and regain his lost will. *A la recherche du temps perdu* here has resonances of its alternate meaning, namely, *temps perdu* as wasted time or a lost life.

Proust's young, naïve narrator believes in absolutes and thinks that he will find in the world the ideal representatives of beauty, love, and social prestige.[1] Instead, as he struggles to find his way through the labyrinth of life, he encounters vanity, cruelty, and other evils that cause him suffering and contribute to his dystopian vision. Among the great reversals that occur in the novel are his loss of will and the discovery that the values of society are the opposite of those held by his mother and grandmother. Values are also reversed in his exploration of the world of sexuality: love becomes torture and temples are the scene of satanic rites. The underworld is the world of his childhood days at Combray turned upside down: "les vrais paradis sont les paradis qu'on a perdus" (III, 870).

Midway through the novel, in the section called *Sodome et Gomorrhe*, the Proustian quest becomes a tour of hell before the Narrator can find his way home again: "Le poète est à plaindre, et qui n'est guidé par aucun Virgile, d'avoir à traverser les cercles d'un enfer de soufre et de poix, de se jeter dans le feu qui tombe du ciel pour en ramener quelques habitants de Sodome" (III, 206). Proust explained to Robert de Montesquiou that his purpose in presenting the different worlds of his human and divine comedy was as follows: *Sodome et Gomorrhe* was intended to be totally different from the volumes that preceded it in order to present "cet émouvant contraste entre une poésie d'éden et une poésie d'enfer."[2]

This descent into the underworld is usually obligatory for every person who undertakes the quest, whether he be named Ulysses, Aeneas, Dante, Leopold Bloom, or simply the Narrator. A voyage into hell is a prerequisite to the joyful ascension at the end of the novel in *Le Temps retrouvé*. The exploration of hell, the elements of which are often thought to be beautiful at first—society will prove to be a wasteland and love a trap—is an essential part of his experience, one that eventually allows him to end his apprenticeship in life and formulate an aesthetics and an ethics as he begins to regain time lost. At the end of the novel, when he regains his will and finally attains the artist's vision, he is capable of converting the negative aspects of his life's experience into the positive forces of creativity.

As we saw in the preceding chapters, the great accelerator of the Proustian universe is desire: desire for women who pass in the street or on the beach at Balbec; desire for cities, which are most often associated with coveted women, such as Balbec in the case of Albertine. The Narrator is driven to seek the unknowable, the *insaisissable*. While still young and at the first stage of his quest, he seeks through physical possession a higher knowledge that belongs to the domains of mind and art. He continues to manifest his displaced vision by seeking absolutes in the real world rather than in art, risking repeating Swann's mistake before eventually discovering the role of desire and suffering in artistic creation. He will finally reach the point—never attained by Swann—of comprehending and transforming his entire experience into knowledge and art.[3]

Manias

Many Proustian characters, including the Narrator himself, exhibit various manias. According to the *Oxford Classical Dictionary*, the word "mania" is derived from the name of a group of punishing deities, kin to the Erinyes, called Maniai because they work by disturbing the mind. In *la Recherche*, maniacal behavior is a form of punishment since such conduct makes it impossible for the person in question to function fully and to realize his or her potential as a human being and, especially, as a creative person. Proust often presents obsessive behavior as the act of being enclosed, tethered, or bound. Throughout the novel, imprisonment and bondage are associated with failure in love and art.

The characters who best illustrate maniacal behavior are Aunt Léonie, Swann, Charlus, and the Narrator.[4] Aunt Léonie is a hypochondriac who refuses to leave her bed and insists on the exact repetition of her safe daily routine: "[Elle] n'avait plus voulu quitter, d'abord Combray, puis à Combray sa maison, puis sa chambre, puis son lit et ne 'descendait' plus, toujours couchée dans un état incertain de chagrin, de débilité physique, de maladie, d'idée fixe et de dévotion" (1, 49). As a result of her obsession with her health, Aunt Léonie has turned her bed into a prison cell.[5]

There is a text in "Journées de lectures" on neurasthenia that can serve as a commentary on the preceding one, especially with reference to Proust's use of "descendait." In the essay, neurasthenia is blamed for the lack of volition and creativity in persons like Aunt Léonie:

il existe certains esprits qu'on pourrait comparer à ces
malades [les neurasthéniques] et qu'une sorte de paresse
ou frivolité empêche de descendre spontanément dans
les régions profondes de soi-même où commence la
véritable vie de l'esprit. . . . [les neurasthéniques] vivent
à la surface dans un perpétuel oubli d'eux-mêmes, dans
une sorte de passivité qui les rend le jouet de tous les
plaisirs. . . . (V, 179)

Swann, with his frivolous behavior and his "paresse d'esprit,"
remains forever the dilettante and cannot descend into himself. At
the end of *Le Temps retrouvé*, once the Narrator is endowed with
the creator's vision, his mind is described as a "riche bassin
minier" that he will exploit for his work (III, 1037).[6]

Aunt Léonie, who can neither rise nor descend, is presented as a machine of perpetual horizontal motion, trapped in
the gears of her weaknesses and manias and unable to set herself
free. Her behavior reminds her nephew of a water lily he always
sees on his walks in Combray. The lily is held fast at the end of its
long stem and is tossed back and forth in the current of the
Vivonne River: "comme un bac actionné mécaniquement, il
n'abordait une rive que pour retourner à celle d'où il était venu,
refaisant éternellement la double traversée" (1, 168). The tethered, perpetual-motion lily, he realizes, represents his aunt and
others like her, caught in the mesh of their obsessions and lacking
the willpower necessary to alter their conditions and lead a productive life. In fact, he discovers an ironic note in their struggle in
that their occasional feeble efforts to correct their behavior supply
the tension that powers the mechanism in which they are caught:
"pris dans l'engrenage de leurs malaises et de leurs manies, les
efforts dans lesquels ils se débattent inutilement pour en sortir ne
font qu'assurer le fonctionnement et faire jouer le déclic de leur
diététique étrange, inéluctable et funeste" (1, 169).

This complete abdication of self to the tyranny of habit
and security is a weakness illustrated by Swann and the hero in
their respective love affairs. In comparing Aunt Léonie to the

mechanical water lily, Proust says that the lily is like the damned
that Dante saw in hell: "[ce nénuphar, pareil à quelqu'un de] ces
malheureux dont le tourment singulier, qui se répète indéfiniment durant l'éternité, excitait la curiosité de Dante . . ." (I,
169). This observation serves as a warning to the young Narrator
to be on his guard against his own foibles and to strengthen his
will. It is a warning that he is unable, for the most part, to heed.
Weaknesses, whether inherited or acquired, are present in us—
potentially at least—and through the insidious workings of habit
they permit the establishment of patterns of mechanical behavior
that are self-perpetuating and destructive to the victim.

Desire, especially when heightened or aggravated by jealousy, also causes obsessive behavior. Swann, Charlus, and the Narrator all struggle to overcome various forms of sexual temptation
and jealous obsession. Charlus is weakened and finally destroyed
by his homosexual lust, just as Swann squanders his energy and
imagination in his relentless pursuit of Odette. Swann's infatuation
is largely provoked by his own irrational jealousy, which prevents
him from dealing effectively with his amorous dilemma, and by
his mistaking eros for aesthetics. The protagonist will eventually
succeed in large part because he is able to free himself from the
sort of obsessive behavior that causes Swann and Charlus to fail as
creative persons. These two older friends and mentors are in
many ways admirable and brilliant men, but they lack the
willpower and vision necessary to prevent them from succumbing
to erotic and social temptations.

A similar debilitative pattern of behavior is found in the
Narrator's relationship with Albertine. Love, and the ruses to
which love forces us to have resort, is presented as a technique, a
machine in whose gears we get caught, making it impossible for
us to escape. As was the case with the water lily, our struggles
only serve to bind us more tightly: "l'amour, suivant une technique infaillible, reserre pour nous d'un mouvement alterné
l'engrenage dans lequel on ne peut plus ni ne pas aimer, ni être
aimé" (1, 927).

In his jealous obsession with Albertine, the Narrator believes that he can possess her fully and at the same time prevent anyone else from doing so if he imprisons her. But the result of this arrangement is only added frustration and boredom, for he becomes her prisoner as much as she is his, since he must be her guard and interrogator: "J'étais plus maître que je n'avais cru. Plus maître, c'est-à-dire plus esclave" (III, 157). Louis Gautier-Vignal, who knew Proust well just after Agostinelli's death, discounts the notion that the chauffeur served as the model for the prisoner, claiming that it was Proust who had become the prisoner of his own health and habits.[7]

During the quest, the protagonist's greatest fear is that he will become like Léonie, totally lacking in will, making it impossible for him to become an artist. At his lowest point in *La Prisonnière*, when the Narrator sees that his vital energy is waning because he has given in to jealous passion and allowed himself to become a sickly recluse, suffering from a disintegration of will and lack of curiosity about anything except the possible betrayals of Albertine, he realizes that he has become Aunt Léonie (III, 79).[8]

Heredity, the biological form of habit, can be one of the most deleterious forces from which it is difficult, if not impossible, to escape. We recall that Swann's lack of will is explained by his inherited weakness of concentration. There is a model whom the Narrator considers to be the perfect embodiment of will and goodness: his grandmother.[9] The grandmother and the mother are said to be the last representatives of the Combray race: "la race de Combray, la race d'où sortaient des êtres absolument intacts comme ma grand'mère et ma mère, semble presque éteinte . . ." (I, 746). But he finds himself linked, through heredity and obsession, to the person of the wrong female relative: Aunt Léonie. She is a total egotist, which is also how he sees himself in his lethargic, jealous dependency upon Albertine. The grandmother, identified with the steeple of Combray and the aviator, is undeterred by the rain as she walks in the garden at Combray, surreptitiously removing stakes from the rose trees. She represents courage, independence, natural distinction, and energy.

There is another example in which a nephew is trapped by the inherited weakness of an uncle. Proust explains Saint-Loup's unexpected conversion to homosexuality, in part, as the result of hereditary factors transmitted through Charlus. Although this is a fanciful bit of genetic theory, it is consistent with Proust's general atavism in the novel. His observation about the kinship of Charlus and Saint-Loup applies just as easily to the Aunt Léonie-Narrator relationship: "On n'est pas toujours impunément le neveu de quelqu'un" (II, 695).

Obsession can even alter one's sex. This is what has happened to Charlus, who was once a virile, athletic[10] homosexual but has now become a woman trapped in a man's body as a result of his constant yearning for other men ("la femme qu'une erreur de la nature avait mise dans le corps de M. de Charlus . . ."). As the Narrator observes,

> le changement que nous marquons ici était d'origine spirituelle. A force de se croire malade, on le devient, on maigrit, on n'a plus la force de se lever, on a des entérites nerveuses. A force de penser tendrement aux hommes, on devient femme, et une robe postiche entrave vos pas. L'idée fixe peut modifier (aussi bien que, dans d'autres cas, la santé) dans ceux-là le sexe. (II, 908-9)

The Loss of Will

The Narrator first knew jealous anguish as a child at Combray when Swann, then a stranger to him, came to dine with his family. Forced to go to bed early on such occasions, the child could hear his mother laughing in the garden with this stranger and knew that she would be unable to come kiss him good night and remain with him for a while in his room, as was her custom. The mother and the grandmother are greatly concerned about the child's delicate health and his overdependence on them. One night when he is especially miserable, he waits up for his mother and implores her to remain with him. She does not want to yield to his nervous anxiety, but the usually stern father tells her to do so. The child is relieved but aware that he has forced his mother to do something wrong. In a kind of premonition, the Narrator predicts that the tears of anguish that burst forth when he was alone with his mother in the bedroom will reverberate throughout his life (I, 37). By forcing his mother to yield to his nervous dependency, he realizes that he is guilty of matricide: "il me semblait que je venais d'une main impie et secrète de tracer dans son âme une première ride et d'y faire apparaître un premier cheveu blanc" (I, 39).[11] He will spend the rest of his life trying to recover the will and energy he lost that night at Combray and to expiate the wrong done to those he loves.[12]

The drama of the good-night kiss is generally thought to be autobiographical and to have taken place at Auteuil, a Paris suburb where a maternal uncle, Louis Weil, had a home at 96, rue La Fontaine. Whether or not such a scene really took place hardly matters; Proust's great affection for and dependency upon his mother is well documented. He spoke of this himself in responding to two questionnaires filled out when he was approximately thirteen and twenty years old.[13]

> Your idea of misery. — Etre séparé de maman. (V, 335)
> [The first questionnaire was in English.]
> Quel serait mon plus grand malheur. — Ne pas avoir connu ma mère ni ma grand-mère. (V, 337)

The Narrator often despairs because he lacks the discipline and power of observation necessary to become a writer. This weakness and lack of confidence is a recurrent theme throughout the novel, sounding right up to the triumphant conclusion. Proust recognized his own lack of will, referring to it twice in the second questionnaire:

Mon principal défaut.—Ne pas savoir, ne pas pouvoir 'vouloir'.
Le don de la nature que je voudrais avoir.—La volonté, et des séductions. (V, 337)

In *La Prisonnière*, the Narrator describes the will as a shield against vices: "Les vices sont un autre aspect de ces existences monotones que la volonté suffirait à rendre moins atroces" (III, 44). Lack of will is the greatest of all vices since it makes resisting the others impossible (III, 836).

Victor Brombert's remark about Baudelaire's claustro-philia applies equally to Proust's and his Narrator's conflicting desires to travel and yet remain cloistered in uterinelike security within his cork-lined room: "Is [Baudelaire's] claustrophilia not largely due to passivity and abdication of will power? The refuge-chamber serves to exclude and protect. It is a correlative of the fear of degradation, of the shame that comes with failure."[14] In a letter written in 1904, the novelist spoke of the importance of discipline to the artist: "Je ne crois pas que la liberté soit très utile à l'artiste . . . la discipline sera comme au névropathe entièrement bienfaisante. Et la discipline est une chose féconde en soi-même quelle que soit la valeur de ce qu'elle prescrit."[15]

After the fall, the madeleine episode and other instances of involuntary memory hold out the promise of eventual salvation—but they are only intermittent and brief. More often than not, he is discouraged. Once the youth loses his will and witnesses the lesbian love scene at Montjouvain, the paradisiacal aspects of Méséglise give way to infernal associations. As Miguet-Ollagnier has observed, "le double châtiment du feu et du déluge commence à dégrader le côté paradisiaque de Méséglise. . . ."[16] Roussainville, the scene of licentious orgies for Gilberte, appears to the Narrator as a biblical city that is chastised or redeemed according to effects created by the weather:

Roussainville, dans les murs duquel je n'ai jamais pénétré . . . tantôt, quand la pluie avait déjà cessé pour

nous, continuait à être châtié comme un village de la
Bible par toutes les lances de l'orage qui flagellaient
obliquement les demeures de ses habitants, ou bien
était déjà pardonné par Dieu le Père qui faisait descendre vers lui, inégalement longues, comme les rayons
d'un ostensoir d'autel, les tiges d'or effrangées de son
soleil reparu. (I, 152)

In *Sodome et Gomorrhe*, when the Narrator dreams of his
dead grandmother and sets out to find her, his descent into the
world of sleep is said to be Hades: "nous nous sommes embar-
qués sur les flots noirs de notre propre sang comme sur un
Léthé intérieur aux sextuples replis. . ." (II, 760).[17] He fails to
find her because he does not know her address; all he knows is
that she who loved the open air and freedom of movement is
enclosed is a small room and cannot budge. In his nightmare
she becomes, in her present circumstances, the opposite of her
former self. Her chief concern remains that he regain his will
and become a productive person. His father appears in the
dream to reassure him that his grandmother still believes that
he is going to write a book: "On lui a même dit que tu allais
faire un livre. Elle a paru contente. Elle a essuyé une larme"
(II, 761).

In an earlier version of this text, the relationship among
the grandmother's death, his will and ability to work, and her
existence in the afterlife is made explicit: "Ma grand'mère était
dans la chambre contiguë, moi je travaillais à ma table, et je me
disais: 'Enfin, elle va me voir travailler, elle qui l'a tant désiré, et
avait fini par désespérer, par renoncer pour toujours.' "[18] There
can be little doubt that such scenes are biographical in origin and
reflect parental anxiety over Proust's inability to select a profession
and lead a productive life. In a letter to Georges de Lauris, Proust
expressed his regret at having accomplished so little before the
death of his parents: "Encore vos succès votre mère pouvait-elle
les prévoir. La mienne est morte en croyant que je ne me
relèverais jamais."[19]

La Recherche is the story of many failures, especially the Narrator's failure to become a writer. His lamentations about his inability to work and his lack of talent occur throughout the novel ("Je ne suis pas romancier. . ." [III, 379]; "Si j'ai jamais pu me croire poète, je sais maintenant que je ne le suis pas" [III, 855]). We read in some of the most poetic prose ever written—in a dazzling tour de force combining acute analysis, poetic metaphors, and profound maxims—about the very things that he cannot observe and describe. A large part of the novel's energy and fascination derives from this mirror trick: we are reading the book he cannot write, although by the end of the novel he is ready to write the ideal version of what we have read. Vladimir Nabokov, who announced back in the fifties that la Recherche was the greatest novel of the first half of the twentieth century, particularly admired this optical trick:

> The book that the Narrator in Proust's book is supposed to write is still a book-within-the-book and is not quite *In Search of Lost Time*—just as the Narrator is not quite Proust. . . . Within the novel, the Narrator Marcel contemplates, in the last volume, the ideal novel he will write. Proust's work is only a copy of that ideal novel—but what a copy![20]

Proust inserts small, tantalizing touches in the novel to heighten the impression that la Recherche is not exactly the book the Narrator will write. At the end of the novel, Odette—now that Bergotte, whom she protected for years, is no longer alive—still hopes to be immortalized in literature. Having heard that the Narrator intends to become a writer, the lady in pink hopes for a part in his drama. She does not make the grade! "Elle était médiocre dans ce rôle [la maîtresse du duc de Guermantes] comme dans tous les autres. Non pas que la vie ne lui en eût souvent donné de beaux, mais elle ne savait pas les jouer" (III, 1020).[21] He indicates that the role she would like to play in his future book is not the one that he is interested in depicting. He intends to "[dégager d'elle] à son insu les lois de sa vie" (III, 1023).

Voyeurism

Voyeurism is part of the Narrator's dystopian experience in that when he resorts to such a vision rather than to artistic modes of seeing, the view obtained is one of hell rather than of paradise. The three major voyeuristic scenes in the novel reveal the secret world of homosexuality, or inverted sex—inverted here both in the homosexual and sadistic sense. Although the encounter between Charlus and Jupien does not contain sadistic behavior, the noises that the protagonist hears before he climbs the ladder to witness the love scene are so violent that he thinks a murder may be taking place: "j'aurais pu croire qu'une personne en égorgeait une autre à côté de moi et qu'ensuite le meurtrier et sa victime ressuscitée prenaient un bain pour effacer les traces du crime" (II, 609). The Narrator witnesses private sexual acts of profanation and sadism by people who have yielded entirely to physical obsessions and who serve as foils or negative examples, in the same way as the water lily. The aesthetic vision he seeks to attain is a transcending one that will enable him to become a creator, whereas acts of voyeurism, especially vicarious participation in sadistic acts, are negative and destructive.

A visual medium—photography—is used in the first and most important of the voyeuristic scenes. Since its invention, photography has often been associated with eroticism and even pornography. In the Proustian universe, normal photographs are used in scenes of sexual encounters that usually involve sadism or other sexual practices then generally considered taboo, such as homosexuality. There are also examples of innocuous photographs used in erotic scenes, uses whose dangers are more subtle but nonetheless real. Swann's habit of embracing a photograph of Botticelli's painting of *Zephora* while imagining that it is Odette he is pressing against his body is an example of a photograph used as an instrument in an erotic ritual with a heterosexual background. A discreet irony exists when Swann places the photograph of *Zephora* on his desk, since it is the pursuit of the living incarnation of this Botticelli creation that prevents him from ever completing his study of Vermeer (I, 225).

The first voyeuristic scene occurs when the young Narrator is out for a stroll in the woods near Combray and chances upon Mlle Vinteuil and her lesbian lover, referred to in the novel only as "her friend." Monsieur Vinteuil, unknown as a composer, dotes on his daughter, making the great sacrifice of abandoning the revision and transcription of his compositions in order to create a happy, respectable future for her (I, 160). Timidly seeking fame as a musician, he instead becomes notorious in the conservative community because of the sexual misconduct of his daughter. When he dies of chagrin because of her actions, she is guilty of parricide. Proust depicts in the figure of the composer a creative person who is destroyed physically by his daughter's sexual misconduct rather than by his own.

Vinteuil's shyness is demonstrated by the fact that although he wants to be recognized for his compositions, he cannot bring himself to admit that it is he who places the sheets of his work on the piano before each visit paid by the Narrator's parents. On these occasions he pretends not to know who put the music there. His remark to this effect becomes a stock phrase in the love ritual between the two girls, who place a photograph of Vinteuil on the table before them as a prelude to their amorous rites, which the prudish father in the picture is forced to witness and which include spitting on the photograph: "Oh, ce portrait de mon père qui nous regarde, je ne sais pas qui a pu le mettre là, j'ai pourtant dit vingt fois que ce n'était pas sa place" (I, 162; see also I, 113).

For a long time, it appears that Mlle Vinteuil has killed both the physical man and his creative legacy. Proust poses the question as to whether the composer will ever get his due (*son salaire*) (I, 160, 163). This remark, too, becomes part of the ritual as the girls mock Vinteuil's ambition to be an artist. The reward for his musical creations is the friend's desecration of the father's

photograph, thus profaning Vinteuil's image.[22] The girls' scandalous behavior is compounded by the fact that they continue to
engage in their erotic rites while in full mourning shortly after his
death. Mlle Vinteuil is a good person, we are told, in spite of herself; she is saved by natural goodness inherited from her father.
For such persons, it is not evil that makes them seek pleasure but
pleasure that seems evil:

> Ce n'est pas le mal qui lui donnait l'idée du plaisir, qui
> lui semblait agréable; c'est le plaisir qui lui semblait
> malin. Et comme, chaque fois qu'elle s'y adonnait, il
> s'accompagnait pour elle de ces pensées mauvaises qui
> le reste du temps étaient absentes de son âme vertueuse,
> elle finissait par trouver au plaisir quelque chose de dia-
> bolique, par l'identifier au Mal.[23]   (I, 164)

Nor is she guilty of what Proust calls "cette indifférence aux souf-
frances qu'on cause . . . [ce qui est] la forme terrible et permanente de la cruauté . . ." (I, 165), indicating that she is remorseful
for having destroyed her father.

Witnessing the love scene between Mlle Vinteuil and her
friend is one of the Narrator's acts for which he feels most guilty.
It is a scene that will return to haunt him and cause him great
anguish when Albertine, thinking that she will please and impress
him because of his admiration for the composer, reveals that she
spent a lot of time with the musician's daughter and her friend
when she was growing up and was practically a sister to them.

Some commentators see *la Recherche* as Proust's own
penance for wrongs done to loved ones. Such a view is supported
by similarities between Proust's life and this incident in the novel.
Mlle Vinteuil resembles her father just as Proust did his mother.
There is also testimony that Proust displayed at a male brothel
photographs of friends who were grandes dames of Parisian society, and that the male prostitutes allegedly spat on the pictures in
Proust's presence. This was the brothel that the novelist helped to
establish and to which he sent some of the family furniture in

another act of profanation. In the novel, furniture inherited from Aunt Léonie is sent to a female brothel (I, 578). There is also a passage where the Narrator has a nightmare in which he performs a sadistic act against his parents; such visions are, he says, inherent in the family picture album (II, 87).

To date, there is no compelling evidence, however, that this scene is biographical in origin. George Painter says that Proust had the act of spitting performed on a photograph of his mother and cites as proof an article by Maurice Sachs written on the occasion of Albert Le Cuziat's death. The latter was one of the chief models for Jupien in that he set up a brothel, with Proust's help, of the type described in the novel as having been created by Jupien for Charlus (III, 867). However, contrary to Painter's assertions, there is nothing in the sources cited by him that states that such a ritual of profanation was performed on a photograph of Proust's mother.[24]

In his book *Le Sabbat*, Sachs writes: "[Proust] faisait préparer un plein carton de photographies d'amies illustres ou chères qu'on présentait à un jeune garçon préalablement sermonné, . . . garçon boucher . . . ou prostitué qui s'écriait: 'alors qu'est-ce que c'est c'te poule-là?' en tirant le portrait de la princesse de C***. . . ." Sachs does not mention Proust's mother as a victim of profanation in either account, but he does speak of *la Recherche* as a shrine to the mother: "[Proust] croyait en un paradis qui se vivait dans le ventre de la mère et jusqu'au sortir de l'enfance, car les délices pour lui n'étaient pas dans une vie à venir, mais dans une vie qui avait été et qui ne pouvait plus être jamais."[25]

In the passage, referred to earlier, where Charlus is described as having a woman's soul within a man's body, Proust speaks of the topic as meriting a special chapter to be called "Profaned Mothers": "peut-on séparer entièrement l'aspect de M. de Charlus du fait que, les fils n'ayant pas toujours la ressemblance paternelle, même sans être invertis et en recherchant des femmes, ils consomment dans leur visage la profanation de leur mère? Mais laissons ici ce qui mériterait un chapitre à part: les mères profanées" (II, 908). We do not know what Proust intended to write in the section he provisionally entitled "Les Mères profanées," but the Vinteuil/Mlle Vinteuil episode is probably a good indication. Traces of this theme are found in the title "Le visage maternel dans un petit-fils débauché," used by Proust in *Le Carnet de 1908*,[26] the first notebook of *la Recherche*. The theme of parents who are saddened or destroyed by their children appears in Proust's earliest work.

Matricide is the subject of two pieces that Proust wrote, one fictional ("La Confession d'une jeune fille" [IV, 85-92]), the other an account of a real matricide ("Sentiments filiaux d'un parricide" [V, 150-59]). In the short story, the heroine combines elements that will be attributed to the Narrator and Mlle Vinteuil: she adores her mother, depends upon her good-night kiss for happiness (IV, 86, 94), and lacks will and resolve (IV, 90). Although she loves her mother and wants to please her, she causes the mother to die of shock as a result of her scandalous sexual conduct. Expressing remorse, after a failed suicide attempt, it seems to her that "je faisais pleurer l'âme de ma mère, l'âme de mon ange gardien, l'âme de Dieu" (IV, 95). What she fears most is that her mother saw her "transfigurée en bête" under the spell of voluptuousness when she looked through the window from the balcony. She feels guilty about her behavior and realizes that she has killed something good within herself as well: "dans tout acte voluptueux et coupable, il y a autant de férocité de la part du corps qui jouit, et qu'en nous autant de bonnes intentions, autant d'anges purs sont martyrisés et pleurent" (IV, 95). She knows that she will die soon from her self-inflicted wounds.

Proust wrote the piece "Sentiments filiaux d'un parricide" for *Le Figaro*. An acquaintance of his, Henri van Blarenberghe, an apparently stable and responsible young man, stabbed his mother to death in a rage and then shot himself. After describing this tragedy and the theme of patricide in classical Greek plays such as *Œdipus Rex*, Proust returns to the general social theme of parents as victims of their children: "nous vieillissons, nous tuons tout ce qui nous aime par les soucis que nous lui donnons . . ." (V, 158).

The theme of the profaned image runs throughout the novel and is connected to Vinteuil's posthumous salvation through art. Near the end of the novel, when the Narrator comes to know Vinteuil's late masterpieces, the sheet of music on the piano stand is said to resemble a photograph of Vinteuil.[27] This "musical" photograph contains the essence of Vinteuil, his inner being (*le moi profond*) and this, rather than the actual profaned photograph, is the real portrait of the composer, a knowledge of whose music is an integral part of the hero's quest to become an artist.

All the voyeuristic scenes involve a profaned image even if a tangible one is not present. Charlus is the male counterpart of Mlle Vinteuil; he ends his days in abject degradation as he continues to waste himself in the pursuit of erotic and sadistic pleasures. By abandoning himself entirely to the pursuit of sadistic sexual gratification, Charlus, whose intelligence, sensitivity, and talent the Narrator admires,[28] represents not only a profaned image of his mother but of the artist, of the great man he might have been and one that the protagonist will later become, having learned from the bad examples of Swann and Charlus.

Vinteuil's music is profaned by Swann and Odette, who turn the little phrase into their national anthem: "le pianiste jouait, pour eux deux, la petite phrase de Vinteuil qui était comme l'air national de leur amour" (I, 218). Swann, who begs Odette to play the little phrase again and again, kisses her constantly as she plays it badly. Many years later, evoking the Swann and Odette of the Verdurin salon, Brichot refers to Swann as the "prince consort embourgeoisé de notre Odette nationale" (II, 894).[29] This fits Proust's scheme of presenting a woman who provokes jealousy as the equivalent of an expanse of time and space. We note again the association of love and geography: the country of their love has its own anthem. The analogy of Odette as a territory and common property indicates, as does the use of the phrase "notre Odette nationale" by other characters, that she was a prostitute. A distinction to be made between the Swann/Odette relationship and the Narrator/Albertine affair is that the younger man never trivializes Vinteuil's music to represent any aspect of their love. On the contrary, when the Narrator is capable of forgetting his jealous obsession, he turns immediately to Vinteuil's music because he realizes that its secrets are far superior to his usual preoccupations.

The key scene in the Narrator's relationship with Albertine occurs at a time when he is bored with her and considers the idea of marriage to be foolish. His earlier suspicions about Albertine's lesbian tendencies have been allayed by her flirtations with Saint-Loup. Balbec has become for him a series of social obligations; if he ever returns to Mme Verdurin's salon, it will be to study the works of a musician whose accomplishments are well known to the hostess. During the train ride back from the Verdurins, he decides to tell Albertine that he can no longer see her. This scene is a turning point in the novel, rivaling the episode of the good-night kiss in its impact upon the Narrator's life.

As he begins to tell Albertine about his plans for the future, he remarks that he has had little pleasure this summer except for the works of this musician. She accepts this tactless remark out of deference to his nervous nature and asks him to name the composer. The superior tone with which he replies enhances the dramatic reversal he is about to experience: "Ma petite chérie, quand je t'aurai dit qu'il s'appelle Vinteuil, en seras-tu beaucoup plus avancée?" (II, 1114). Albertine, thinking she will gain favor in his eyes, cannot wait to tell him that she knows Mlle Vinteuil and her friend, who was, in fact, practically a sister to her. The sudden shift in his position is ironic and cruel. The Narrator, who thought he was about to enter the world of self-reliance and explore the cosmic and exhilarating world of Vinteuil's music, is instead plunged straightaway into the other Vinteuil world, the dark planet of homosexuality and unending jealousy. The world of Balbec is joined to that of Combray by the dark and troubled passageway of homosexuality and sadism rather than through the luminous and

joyous portal of art. The image of the scene at Montjouvain, held
in reserve for so long, works its vengeance upon him like Orestes
come to avenge the murder of Agamemnon. He probes his con-
science and believes that he is being punished for having allowed
his grandmother to die.[30] He is aware that a terrible, new, and fully
deserved life is beginning for him:

> les funestes conséquences que les actes mauvais engen-
> drent indéfiniment, non pas seulement pour ceux qui
> les ont commis, mais pour ceux qui n'ont fait, qui
> n'ont cru, que contempler un spectacle curieux et
> divertissant, comme moi, hélas! en cette fin de journée
> lointaine à Montjouvain, caché derrière un buisson, où
> (comme quand j'avais complaisamment écouté le récit
> des amours de Swann)[31] j'avais dangereusement laissé
> s'élargir en moi la voie funeste et destinée à être
> douloureuse du Savoir. (II, 1115)

The Narrator is so shocked by the unsuspected relationship
between Albertine and Mlle Vinteuil that he determines to make
Albertine his prisoner and, if possible, his wife to prevent a recur-
rence of such behavior. He recalls the scenes that provoked his
jealousy and fear of women partaking in "inconcevables joies" (II,
1121): his mother talking and laughing with strangers in the garden at Combray during his childhood; Swann looking desperately
for Odette in nighttime Paris; and now his own suspicions about
Albertine and Mlle Vinteuil's days together in Trieste. As he
focuses his jealous wrath on Trieste, it becomes a city he wishes
to destroy, "une cité maudite que j'aurais voulu faire brûler sur-le-
champ et supprimer du monde réel. Cette ville était enfoncée
dans mon cœur comme une point permanente" (II, 1121).

He accepts the revelation of Albertine's possible lesbianism
as punishment for past sins: unkindness to his grandmother and his
guilt at having listened unsympathetically to Swann's story of his life
with Odette, during which the Narrator denied that he understood the nature of jealousy. Also returning to haunt him is the guilt
he felt at being a voyeur when he witnessed the scene of profane

love between Mlle Vinteuil and her friend, who are especially avenged in the person of Albertine. Once the terrible discovery about Albertine and Mlle Vinteuil's friendship has been made, a cataclysmic reversal takes place and the entire planet becomes a vision of hell, where all space is occupied by jealous obsession:

> Albertine amie de Mlle de Vinteuil et de son amie, pratiquante professionnelle du Saphisme, c'était, auprès de ce que j'avais imaginé dans les plus grands doutes, ce qu'est au petit acoustique de l'Exposition de 1889, dont on espérait à peine qu'il pourrait aller du bout d'une maison à une autre, les téléphones planant sur les rues, les villes, les champs, les mers, reliant les pays. C'était une *terra incognita* terrible où je venais d'atterrir, une phase nouvelle de souffrances insoupçonnées qui s'ouvrait. (II, 1115)

Infinite desire becomes infinite pain as he is mired in his jealous suspicions, which become omnipresent: "Gomorrhe était dispersée aux quatre coins du monde" (III, 23). His attempts to possess Albertine during her imprisonment will lead him to experience a solitude that is cosmic: "L'homme est l'être qui ne peut sortir de soi, qui ne connaît les autres qu'en soi, et, en disant le contraire, ment" (III, 450).

The greatly accelerated movement created by his desire for the girls on the beach and his exploration of society now comes to a halt. Images of bondage predominate. He is overwhelmed by the implications of the Albertine-Vinteuil connection. By comparing his worst fears about Albertine's lesbianism to the primitive and unlikely telephone displayed at the Exposition of 1889, which rapidly developed into a global network, we see that instead of possessing the time-space coordinates of an enviable past, he is confronted with a proliferation of sexual and perhaps even sadistic contacts that ignite his jealous suspicions. Just before the moment of revelation at Parville station, he had intended to abandon Albertine forever, but when she takes a few steps away from him and opens the door of the train, it is as though she ripped a hole in his heart and walked into it, so total is his involvement with her now. It is she who has entered into total possession of his being: "cette séparation spatiale . . . n'était qu'une apparence . . . il eût fallu placer maintenant Albertine, non pas à quelque distance de moi, mais en moi" (II, 1116).

The image of the door is repeated later: "depuis ma blessure de Balbec, c'était dans mon cœur, à une grande profondeur, *difficile à extraire*, qu'était le double d'Albertine" (III, 253; emphasis added). It was his intention to choose the moment of rupture in order to maintain within himself the sense of happiness and the last vibrations of the voice he had rendered amorous (II, 835). Instead, he is shaken by the infernal reverberations of the train door.[32]

As he relives in his memory the scene of Mlle Vinteuil and her friend at Montjouvain, it is now Albertine who falls into Mlle Vinteuil's arms: "Derrière Albertine je ne voyais plus les montagnes bleues de la mer, mais la chambre de Montjouvain où elle tombait dans les bras de Mlle Vinteuil avec ce rire où elle faisait entendre comme le son inconnu de sa jouissance" (II, 1117). The infernal laughter and the sadistic chamber that has replaced her normal habitat—the spacious mobile blue mountains of the sea—indicate the transformation of Albertine from sea goddess to Fury: "Comme par un courant électrique qui vous meut, j'ai été secoué par mes amours . . ." (II, 1127). Now just when he is about to assert his independence and begin to work seriously, the knowledge that Albertine knew Mlle Vinteuil and her friend provokes a relapse of the loss of will he suffered as a child at Combray (II, 1130-31). The brief fourth chapter ends with his determination to marry Albertine. After he imprisons her, he will be as dependent upon her presence and caresses as he was upon his mother's at Combray: "C'était un pouvoir d'apaisement tel que je n'en avais pas éprouvé de pareil depuis les soirs lointains de Combray où ma mère penchée sur mon lit venait m'apporter le repos dans un baiser" (III, 77).[33]

The Temple of Dishonor

Charlus's attempts to set up sadomasochistic encounters with soldiers or butcher boys become scenes of black humor as a result of the discrepancy between his brutal desires and reality.[34] He and Jupien— two purveyors of male flesh at work in wartime Paris, only miles from where one of the largest slaughters in military history was taking place—cannot find a real brute to torture Charlus and hurl insults at him. They can only find tender young men who half-heartedly perform the task of flogging him in order to earn enough money to send home to help their poor mothers, as Charlus learns much to his disgust. The tragic element derives from the fact that this "homme spirituel" has given himself over entirely to concupiscence and masochism. By renouncing things of the spirit for pursuit of the flesh, Charlus has accepted his destruction by becoming a willing victim to his lust: "ce Prométhée *consentant* s'était fait clouer par la Force au rocher de la pure Matière" (III, 838; emphasis added).[35]

This abandonment of will and self-respect makes of Charlus a dystopian version of Prometheus. According to Chantal Robin, Charlus

> exprime avant tout le drame de l'homme livré aux puissances du mal, des passions et de la destruction. L'image du Prométhée civilisateur, bienfaiteur de l'humanité s'inverse. Proust associe au mythe prométhéen le malheur de l'humanité attachée au monde matériel et périssable. . . . Charlus, au fond des enfers . . . personnifie toutes les forces du mal.[36]

Proust presents Charlus's yielding to his obsession as "une démence complète" (III, 838). This deplorable state was reached by allowing the habit of physical gratification to stifle the voice of morality within him. In his final word on the Guermantes brothers, Proust says that all their troubles with mistresses and lovers stem from the same laziness and lack of will, although these deficiencies manifest themselves differently in each: "Ainsi les deux frères, si différents dans leurs goûts, étaient arrivés à la déconsidération à cause d'une même paresse, d'un même manque de volonté . . ." (III, 1016*).

Proust paid Albert Le Cuziat to let him witness a flagellation at the brothel. When the writer returned home that night and recounted his evening to Céleste Albaret, she was horrified by what he told her:

> Ma chère Céleste, ce que j'ai vu ce soir est inimaginable. J'arrive de chez Le Cuziat. . . . il y avait un homme qui se rend chez lui pour se faire flageller. . . . une espèce de sale individu . . . et qu'on paie pour cela, lui tape dessus à coups de fouet, jusqu'à ce que le sang gicle de partout. Et c'est alors seulement que le malheureux a la jouissance de tous ses plaisirs. . . . [37]

Céleste expressed her disgust with Le Cuziat, saying he deserved to die in prison. Proust, who found redeeming qualities in everyone, pointed out that Le Cuziat adored his mother and did everything possible for her when she was alive. Proust evidences the same compassion for his characters.[38] The Narrator attributes this virtue in himself to the influence of his mother and grandmother: "je tenais de ma mère et de ma grand'mère d'être incapable de rancune . . . et de ne jamais condamner personne" (I, 746). In spite of his homosexuality, Charlus worshiped his wife, although he later boasted that, during her funeral service, he obtained the name and address of a choirboy he hoped to seduce, thus profaning her memory while in the act of commemorating her demise (II, 954).[39] During the protagonist's explorations of the brothel, he makes additional discoveries about human depravity and social hypocrisy; it is here that Saint-Loup loses his Croix de guerre. One of the regular worshipers in Jupien's temple of sexuality is a priest who is always asked to contribute to the collection plate (III, 829).

Proust calls homosexuals "une race maudite," but it is to be noted that the experience of erotic love, whether heterosexual or homosexual, leads nowhere. Swann, whose heterosexuality is never doubted, pursues Odette, squanders his talents, and ruins his life.[40] The abandonment of one's true goal, not a condemnation of homosexuality, is the moral lesson *la Recherche* teaches. Proust's reason for using the designation "accursed race" seems to be a recognition of society's persecution of homosexuals since ancient Greece rather than an ethical judgment.[41] This is borne out by a number of passages in the novel and by Proust's coupling the Jews with homosexuals as victims of prejudice.

World War I is depicted in *Le Temps retrouvé* in what was originally intended to be a section of *Sodome et Gomorrhe*. The episode where the homosexuals from Jupien's establishment take refuge in a subway tunnel during an air raid, as well as the last voyeuristic scene immediately following, where Charlus, chained naked to an iron bed in the brothel, is being flogged by a young butcher boy, are all apocalyptic scenes.[42] "Tu n'as qu'à penser quelle chose cosmique serait une guerre aujourd'hui. Ce serait plus catastrophique que le *Déluge* et le *Gotterdämmerung*" (II, 412). War, the ultimate evil, becomes global for the first time in history.

During the air raid, which evokes Wagner's "Ride of the Valkyries," the homosexual lovers continue their trysts in the darkness of the underground métro, where they have sought shelter from the German bombs. Proust makes allusions to Pompeii, another city associated with eroticism and destruction by fire. In fact, at Jupien's brothel Charlus links Sodom and Gomorrah and Pompeii when he points out that the names of those two biblical cities were inscribed on the wall of a house in Pompeii (III, 807). A few pages later the allusion is concretized when the Narrator enters the brothel and notices that the walls are covered with "peintures pompéiennes" (III, 837*), which nicely reverses the order: now the temple of Sodom has Pompeiin images scrawled on its walls, making the same point, namely, that people who abandon themselves entirely to lust risk moral and physical destruction.

Jealousy and Suffering

*nous ne vivons qu'avec ce que nous n'aimons pas, que nous n'avons fait
vivre avec nous que pour tuer l'insupportable amour, qu'il s'agisse d'une
femme, d'un pays, ou encore d'une femme enfermant un pays.* (III, 98)

each man kills the thing he loves. . . .
  —Oscar Wilde

Erotic love of whatever kind is always a source of anguish in *la
Recherche*. It seems that Proust might have had a demonstration of
La Rochefoucauld's maxim (LXXII) in mind as he developed his
own theory of love: "Si on juge de l'amour par la plupart de ses
effets, il ressemble plus à la haine qu'à l'amitié."[43]

Although the problem of desire and sexuality is apparent
throughout the novel, homosexual and sadistic manifestations are
concentrated in the volume entitled *Sodome et Gomorrhe*. Proust
chose the title as a direct reference to the biblical cities that were
destroyed by fire because of the wicked acts of their inhabitants.
Desire, sexuality, and jealousy are associated by the author with
the Judeo-Christian concept of hell, the main elements of which
are cruelty, guilt, suffering, and despair. In the Narrator's case, as
we have seen, suffering takes the form of intense jealousy at
Albertine's presumed betrayals and the guilt he feels for both his
grandmother's and Albertine's deaths, although he was powerless
to prevent them. The terrible jealousy from which he suffers in
Sodome et Gomorrhe, *La Prisonnière*, and *La Fugitive* is, as the various titles indicate, an infernal experience. Swann's jealousy is also
depicted as a fall into the underworld (I, 367). Those whom we
desire flee us. This flight and betrayal—real or imagined—greatly
increases our desire, and the only relief is to imprison the desired
person. But, alas, this captivity leads to an emotional and moral
hell.[44] Jealousy, which caused the Narrator's fall and loss of will at
Combray, is a manifestation of Satan:

> La jalousie est aussi un démon qui ne peut être exor-
> cisé, et reparaît toujours, incarné sous une nouvelle

forme. Puissions-nous arriver à les exterminer toutes, à garder perpétuellement celle que nous aimons, l'Esprit du Mal prendrait alors une autre forme, plus pathétique encore, le désespoir de n'avoir obtenu la fidélité que par force, le désespoir de n'être pas aimé. (III, 103)

Even before Albertine's imprisonment, the obsessive lover had understood that the degree of his desire depended upon qualities his own imagination had bestowed upon her. In his more lucid moments he realizes that in seeking to gain access to the mystery of Balbec by possessing Albertine physically, he abandoned the pursuit of the artist's vision for that of vain eroticism, "le désir d'elle étant lui-même une forme paresseuse, lâche et incomplète de posséder Balbec, comme si posséder matériellement une chose, faire sa résidence d'une ville, équivalait à la posséder spirituellement. . . ." The Narrator is aware that in his attempts to possess Albertine he is using her as a medium through whom he hopes to gain access to Balbec and his past. He considers her a magician, embodying the essence of Balbec: "Elle semblait une magicienne me présentant un miroir du Temps.[45] . . . Il suffisait . . . qu'elle était passée chez moi pour que je la revisse comme une rose au bord de la mer" (II, 352).

If homosexuality and sadism are elements of an inverted or dystopian world that the Narrator glimpses when he observes others, he himself experiences the hell of jealousy when he discovers Albertine's lesbianism. Even at the beginning of her confinement, he was aware that she was only capable of causing suffering, not joy, and he sought to loosen the chain that bound them (III, 28). Love, which he still pursues as an idealistic, absolute quality, is transformed into scenes of torture—usually cruel interrogations by the jealous lover. We again see the importance of the profaned-image motif in the novel. Albertine, the rosy-cheeked girl who, as the embodiment of Balbec, is the creation of the Narrator's own imagination, becomes a profaned angel during scenes of jealous interrogation: "la stabilité de nature que nous lui prêtons n'est que fictive. . . . la rose jeune fille nous tient, la seconde fois, les propos d'une lubrique Furie" (III, 64-65). Love is described as a torrent of sulfur and brimstone, and his life with Albertine is characterized as a secret hell (III, 80) and mutual torture: "J'appelle ici amour une torture réciproque" (III, 109).[46]

From the moment Albertine reveals her connection with Mlle Vinteuil—just at the point when the protagonist was trying to decide how to break with her—and his immediate resolve to imprison her, their relationship first consists of jealousy and torture, then boredom, followed by meditations on art as he begins to think of abandoning her. The degree of his ability to concentrate on aesthetic thoughts is an indication of the extent of his recovery from his obsession with her, of a move toward utopia—freedom, energy, aesthetic curiosity, and above all, the urge and determination to create: "La musique, bien différente en cela de la société d'Albertine, m'aidait à descendre en moi-même, à y découvrir du nouveau. . ." (III, 159). But just at the moment when he is about to leave Albertine to pursue his artistic vocation, a new revelation or suspicion will surface concerning her past, present, or future behavior, and the cycle of reciprocal torture will begin again as the Narrator abandons art for eros. As we have seen, his desire to occupy all of the time-space coordinates of Albertine's being is monstrous. This impossible, megalomaniacal desire interferes with his artistic meditations and prevents him from working. Thus, the creation of works of art—often described as separate, integral worlds or planets—is menaced by the fire of eros and jealousy.

As a result of his experience with Albertine, a relationship is established between fugacity and jealousy that becomes a fundamental aspect of Proustian desire and suffering: "quand . . . je la voyais prendre sa bicyclette et filer à toute vitesse, je ne pouvais m'empêcher de penser qu'elle allait rejoindre celle à qui elle avait à peine parlé" (II, 853). In a text entitled, "Dialogues," Proust gives the following definition of jealousy: "être jaloux, c'est imaginer le plaisir d'une femme que nous aimons" (V, 434). Flight from the Narrator becomes haste to join another, the rival who will enjoy pleasures that he will never know. A further explanation for the impossibility of knowing the loved one is the mythological division[47] of the androgyne into two separate and isolated sexes: "*Combien je souffrais de cette position où nous a réduits* l'oubli de la nature qui, en instituant *la division des corps,* n'a pas songé à rendre possible l'interpénétration des âmes!" (III, 386; emphasis added). The isolation of an individual, especially an obsessively jealous person, within a single sex and soul results in torture and confinement. The problem of jealousy is further complicated by the Proustian conception of successive selves, since the Narrator finds that there are many different Albertines about whom he can be jealous. This complexity is represented by Proust through pictorial analogies, snapshots, and profiles:

> le nom de Léa m'avait fait revoir, pour en être jaloux, l'image d'Albertine au casino près des deux jeunes filles. Car je ne possédais dans ma mémoire que des séries d'Albertine séparées les unes des autres, incomplètes, des profils, des instantanés; aussi ma jalousie se confinait-elle à une expression discontinue, *à la fois fugitive et fixée,* et aux êtres qui l'avaient amenée sur la figure d'Albertine. (III, 149; emphasis added)

After Albertine's death, she survives in his memory in a vital way because of the jealousy that continues to plague him as it had when she was his prisoner. He dispatches an agent, Aimé, to Balbec in order to confirm his suspicions about her lesbian affairs; Aimé reports that Albertine did have relations with some of the women at the bathing establishment. As the Narrator, in his sorrow, muses over these betrayals, he sees Albertine in the company of her friends, who might have been her sexual partners at various Balbec locations. Instead of being the paradise he had hoped to find, the coastal city of Balbec now belongs to the geography of hell: "c'était le fragment d'un autre monde, d'une planète inconnue et maudite, une vue de l'Enfer. L'Enfer c'était tout ce

Balbec,[48] tous ces pays avoisinants d'où . . . elle faisait venir souvent les filles plus jeunes qu'elle amenait à la douche" (III, 518).

Now that she is dead, sea imagery predominates in his visualizations of the Albertine of Balbec. He has often imagined her as a piece of sculpture; now he sees her and the young washerwoman in a nautical bas-relief. A memory of her as she was in his bed, especially the configuration of her thigh, reminds him of *Leda* by Leonardo. Imagining Albertine and the young washerwoman in a strong embrace, the Narrator compares these visions to an electrical current running from his brain to his heart, a current that burns his heart as he suffers for his and Albertine's sins: jealousy, betrayal, and guilt at having glimpsed the forbidden.

Proust employs electricity in an analogy to illustrate the speed of rapid communication and the fire associated with the tortures of jealousy: "mon énervement . . . rencontrait chez elle la force électrique d'une volonté contraire qui le repoussait vivement; dans les yeux d'Albertine j'en voyais jaillir les étincelles" (III, 91). The first such analogy, quoted earlier, was used in the Parville station scene (II, 1127). The memory of Albertine is like an electrical wire connecting her to his heart, where the slightest reminder of anything they shared in common is enough to reestablish contact: "Et même une syllabe commune à deux noms différents suffisait à ma mémoire—comme à un électricien qui se contente du moindre corps bon conducteur—pour rétablir le contact entre Albertine et mon cœur" (III, 538*). Here is his earlier jealous reaction upon hearing Saint-Loup's description of Albertine's life in Touraine after she abandons him:

> A ces mots de hangar, de couloir, de salon, et avant même qu'ils eussent fini d'être prononcés, mon cœur fut bouleversé avec plus de rapidité que n'eût mis un courant électrique, car la force qui fait le plus de fois le tour de la terre en une seconde, ce n'est pas l'électricité, c'est la douleur (III, 472).

Proust again emphasizes the rapidity of the reaction and the cosmic nature of the event. Space, which was once filled with his ardor for Albertine, is now replete with suffering.

The scene in the bathing establishment and others like it are a pendant to the Narrator's first voyeuristic scene involving Mlle Vinteuil and her friend. Unlike the latter, the later voyeuristic scenes are imagined or staged, a practice that seems masochistic. In one such incident he has two laundry girls brought to a house of assignation, where they perform the same amorous rites they allegedly engaged in with Albertine (III, 550).

During periods of intense jealousy, such sparks form a live wire connected directly to his heart, causing him to feel the infernal flames as his being is racked by disappointment and suffering. Such is the case when the laundry girl recounts an incident for the Narrator where her caresses made Albertine swoon:

> cent fois par heure le courant interrompu était rétabli et mon cœur était brûlé sans pitié par un feu d'enfer, tandis que je voyais Albertine, ressuscitée par ma jalousie, vraiment vivante, se raidir sous les caresses de la petite blanchisseuse à qui elle disait: "Tu me mets aux anges." (III, 528)[49]

There is an irony in Albertine's remark in that by witnessing her heaven of sensuality the Narrator creates his own hell. The irony is increased if we recall earlier associations between Albertine and mythological winged creatures. The Narrator constantly seeks erotic fulfillment in the possession of Albertine and others like her, but to no avail. Possession of Albertine does not reveal to him the secret of Balbec's beauty; revelations after her death about her activities at the seaside resort—activities unknown, even unsuspected—turn his view of Balbec into the reverse of the paradise he had imagined.

There is no tangible profaned image in the imagined and staged voyeuristic scenes, but what the Narrator beholds is worse: a profanation of his desire to possess Albertine. She appears to be enjoying with someone else what he and she apparently never shared: a sexually fulfilling experience. The Narrator seems to have experienced moments of erotic pleasure with her, but not the fulfillment of his misplaced desires. In any case, his jealous obsession demands exclusivity: "L'amour, dans l'anxiété douloureuse comme dans le désir heureux, est l'exigence d'un tout" (III, 106). As we have seen, the tyranny of love was first felt by the Narrator when, as a child, he was jealous of the time his mother spent with Swann.

In his Freudian reading of the text, Serge Doubrovsky explains the Narrator's jealousy of Swann in terms of sibling rivalry: "n'oublions pas que la 'scène du coucher' s'articule à la 'scène du dîner', où la mère est précisément en train de nourrir un autre que soi: *Swann*, torturante gémellité phonétique qui survit à l'élimination du 'frère' de Jean Santeuil—et de Marcel Proust."[50] At Balbec, the Narrator compares the paradise of the grandmother's presence to that of a suckling baby and a celestial chorus (I, 668, 670). The possession of Albertine-maman by another creates a demonic version of this scene.

The jealous, obsessive lover sees potential rivals everywhere. Swann and the Narrator both fluctuate between desire and boredom, depending on the availability and presumed infidelity of the woman. Both wish for a cataclysmic event, such as the accidental death of their mistresses, that would liberate them from the prison of passion. These death wishes are indicative of the severity of the anguish they suffer and their frustration at not being able to escape from it. Aunt Léonie expresses a similar wish for a calamity in the family that would free her from the routine imposed by obsessive behavior (1, 116).

The Narrator experiences such calamities in the deaths of his grandmother and Albertine. He learns that, shattering though they may be, such occurrences do not make us change our lives because we still remain trapped in those patterns we have allowed habit to weave around us. Catastrophies may shake us, but they will not in and of themselves free us from the web of habit. The flaws within us still hold us fast, just as the water lily is held back by its own stem, no matter how the course of the river may change.[51] Albertine's death does not bring an end to the jealousy that plagues the Narrator since his obsessive desire to know her actions and his attempts to find out whatever he can about them do not cease with her demise. (Proust engaged in the same pattern of behavior after Agostinelli's death.)

As we have seen, the Narrator's definition of jealousy is to imagine the woman we love experiencing pleasure with someone else. It is true that the Narrator expects too much of desire, just as he expected too much of the theater, of the Guermantes, of Balbec, and so forth, but what he fears especially is that another person will usurp what he desires most, thereby rendering him useless and impotent. On the aesthetic plane, this corresponds to his fear of remaining sterile as an artist. Near the end of his quest, he says that art is the true last judgment (III, 880). The implication is clear: failure to achieve his ambition to become a writer will be the equivalent of hell for him.

Escape from the web of habit will depend upon a change even more fundamental than the death of loved ones, namely, the Narrator's eventual recovery of will and his realization that the way to recapture lost time is through the creation of a work of art. This moment of lucidity occurs much later in the novel, when the Narrator finally understands the true meaning of his experience with Albertine and how to make use of it in relation to will and creativity.

Dystopia: The Wasteland

No group comes off worse in Proust's exploration of human vanity than aristocrats and society people. Proust depicts them as arrogant, ignorant, illiterate, vain, unfeeling, and cruel. Pleasure, whether sexually or socially gratifying, is suspected of being evil because it distracts us from a higher goal. Swann falls into the twin traps of sexuality and society when he tries to create a salon for Odette so that she and his daughter will have a social position that approaches respectability. Swann, in turn, is the victim of a form of parricide when Gilberte profanes his memory by denying him and changing her name (III, 573-77). There is an earlier pendant scene where the duchesse de Guermantes, supposedly Swann's best friend, denies the terminally ill man's request to meet his daughter just once in private. Another scene between Swann and Oriane—the famous episode of the red shoes—indicates the cruel indifference of society people to the needs and suffering of others (II, 596-97).[52] One of the great ironies of the novel, of course, is that after Swann's death Gilberte becomes a Guermantes through her marriage to Saint-Loup. Swann is saved from oblivion by the Narrator, who recognizes him as his spiritual father and the source of his book (III, 915).

Society represents the reverse of art and ethical values. The Narrator discovers that there is no real substance in social gatherings; when he is there, he is living a sterile, empty, superficial existence: "durant ces heures mondaines où j'habitais mon épiderme . . ." (II, 527-28).[53] Social rituals are mechanistic, habitual, obsessive, and motivated by vanity; they are futile at best, and are often destructive. Those who frequent the salons of the faubourg Saint-Germain are tainted with snobbism, pettiness, and dilettantism. Swann is the art expert who cannot gaze inwardly. According to the duc de Guermantes's inverted system of values, works of art are important if they are among those he has seen: "Si c'est à voir, je l'ai vu" (II, 524). When he calls on the Narrator's family during the grandmother's last hours, he expects them to be sensitive to the great honor he is bestowing upon them (II, 338). His main concern is how they receive him, not their sorrow over a beloved relative's death.

Swann is at first seduced by the charms of the Verdurin salon: "Quel charmant milieu, se disait-il. Comme c'est au fond la vraie vie qu'on mène là! . . . Comme Mme Verdurin, malgré de petites exagérations un peu risibles, a un amour sincère de la peinture, de la musique . . . !" (I, 248). Only later does he discover its infernal aspects: "En somme, la vie qu'on menait chez les Verdurin et qu'il avait appelée si souvent 'la vraie vie' lui semblait la pire de toutes, et leur petit noyau le dernier des milieux. 'C'est vraiment . . . ce qu'il y a de plus bas dans l'échelle sociale, le dernier cercle de Dante'" (I, 287). The salon is the profane version of the artist's studio; in fact, Biche (or Tiche) can only become the artist Elstir after he escapes from the clutches of Mme Verdurin.[54]

Mme Verdurin, obsessed with her position in society, is the social equivalent of the insanely jealous lover and exhibits the same fury whenever anyone usurps her position within the little clan: "[M. de Charlus déchaînait chez elle] ce sentiment haineux qui n'était chez elle qu'une forme particulière, une forme sociale de la jalousie" (III, 278). Her obsession is the absolute inviolability, the fidelity of the members of the little clan, who are often referred to as "the faithful." Note the religious tag for those who worship at the profane shrine where Mme Verdurin ("la patronne") is the idol to be revered.

In order to gain admission to her salon, one must adhere strictly to the credo, which basically states that the artists and professional people being protected by Mme Verdurin are the best in the world (I, 188). Once admitted to the Verdurin circle, rules must be obeyed. Those who do not, such as Swann and Charlus, are "executed." Mme Verdurin's devotion to the faithful does not extend beyond the grave. Once dead or dying and hence no longer of use to her—indeed, the dying and recently dead are a threat to the convening of her regular soirées—the former faithful are as anonymous as paupers buried in a common grave.[55]

Although the Verdurin salon functions as a prison, many of the faithful are flattered by the iron hand with which Mme Verdurin rules them. Should some of the members of the little clan wish to travel apart from the group, she either convinces them that they risk life and limb by doing so or, if that argument fails, she changes her plans so that they can all go together.[56] At Balbec, her "prisoners," who would rather rest after dessert, coffee, and liqueurs, are forced to go on excursions, "installés de force en voiture [et emmenés] malgré eux vers l'un ou l'autre des points de vue qui foisonnent autour de Douville" (II, 998). In their comings and goings to and from la Raspelière, they are allowed to move about only in vehicles provided or designated by "la patronne." She even commandeers the adjoining land, making the landscape part of the group's domain. It cannot be seen at its best without her presence and at a time approved by her. Her passion takes on the monstrous aspects of the jealous lover as she becomes a queen of time and space: "Mme Verdurin faisait visiter [les sites] aux étrangers un peu comme des annexes . . . de sa propriété . . . qu'on n'aurait pas connus si on n'avait pas été reçu chez la Patronne." The Narrator notes her "prétention de s'arroger un droit unique sur les promenades comme sur le jeu de Morel . . . et de contraindre les paysages à faire partie du petit clan . . ." (II, 998).

Seen from afar, society, like our planet, may appear to have the luster of a star in the night, but up close it reveals itself to be ugly and sterile. This image is similar to an earlier planetary image involving Saint-Loup's passion for the actress Rachel. The Narrator, an objective observer in this case, sees at close range that Rachel's face is pockmarked "like the moon." Saint-Loup, who sees her for the first time in the limelight of the stage, considers her to be a celestial beauty. The objective viewer sees the "truth" in the ugliness of the actress-prostitute's face but lacks the poetry of experience. This stigmatizing of a woman's face occurs throughout la Recherche.[57] In the scene where the child's behavior forces the mother to relent and spend the night in his room, the boy feels guilty for tracing the first wrinkle on his mother's soul in an act approaching matricide. He has wounded something within her by stigmatizing her code of ethics relative to his behavior.[58]

The blemishing process taints society as a whole. Most of what glitters and attracts when we are young turns out to be ugly or, at best, of no value when seen up close. At first the Narrator does not realize the danger such a company of idle and haughty people pose to his artistic vocation because he is so fascinated by the apparent brilliance of that milieu. So eager is he to belong to it that an invitation he receives to a great social event is compared to a meteorite dropped by one of the queens of society as they follow their stellar paths across infinite distances (II, 377-78).[59] As he moves through society and comes to know "le beau monde" as it really is, he finally sees that it is superficial, petty, and empty. To illustrate this, he quotes a line from Victor Hugo's *Châtiments:* "Et que tout cela fasse un astre dans la nuit!" (III, 718). Proust, who usually quotes from memory, has done so here and slightly altered the ending of Hugo's line; the original reads "dans les cieux." Proust's variation, insisting on the darkness of space, heightens the contrast of the apparent glitter and the surrounding void. At the matinée given by the princesse de Guermantes, the Narrator discovers that the denizens of the feast of the gods (II, 272) have become fat, mechanical dolls, caricatures of their former selves (III, 924, 948).

The reverse holds true for artists; it is only when seen up close through the optics of their work that they are interesting and attractive. The Narrator is surprised at the writer Bergotte's rather ugly appearance when he meets the man whose books he admires. The same is true of Vinteuil, but here Proust reverses the order of presentation: we first encounter him as the ordinary, prudish piano teacher at Combray, with no expectations that he will become a great composer.

The opposite poles of the protagonist's world are Combray-Eden and Balbec-Hell. In addition to serving as the site for the disillusionments of love, Balbec is depoetized in another sense. Because he now knows so many inhabitants of the region—both permanent residents like the Cambremers or vacationing ones like the invasive members of the Verdurin clan—Balbec has become an immense, stuffy salon, "cette vallée trop sociale" (II, 1112); it is the opposite, in fact, of the wild, unspoiled seacoast he had envisaged before going there. His experience with respect to geographical possession is the same as that of physical possession—a total disappointment.[60] He finds himself in a vast wasteland, far from the primeval sea and medieval art he had hoped to discover.

He does not know yet how to convert the spectacle of mediocrity that surrounds him into art.

Not only have all the places the Narrator has dreamed of turned out to be disappointing—and, in the case of Balbec, far worse—but later Combray, the paradise of his childhood, will also undergo depoetization. On a return visit there as a mature man but despairing artist, he discovers that the source of the Vivonne River, which as a child he imagined to be as extraterrestrial as the entrance to hell, is only the size of a small laundry basin where bubbles float to the surface. Gilberte also shows him how the two paths, Swann's way and the Guermantes way, are connected, thus destroying a cherished myth of his childhood. He had always thought the walks represented two separate realms that could not be visited on the same day; now he sees that they form a circuit. This revelation anticipates metaphorically the coming together, or unification, of his entire life experience, which will result in the book we are reading. But for the moment he is discouraged and does not even bother to visit Combray's church, which epitomized all the positive elements of the place and was for him an important symbol connected with absolute love (primarily love for his grandmother and those qualities for which she stood), independence of spirit, and natural distinction. He sees in his lack of interest in Combray and his general dysphoria additional proof that he will never become a writer (III, 691).

Thus, the Narrator, who seeks to rediscover the lost paradise of his childhood at Combray, finds instead dystopian visions of love and society. This depiction of society follows the usual Proustian progression in his hero's odyssey, namely, from anticipation to disappointment and, finally, discovery of society's relationship to the book he will write. In giving us this acerbic portrait of the vain pursuits of love and society, Proust places himself firmly in the lineage of the great French moralists. *A la recherche du temps perdu* may be understood as a vast sermon on vanity.[61]

We have seen that the ideal lost world the Narrator seeks contains its opposite. This is in keeping with Proust's theory that each thing contains its own contradiction: "Il n'y a pas une idée qui ne porte en elle sa réfutation possible, un mot le mot contraire" (III, 602). In an early text, Proust says that our sorrows are the reverse of our pleasures: "nous décidons nous-même nos chagrins, en choisissant nos plaisirs, car les uns ne sont que l'envers des autres" (*"Dialogue,"* [V, 434]). There is only a slight phonemic difference in French between reverse and hell: *envers/enfer.* Charlus remarks that he is not an angel (III, 829) and that Jupien's establishment represents a reversal of traditional values: "Ici c'est le contraire des Carmels, c'est grâce au vice que vit la vertu" (III, 830). As the Narrator remarks at the end of his quest, society is a place where values are reversed, "ces festins de barbares . . . où . . . les valeurs sont si renversées . . ." (III, 1039).

The hot, suffocating, false world of hell is represented in Proust's universe by fire, weight, gravity, being bound and flogged or tortured by jealous interrogations. Albertine, who while free and desired was alternately a winged creature—elusive, fugacious, and mysterious—Venus, and the sea incarnate, becomes an ordinary person—worse, a burden—once she is imprisoned and possessed. The presence of desire can animate a woman who was immobile and, conversely, its lack can cause a woman endowed with speed to become static and dull. Albertine at Balbec is a creature of flight, but when the Narrator imprisons her in his Paris apartment, she is no longer desirable, having become a burdensome slave, a prisoner of gravity from whom he longs to be free:

> Ce n'était plus la même Albertine, parce qu'elle n'était pas, comme à Balbec, sans cesse en fuite sur sa bicyclette. . . . Parce que le vent de la mer ne gonflait plus ses vêtements, parce que, surtout, je lui avais coupé les ailes, elle avait cessé d'être une Victoire, elle était une pesante esclave dont j'aurais voulu me débarrasser. (III, 371)

Albertine undergoes a marked change as a prisoner when we compare the now burdensome slave to earlier epithets used to describe her: une grande déesse, une grande actrice de la plage en feu, la chatoyante actrice, ange, péri, muse orgiaque, bacchante à bicyclette, and so on. Imprisoned, she becomes the opposite of an "être de fuite," for she is now "une grise prisonnière" (III, 173). Her clipped wings make her the antithesis of a girl in motion.

Albertine as a prisoner is the dystopian counterpart of the experience of art as described in Swann's meditation on Vinteuil's sonata. Comparing the music to all great discoveries in art and science, he described such revelations as "divine captives." In the Narrator's apartment, Albertine becomes an infernal captive, a creature who is the opposite of what seemed promised to him by possession of the girl first sighted pushing a bicycle along the beach at Balbec.[62] She is a weight rather than a blessing, in more ways his jailor than he is hers; with her his life becomes "une servitude éternelle." He realizes that she is "un trésor en échange duquel j'avais aliéné ma liberté, la solitude, la pensée" (III, 331). What he sacrifices in order to imprison her are the elements necessary for creativity.

It is only after the Narrator comes to understand the true role of regret and suffering in his life that he will be ready to assume his vocation as a writer. For a long time he does not understand the relationship between the destruction of the "shards" of his being through the fire of jealousy to the work that he is trying to create. This moment of illumination will make it possible for him to convert the apparently negative aspects of his relationship with Albertine into a great positive force, enabling him to become a creative person. By transforming the destructive forces of the torture chamber into a creative darkroom, the Narrator will open a window onto the cosmos.

Death of an Aviator

As Proust elaborated his novel, the aviator emerged as one of the dominant symbols of the creative person. When Alfred Agostinelli reappeared in Proust's life in late 1912 or early 1913 and was hired as his secretary, the writer quickly became infatuated with the young man. It will be recalled that Agostinelli died in an airplane crash not long after fleeing Proust's apartment. Since the writer subsequently borrowed a number of incidents from his relationship with Agostinelli and used them in describing the Narrator's experience with Albertine, much has been written about the role of Agostinelli in Proust's life and his influence on the novel. Many of the assumptions upon which a number of commentators based their conclusions are not borne out by the textual and biographical documents at our disposal. This chapter and the next attempt to determine exactly what Agostinelli contributed to the novel, especially to the character of Albertine and the symbol of the aviator. Tracing the development of the aviator as representative of the Proustian artist and his elevated vision will ultimately lead us to the concluding chapter in the Proustian quest.

1907: Agostinelli, "artisan de mon voyage"

The year 1907 was, for many reasons, a crucial one for Proust. In the closing days of 1906, he had moved to 102, boulevard Haussmann, where he would write virtually all of *la Recherche*. This would remain his home until 1919, when the apartment was sold from under him. Although still in mourning over the deaths of

both his parents—especially his mother, who had died in 1905—
Proust seems to have been through the worst days of his grief. In
the letters of this year we find him sobered by his experience and
taking a renewed interest in life as he describes for his correspondents various works of art and the mannerisms of friends observed
in society. He also recounts anecdotes that he would eventually
incorporate into the novel. This is also the year that Henri van
Blarenberghe, a young man with whom Proust was slightly
acquainted, murdered his mother and then committed suicide, a
tragedy that prompted Gaston Calmette, editor of *Le Figaro*, to ask
Proust to write an article about the crime. The piece he wrote,
"Sentiments filiaux d'un parricide," was published in *Le Figaro* on
February 1, 1907. In describing the love-hate relationship that he
supposed must have existed between van Blarenberghe and his
mother, Proust alludes to the tragedy of *Œdipus, King of Thebes*.[1]
He also wrote "Journées de lecture" and "Impressions de route en
automobile"; the importance of these works for the future novel
may be seen in retrospect.

Proust's brother, Robert, was an early car enthusiast.[2] So
was Jacques Bizet, one of Proust's closest friends and the son of
the illustrious composer and Geneviève Halévy, who would
later become Mme Emile Straus, Proust's great friend, confi-
dante, and the primary model for the duchesse de Guermantes.
In the early days before he became a victim of drugs, Jacques
was an enterprising young man, a director of one of the first
car-rental agencies in Paris, Taximètres Unic.[3] The company
rented Unic automobiles in Paris and served vacationers in
Cabourg in the summer and in Monaco during the winter. It
was through his hiring of Bizet's drivers that Proust first met
Agostinelli.[4] Another of Bizet's drivers, Odilon Albaret, later
became Proust's regular chauffeur, a service that was inter-
rupted only when Albaret was mobilized in August 1914,
along with the other Paris taxi drivers, prior to the first battle
of the Marne. It was as a result of the mobilization of all
able-bodied men that Albaret's young wife, Céleste, became

Proust's housekeeper; she was to remain his faithful servant and friend for the remaining eight years of his life.

In August 1907, Proust made what turned out to be a momentous decision. Having first considered going to Touraine, Brittany, and even Germany, or just remaining in Paris for the rest of the summer, he finally elected to stay at the new Grand-Hôtel in Cabourg, which he would transform into Balbec in the novel. Because Proust wanted to visit the architectural sites of the region, especially those described by Ruskin, he hired Agostinelli to take him in his red taxi on various excursions.[5]

The 1907 motoring trips with Agostinelli along the coast were in many respects like a resurrection for Proust, who for the last six years had been leading a reclusive life; his health had been particularly poor earlier that year.[6] His Cabourg sojourn brought about a sudden change of routine for Proust, who up until then had only gotten out of bed once a week and even then without dressing. He described the dynamics of his new seaside life as that of a cannonball ("la vie de boulet de canon").[7] As Agostinelli drove him from one medieval church to another, Proust jotted down his impressions, which would prove of great importance to the novel he would begin writing the next year.[8]

Although Cabourg outwardly seemed to reflect a positive change for Proust, he confided to his correspondents that the opposite was the case: "je n'ai jamais été si malheureux."[9] The painful memory of past vacations with his mother at Cabourg and other places along the Normandy coast was a fresh reminder of all that he had lost as a result of her passing on. This is probably the inspiration for the famous "Intermittences du cœur" episode (II, 751-81). The incident occurs when the Narrator returns to the Grand-Hôtel at Balbec and leans over to unbutton his boots, as his grandmother had done for him in that same room, with the result that she is suddenly restored to him through an act of involuntary memory so vivid that his grief becomes almost unbearable. He is forced to cancel all engagements and enters into a period of grieving and reflection on memory, loss, and death. In the novel, this withdrawal represents the Narrator's final, intense period of grieving for his grandmother. For Proust, too, the period of profound grief seemed to end with the Cabourg trip in 1907. Active, curious, and more determined than ever to write in spite of the great fatigue he still felt, Proust was about to enter a mature creative period that would last the rest of his life and produce what many consider the major novel of the twentieth century.

During the Cabourg excursions, with Agostinelli at the wheel, Proust himself became "un fervent de l'automobilisme."[10] The purpose of these outings was primarily to study Gothic architecture, with incidental social calls on members of Paris society who owned or rented villas near Cabourg.[11] Proust knew which churches he wanted to see from his readings and translations of Ruskin's critical writings, but he also wrote to the distinguished art historian Emile Mâle, asking him to recommend the best examples of religious and secular medieval architecture.[12] Among the sites visited that summer were Bayeux, Caen (whose steeples would be described in la Recherche as those of Martinville), Balleroy, Dives, Lisieux, Pont-Audemer, Evreux, and Conches (whose stained-glass windows Proust admired).

None of Proust's writings prior to these excursions contain the impressions of speed and parallax vision that would become important features of his presentation of multiple perspectives and relativity in the novel. The intensity of the impressions received was probably due not only to the new kinetic experience of moving rapidly through space in an automobile but also to Proust's preparations preceding each trip. Before setting off, he would drink an incredible amount of coffee—as many as seventeen cups—because he believed the caffeine suppressed or diminished any incipient asthma attack. At the Clermont-Tonnerres' chalet, Proust was so shaky from the caffeine that, when ready to depart, he required assistance to descend the stairs.[13] The automobile ride, with the speed-worshiping Agostinelli at the wheel, made quite an impact on the normally supine and supersensitive Proust, especially after so many cups of coffee. Under such conditions, what would have been an extraordinary experience for anyone in the early days of car travel—the play of hill, valley, and steeples in a vehicle that seemed to fly along the road—must have been greatly magnified for Proust. Such outings called for an adventuresome spirit as well, since the roads were rough and accidents were frequent.[14] The car, in its early days, was considered as much a sport for the wealthy as a mode of transportation. Proust credited Agostinelli's skill as a driver as making possible the daily and even nightly excursions to see the medieval architecture of the region.

These trips were described by Proust in a newspaper article entitled "Impressions de route en automobile" (*Le Figaro*, November 19, 1907), parts of which were later worked into various passages of *la Recherche*, most notably the passages on the steeples of Martinville (I, 179-82) and Albertine at the pianola (III, 381-84).[15] This was probably Proust's finest piece of writing to date. In the Martinville episode, the young Narrator is seated in a carriage, but the sensations he describes are those witnessed at Caen, where Proust saw the steeples of the cathedral shift position as he approached them in the car with Agostinelli. Some of these descriptions appear in the outings the Narrator takes with Albertine in the Balbec region. After that summer at Cabourg, Agostinelli would not play a major role again in Proust's life for another six years.

1913: Albertine, "compagnon de ma captivité"

At the urging of Mme Emile Straus, Proust, who seldom went out while writing *la Recherche*, subscribed to a precursor of the radio called the "théâtrophone" over which plays and concerts were periodically broadcast from various theaters, the Opéra, the Opéra-Comique, and a few other concert halls.[16] In 1913, during Agostinelli's last autumn with him, Proust purchased an Aeolian automatic piano player, which was adapted to the grand piano he kept in his room.[17] Much to the exasperation of the piano-roll suppliers, Proust began to ask for pieces that had never been

requested before, such as the piano transcription of Beethoven's
Quartet no. 14:

> Quand je ne suis pas trop triste pour en écouter, ma
> consolation est dans la musique, j'ai complété le
> théâtrophone par l'achat d'un pianola. Malheureuse-
> ment on n'a pas justement les morceaux que je
> voudrais jouer. Le sublime XIVᵉ *quatuor* de Beethoven
> n'existe pas dans leurs rouleaux.[18]

During the last years of the war, Beethoven's late string
quartets were among the selections that Proust hired the Quatuor
Poulet to play for him in the early morning hours. Proust would
model Vinteuil's last works, in part, on these quartets. But in
1913, the théâtrophone and the pianola provided him with
music.[19] In *La Prisonnière*, the Narrator and Albertine own a
pianola. During periods of calm he often asks her to play for him
both as a distraction from his jealous obsession and in order that
he may study and better comprehend musical works of which he
has only a rudimentary or imperfect knowledge. He conducts his
research by having Albertine play the music on the pianola as he
reclines and listens. During the performance of the music, the
instrument becomes a magic lantern, projecting images appropriate to the music on the walls of the room:

> le pianola était par moments pour nous comme une
> lanterne magique scientifique (historique et géo-
> graphique), et sur les murs de cette chambre . . . je
> voyais, selon qu'Albertine jouait du Rameau ou du
> Borodine, s'étendre tantôt une tapisserie du XVIIIᵉ siè-
> cle semée d'Amours sur un fond de roses, tantôt la
> steppe orientale où les sonorités s'étouffent dans l'illi-
> mité des distances et le feutrage de la neige. (III, 382)

In the Proustian universe machines undergo metamorphosis as readily as do natural things, as in the case of the pianola
becoming a projector of images. The Narrator's constant search
for the meaning of each experience in its totality is apparent when

he speaks of the projector as being scientific (knowledge), historical (time), and geographic (place); thus, the artist's vision constitutes time, space, and knowledge. Such projections represent an elaborate form of synesthesia whereby the auditory becomes visual. That is to say, the sounds do not merely suggest color but entire paintings or tapestries appropriate to the national origin of the music; these images are projected onto the walls of the Narrator's room so that he can analyze them in order to discover the truths they contain.[20] Albertine, serving as program director and organist, senses the precise moment when he has fully grasped the secret of each piece; she then returns the roll and rents another.

An addition to the text tells us that Vinteuil's music—though not the septet—was featured among the selections played on the pianola for him by Albertine. As we saw in "The Prison," Vinteuil's music is closely interwoven with the theme of sexuality. In the pianola passage, however, the Narrator believes that Albertine is no longer seeking to contact Mlle Vinteuil; her father's music is freed from the emotion of jealousy, sanitized, as it were, so that he can attempt to learn its secrets "sans souffrance" (III, 371*). Because he is less familiar with these pieces by Vinteuil, the music is characterized by "les lignes fragmentaires et interrompues de la construction, d'abord ensevelie dans la brume. . . ." Proust repeats the word "nébuleuse" or its variant twice in this passage ("ce travail de modelage d'une nébuleuse encore informe" and "le modelage de ces nébuleuses" [III, 372]). The word was also among those used to describe the little band of girls at their first appearance on the beach at Balbec, (I, 832), and as they continue their procession, Proust describes them as various statues and friezes belonging to architectural details (I, 788ff.). This is but another example of the linking of the theme of the "passantes" to music, which will be resolved when the Narrator understands the relationship of jealousy and suffering to the production of art. In the pianola passage, Albertine is the "passante" he believes he has captured and tamed

("Ange musicien") as he attempts to comprehend her and the music through the total possession of each:

> De même que le volume de cet Ange musicien était constitué par les trajets multiples entre les différents points du passé que son souvenir occupait en moi et les différents signes, depuis la vue jusqu'aux sensations les plus intérieures de mon être, qui m'aidaient à descendre jusque dans l'intimité du sien, la musique qu'elle jouait avait aussi un volume . . . selon que j'avais plus ou moins réussi à y mettre de la lumière et à rejoindre les unes aux autres les lignes d'une construction qui m'avait d'abord paru presque tout entière noyée dans le brouillard. (III, 372)

Albertine's understanding of his aesthetic needs proves her superiority over Odette, who is never able to assist Swann in his artistic development. The fact that Odette's intelligence and taste never advance beyond those of a not very bright cocotte is indicated by the Narrator at the reception held by the princesse de Guermantes when he compares her to a mechanical doll (III, 948) and a sterilized rose (III, 950).

It is good that Albertine is so compliant as a projectionist, since she is largely responsible for the bareness of his walls: "ces décorations fugitives étaient . . . les seules de ma chambre." Although he had promised himself that when he obtained his inheritance from Aunt Léonie, he would amass an art collection like Swann's, in his desperation to keep Albertine near him at all costs, he has squandered his money on her: "tout mon argent passait à avoir des chevaux, une automobile, des toilettes pour Albertine" (III, 382).[21]

Synesthesia is also found in a passage that occurs much earlier in the novel. The two passages are related through imagery and the aesthetic dilemma the Narrator tries to resolve, namely, to discover the secret of beautiful things. During his childhood days spent at Combray, the boy's view of the hawthorns that appear sporadically on his walks is compared to musical intervals, but at that point in his life the flowers do not yield up their secret; the Narrator compares them to "ces mélodies qu'on rejoue cent fois de suite sans descendre plus avant dans leur secret" (I, 138).

As he reviews the numerous rolls of music with Albertine, the Narrator's method reveals a systemization of a standard Proustian metaphor: music as visual image, or the artist and his works as magic lantern. He now has a deeper understanding of life and art than he formerly possessed in his youth, when he was dazzled by the impenetrable beauty of the hawthorns. But the passage does not carry any deep conviction, so far as aesthetic revelations are concerned, because Proust gives us no indication of precisely what it is the Narrator has learned, nor does he particularize the music beyond the well-known fact that art reflects a given time and place. This is not to deny the skill of the writer and the aptness of the images. Proust's purpose here is not to make any major revelations but to describe the process of aesthetic contemplation and Albertine's role as mediator, a role that Agostinelli was perhaps the first to fill. For passages that do convince us of the greatness of music and the exact nature of the Narrator's own aesthetic convictions, we must turn to the pages on Vinteuil's and Wagner's music.

Proust connects the Narrator's initial sighting of Albertine and the last vision he has of her at the pianola. As we have seen, one of his first epithets for her was "la bacchante à bicyclette" (I, 873). This phrase was coined before he met her or knew anything about her; he had instinctively sensed her sexual attractiveness and presumed to see in her something wild and fleeting in nature. These impressions were created in particular by the bicycle she was pushing, as well as the theme of speed that is always associated with Albertine. The connections between Albertine and the themes of speed and fugacity deepen as the Narrator attempts to know her and finally decides to imprison her.

While watching Albertine at the pianola, as her legs "pedal" the musical instrument, the Narrator recalls the first time he saw her with her bicycle: "Ses belles jambes, que le premier jour j'avais imaginées avec raison avoir manœuvré pendant toute son adolescence les pédales d'une bicyclette, montaient and descendaient tour à tour sur celles du pianola . . ." (III, 382).

There is a barely sublimated recognition here of the relationship between, on the one hand, pleasure ("ses belles jambes") and the suffering caused by jealousy that he usually experiences and, on the other, the creative power of the artist as her legs operate an instrument (pianola) that produces complex art (music and light, which become paintings on the walls). We find a similar analogy in the passage on reading in the garden at Combray, where the book (literary art) becomes in the Narrator's mind a film that projects visual images before him (I, 83ff.). In both passages, the use of simultaneous perceptions is typical of Proust. In the pianola passage, he is conscious both of Albertine's beauty and the beauty of the music, perceiving the images projected by both.

Albertine, whose beauty and sexuality usually represent a threat to his becoming an artist, has been tamed ("une bête sauvage domestiquée" [III, 382]), or so he believes at such moments; those beautiful legs that, along with her other attributes, caused him to feel such ardent desire and jealous passion are now beatified as they produce art in the form of musical paintings for his contemplation. Albertine's legs may be said to embody the many landscapes through which she has pedaled.[22] This is yet another variation on the main Proustian theme of women-as-countries (les femmes-pays). Albertine has always represented for him the female equivalent of Balbec. As she metamorphoses into an angel and Saint Cecilia, she becomes many countries, depending on the music being played. Because of the connection between physical beauty and aesthetic experience, the Narrator is tempted to regard Albertine as a work of art as she plays the pianola. Visualizing her as a sculpted angel, and perhaps a bit carried away by the grandeur of his analysis of her beauty, he is at the point of calling her a work of art when, remembering Swann's similar mistake with Odette, he catches himself abruptly and rejects the idea of

cet ange musicien, œuvre d'art qui, tout à l'heure, par
une douce magie, allait se détacher de sa niche et offrir
à mes baisers sa substance précieuse et rose. Mais non;
Albertine n'était nullement pour moi une œuvre
d'art. . . . j'avais connu Swann. . . . Rien de tel chez moi.
(III, 383-84)[23]

In the final, grand recognition scene—where the Narrator, now grown old, realizes that he will be an artist if he can live long enough to give birth to the work he carries within him—the relationship between vanity and art, involving suffering, mistakes, regrets, and creation, is made explicit (III, 897). The future redemptive nature of his relationship with Albertine, and of his experience in society, is prefigured in the pianola passage, where the former "bacchante" and present "pesante esclave" becomes, as she plays the instrument, Saint Cecilia (III, 382) and an "ange musicien" (III, 384), where music, light, and painting combine to form a vivid aesthetic experience through metaphor and synesthesia. At the end of his quest, the Narrator will learn how to transform the common elements of everyday life into the beauty and magic of art in order to produce his own magnum opus.

The parties Proust attended during his youth are among the biographical sources for the pianola/magic lantern episode. On occasion during musical performances, images were projected onto a screen or wall. At a party Madeleine Lemaire hosted in 1894, a tenor from the Opéra-Comique sang poems from Robert de Montesquiou's *Chauves-souris,* set to music by Léon Delafosse: "Pendant que Delafosse jouait un prélude . . . on voyait des projections de chauves-souris. . . ."[24] In a description of princesse Edmond de Polignac's salon, first published in *Le Figaro* in 1903, Proust remembered that the prince composed music inspired by the forest on his estate at Fontainebleau. While the prince's music was being played, one noticed "[passant] derrière l'orchestre une sorte d'immense agrandissement lumineux de photographies prises dans la forêt" (V, 467). These early examples of "son et lumière" reinforced Proust's deeply held belief in the synesthetic value of all art.

In its role as inspirer, the forest did "create" the music through the person of the prince. Once the music was written down by the prince and performed, it was capable of recreating and projecting images of the forest. Such a process underscores the predominance of vision as the catalyst of art in *la Recherche*. Vision as source or as end result lies behind every aspect of Proustian art. The entire novel could be viewed as an object lesson in how to see or—when negative examples are provided, as such correctives often are throughout the text—how not to see.

Light is the main purveyor of vision from one person or object to another. The concept of artists and works of art as projectors of light produces one of the richest constellations of metaphors in Proust's novel. This is true not only of the magic lantern itself but of related images; for example, Elstir's head is compared to a projector (II, 419), as is Vinteuil's through "[sa musique,] mode sur lequel il 'entendait' et projetait hors de lui l'univers" (III, 375). In the Proustian cosmos, artists are frequently represented as mirrors or planets, these last being, in essence, giant reflectors of light. The artist becomes a sharp focal point of light when the universe enters through his sensory perceptions (primarily visual), is concretely converted into a work of art (a conversion made possible by the artist's vision plus his craftsmanship), and is projected back into the universe. Proust, in a passage on the writer Bergotte, defined genius as "le pouvoir réfléchissant" (I, 555). The projection back into the universe is the central point of Proust's ethics, all genuine creation being altruistic. At that point, the artist has conquered vanity and redeemed himself from past mistakes and shortcomings.

The comparison of Albertine to Saint Cecilia is taken directly from Proust's description of his motoring trips through Normandy and Brittany with Agostinelli. In referring to this passage in his introduction to Proust's correspondence for the year 1907, Philip Kolb, who usually immediately senses the links between Proust's life and *la Recherche*, finds it "curious" that Proust compares Agostinelli at the wheel with Saint

Cecilia playing the organ.[25] Agostinelli in his motoring coat first reminded Proust of a pilgrim or nun of speed and then of Saint Cecilia.

Saint Cecilia was the patron saint of music—especially church music—and, according to tradition she was also the inventor of the organ.[26] We recall that Proust and Agostinelli were en route to see the architecture and sculpture of the medieval churches in the region. As was already noted, Proust often "sees" music in terms of art and architecture, of which the pianola passage is but one example.[27] In "Impressions de route en automobile," Proust describes the automobile as a kind of musical vehicle, with Agostinelli pulling out all the stops as he drives the writer from one church to another.

> De temps à autre—*sainte Cécile* improvisant sur un *instrument* plus immatériel encore—[Agostinelli] *touchait* le *clavier* et *tirait* un des jeux de ces *orgues* cachées dans l'automobile et dont nous ne remarquons guère la *musique,* pourtant continue, qu'à ces changements de *registre* que sont les changements de vitesse; *musique* pour ainsi dire abstraite, tout symbole et tout nombre, et qui fait penser à cette *harmonie* que produisent . . . les sphères. . . . (V, 67; emphasis added)

Rather than being unusual or curious, the association of machine, speed, and music occurs throughout the novel.[28] One of the most striking examples involves the same locale, namely, the hotel at Balbec—we recall that Proust and Agostinelli set out from the Grand-Hôtel de Cabourg—and somewhat similar circumstances. The Balbec hotel is said to be as high as a church tower, and the elevator boy ("lift") is compared to an organist: "un personnage encore inconnu de moi, qu'on appelait 'lift' (et qui au point le plus haut de l'hôtel, là où serait le lanternon d'une église normande, était installé . . . comme un organiste dans sa chambre) . . ." (I, 665).

This is the Narrator's first elevator ride, an experience involving speed, of being transported, where the person who operates the machine is seen as an organist. Although he has not yet met Albertine, the images used to describe his elevator ride with the "lift" anticipate his experience with the girl who will become his organist and merit fully the title "compagnon de ma captivité."[29] In the following quote, my italicization of certain words describing the elevator ride are similar to the ones used in Proust's descriptions of his excursions with Agostinelli in Normandy and Brittany, as well as in the Narrator's apartment, where Albertine is a prisoner at the pianola: "j'adressai la parole au jeune *organiste*, *artisan* de mon *voyage* et *compagnon* de ma *captivité*, lequel continuait à *tirer* les *registres* de son *instrument* et à *pousser* les *tuyaux*" (I, 665). Albertine as Saint Cecilia will provide a full development of the themes that are sketched out here.

Just as the mechanized elevator becomes a mobile organ lifting the protagonist to the top of the hotel-church, so the automobile with Agostinelli-Saint Cecilia at the wheel becomes an organ moving Proust through space from one medieval church to another as he explores the past through its architecture.[30] The hotel-church of the novel reminds us of the purpose behind the excursions that Agostinelli made with Proust; Agostinelli was the "artisan de mon voyage" in 1907, long before he became the "compagnon de ma captivité" in 1913.

Arriving at Lisieux after nightfall, Proust despairs of being able to see the cathedral facade described by Ruskin. Suddenly the statues leap out from the darkness as the "ingenious" Agostinelli trains the headlights on the portals. Proust appreciates both the modern (the automobile) and the ancient (the cathedral) as past and present meet and illuminate each other: "Agostinelli . . . envoyant aux vieilles sculptures le salut du présent dont la lumière ne servait plus qu'à mieux lire les leçons du passé . . ." (V, 66). Past and present are thus seen in each other's light. The unexpected flood of light, creating a long-awaited aesthetic experience as the statues leap out from the void, is like Albertine's projection of pictures from the pianola. Proust is reading the lessons of the past at Lisieux like the "paintings" projected onto the wall by the pianola, the only difference being that in the lived experience there was no synesthesia. Agostinelli projected light onto real works of art—the portals of churches. With the pianola, Proust provides a metaphorical projection of transposed art: the music becomes light, which contains the plastic vision.

While Proust was looking at the sculpture at Lisieux, curious children gathered around the automobile. In his description, Proust further enriched the scene by having the reflected light from the cathedral fall on the children and create a tableau vivant of the nativity. Then he reversed the source of the light, with the artificial light from the car becoming divine light emanating from the cathedral:

> Et quand je revins vers la voiture je vis un groupe d'enfants que la curiosité avait amenés là et qui, penchant sur le phare leurs têtes dont les boucles palpitaient dans cette lumière surnaturelle, recomposaient ici, comme projetée de la cathédrale dans un rayon, la figuration angélique d'une Nativité. (V, 66)

The confrontation of automobile and cathedral as present and past in both an ordinary and aesthetic context is an early example of Proust's technique of layering (*épaisseur*).[31] The past is shown to live in the present, and the children become living stone repeating the scene of the nativity. The children are descendants of generations now long gone, descendants not only of those who were models for the statues but also representatives of all generations that have repeated and will continue to repeat the nativity scene.

For Proust, the use of synesthesia is not simply an element of literary technique but a way of expressing his profound belief in the unity of all experience. The artist's function is to seize fleeting impressions, analyze them, and preserve for others, through his art, moments that would otherwise be lost forever. Proust endowed his book with an active title, the motto of the Proustian explorer: *A la recherche*. He created a work that had to be long enough to convey convincingly the shape of time. In fact, the Proustian quest never ends; like the cosmos itself, according to the most credible theory, it is always expanding: light into music, music into painting, life into art, and art into life. The Proustian universe is designed to be a fictional world without end, the literary equivalent of the cosmos. The explorers of this open universe, as we shall see in the next chapter, are the artist-aviators.

1914: "la mer sera mon tombeau"

Although Proust valued Agostinelli's service as a chauffeur and later as a secretary, when the Agostinellis moved into Proust's apartment, in the spring of 1913, they inevitably disrupted the writer's bizarre but highly organized life. Anna, whom the new secretary was said to have married after she had been his mistress for some years, has been described as ugly and unpleasant. The photograph of her published in Céleste Albaret's memoirs shows a woman who, although clearly squinting at the sun, nevertheless appears rather plain, with coarse features.[32] Proust, who also found her ugly and disagreeable, says that she was insanely jealous and would have killed Agostinelli had she been aware of his many infidelities. The writer found it difficult to understand how the handsome young Italian could have fallen in love with such a harsh, unattractive woman, even though this fact confirmed his theory about the subjective nature of love: "Son premier amour pour elle est inexplicable, car elle est laide, mais enfin il ne vivait que pour elle. . . ."[33] Proust's letters written in the spring and summer of 1913 contain veiled references to the kinds of sorrows he experienced when in love, for by that time Proust had become infatuated with his rash young chauffeur-secretary. He wrote to Mme Straus in mid-March: "il me semble que toutes les peines que j'ai seraient peut-être moins cruelles si je vous les racontais. Et elles ont un caractère assez général, assez humain pour peut-être vous intéresser." He wrote to Mme de Noailles in the summer: "de grands chagrins que j'ai eus cette année et que j'ai encore, me semblent comme une préparation à ressentir plus entièrement certaines pièces de ce livre."[34]

Proust had hired Agostinelli to finish preparing the typescript of *Du côté de chez Swann*. At this time, *la Recherche* consisted of three volumes: *Du côté de chez Swann*, which would be published on November 14, 1913, and two other projected volumes, *Le Côté de Guermantes* and *Le Temps retrouvé*. The strain of hard work and having the Agostinellis under the same roof was almost too much for Proust to bear. He confided to Lucien Daudet that he had lost an incredible amount of weight: "Mon cher petit, j'ai voulu vous écrire mais je ne vous écrirai plus parce qu'il faudrait que je reprenne 30 kilos (!)...." He also wrote to Georges de Lauris about his health, explaining why he found it so difficult to work and saying that the book about to be published resembled "La Fin de la jalousie . . . mais en cent fois moins mal et plus approfondi."[35]

It was only because of his fascination with his new secretary that Proust tolerated Anna's presence. He showered Agostinelli with money and privileges. In his letters written at this time, he urges friends not to mention money matters when writing to him, such as his intention to have his novel published at his own expense.[36] Although Proust was very generous to the Agostinellis, he did not want them to know anything about his finances, apparently for fear that they might demand even more of him. Agostinelli soon became passionately interested in aviation, a trait given to Albertine in the novel. As we have seen, she generally shares Agostinelli's predilection for sports and machines of speed.[37] Albertine and the Narrator make their last excursion together to an airfield:

> Comme il n'avait pas tardé à s'établir autour de Paris des hangars d'aviation . . . le but de nos sorties—agréable d'ailleurs à Albertine, passionnée pour tous les sports—fût un de ces aérodromes.... [Après le décollage d'un avion] Albertine ne pouvait contenir sa joie et elle demandait des explications aux mécaniciens....
> (III, 105-6).

The year 1913 is known in French aviation history as the "Année glorieuse," for that year French flyers flew nonstop from Nancy to Cairo and as far away as Algeria. Roland Garros was the first aviator to fly across the Mediterranean. A new speed record of 126 miles per hour was set and pilots reached altitudes of twenty-thousand feet. Aerodromes were opened at Buc, near Versailles, and Issy, drawing crowds of the curious, the idle rich, and brave young men like Agostinelli and Jacques-Henri Lartigue, who saw a new frontier opening up before them and were eager to fly the new machines.[38] (See p. 151). Proust tried to dissuade Agostinelli from taking flying lessons, but his objections were overruled by Anna's determination; she thought the couple would become fabulously wealthy if her husband could learn to fly an airplane.[39] Proust had warned them to expect no aid from him should Agostinelli be involved in an airplane accident: "Si jamais le malheur voulait que vous eussiez un accident d'aéroplane, dites bien à votre femme qu'elle ne trouvera en moi ni un protecteur, ni un ami et n'aura jamais un sou de moi."[40]

Céleste learned of Agostinelli's passion for sports and his daredevil nature through her husband, Odilon, who had been working with Agostinelli periodically for years: "J'ai . . . su par Odilon qu'il [Agostinelli] avait la folie de la mécanique et que cette folie s'est tournée de l'automobile vers l'aviation. . . . Il était aussi audacieux et casse-cou."[41] In his last letter to Agostinelli, which the young man did not live to read, Proust refers to his secretary's love of sports, which, as we have seen, is one of Albertine's distinguishing characteristics: "Puisque vous vous intéressez à *Swann* et aux sports, je vous envoie un article paru sur *Swann* dans un journal de Sports."[42] Thanks to Proust's generosity—the couple were still living in the novelist's apartment on the boulevard Haussmann—Agostinelli was able to take flying lessons at Buc, where Roland Garros had an aviation school. Since Agostinelli no longer owned a car, Proust paid Odilon to drive him to and from the airfield.

During November 1913, the relationship between Proust and his secretary apparently became strained. On December 1,

Jacques–Henri Lartigue, Maurice Farman in his Biplane,
Buc, November 1911 (© Association des Amis
de Jacques–Henri Lartigue).

Agostinelli and Anna fled Proust's apartment for the Riviera.[43] Distressed and angry, Proust sent Albert Nahmias to Nice to bring them back. The jealous writer tried everything to recapture Agostinelli, hiring a private detective agency to follow the fugitive and having Nahmias enter into negotiations with Agostinelli's father, to whom Proust offered a secret monthly payment if he could guarantee that his son would return to Paris and stay there until April 1914. All Proust's attempts failed, and Agostinelli did not come back. In the novel, Saint-Loup, who plays the same role that Nahmias filled in real life, also fails in his mission, and Albertine never returns.[44]

At the end of March 1914, Agostinelli, aged twenty-five, enrolled in the aviation school run by the Garbero brothers at La Grimaudière, near Antibes, under the name Marcel Swann. After two months of training, during which he made rapid progress, he was ready for his second solo flight. Around five in the afternoon on Saturday, May 30, Agostinelli took off in a monoplane. (See p. 153.) Anna and Emile, Alfred's brother, who was also an apprentice pilot, were watching as Agostinelli went through his maneuvers. Elated by his success, the impetuous young man ignored the warnings of chief pilot Joseph Garbero and left the designated flying area, heading the plane out over the Bay of Angels. Attempting a turn, the inexperienced pilot forgot to increase his altitude and the right wing skimmed the water, pulling the aircraft into the sea as Anna, Emile, and other pilots from the Garbero school watched in horror. Once Agostinelli had recovered from the shock of finding himself unexpectedly plunged into the water, he noticed that although the plane was three-fourths submerged, it seemed to be floating. He stood atop the pilot's seat and screamed for help. Those on shore quickly found a boat and rescuers began rowing frantically toward the downed aviator. But suddenly the plane went straight down, taking Agostinelli with it. He was known to be a good swimmer, and his friends were later puzzled as to why he disappeared without a struggle.[45] Some said that sharks had been seen in the area,

Alfred Agostinelli in his Monoplane
(Private collection of Céleste Albaret).

while others claimed that the spot where he went down was
known to have swift currents. Search boats continued to ply the
waters in the bay until dark. Whatever had happened to make
him disappear so quickly, Agostinelli was not seen again until
fisherman found the body eight days later.[46]

Le Figaro carried the news of the accident the next day.
Proust had learned of the tragedy on the evening of the thirtieth
when he received a telegram from Anna.[47] On Sunday morning,
a boat succeeded in locating the sunken plane, but the body was
no longer there. The family gave the newspapers a description of
what Agostinelli had been wearing: a khaki one-piece flying suit,
a brown rubber helmet, gray shirt, black pants, black shoes, and a
signet ring with the initials AA.[48] In addition to the heavy clothing, Agostinelli had on his person all his money—about five or six
thousand francs, which represented the remainder of what Proust
had given him—probably because he did not trust Anna and his
brother. Agostinelli's father and brother both realized that if the
body were found, all the money would go to Anna, since everyone thought that she was the pilot's legal wife; they allegedly
turned against her and sent a wire to the prince de Monaco telling
him of Anna's true status as the mistress of the dead aviator.[49]

On June 1, La Nouvelle Revue Française published extracts
from Le Côté de Guermantes, which was originally intended as the
second volume of the novel, for which Proust now began to
receive proofs, but he was too upset to work.[50] He also had Anna
and Emile to worry about. After the funeral, they had come running back to Paris, confident that he would help them in spite of
the earlier warnings that they would never receive a penny from
him should Agostinelli die in a plane crash. Proust, as was his
nature in such circumstances, relented and did everything he
could to help, trying to find them employment, enlisting the aid
of friends such as Emile Straus on their behalf, and even writing
to the prince de Monaco to see if Anna could inherit anything
from Agostinelli even though she was not legally his widow. In
the weeks following Agostinelli's death, Anna tried several times

to commit suicide, and Proust was afraid that if her situation grew desperate enough, she might succeed in killing herself.[51] Proust himself was not immune to death wishes. Later that fall, he confided to Lucien Daudet that during the days following Agostinelli's accident he had longed to die: "moi, qui avais si bien supporté d'être malade, qui me trouvais nullement à plaindre, j'ai su ce que c'était, chaque fois que je montais en taxi, d'espérer de tout mon cœur que l'autobus qui venait allait m'écraser."[52]

On May 28, two days before Agostinelli's fatal accident, Proust had gone to arrange the sale of some stocks in order to raise enough money to buy an airplane as a surprise gift for Agostinelli.[53] On May 30—the very day of Agostinelli's death— Proust wrote a long letter to the young man, telling him that he had spent twenty-seven thousand francs to buy an airplane for him. Proust began by thanking Agostinelli for his letter and quoting briefly from it: "Je vous remercie beaucoup de votre lettre (une phrase était *ravissante* (crépusculaire etc.). . . ."[54] Proust would later use passages from Agostinelli's letters in the last ones Albertine writes to the Narrator in *La Fugitive:* "Croyez que de mon côté je n'oublierai pas cette promenade deux fois crépusculaire (puisque la nuit venait et que nous allions nous quitter) et qu'elle ne s'effacera de mon esprit qu'avec la nuit complète" (III, 468).[55]

Proust had asked Agostinelli to send back all his letters and had given him specific instructions about how to do so. Proust's letters to Agostinelli were destroyed by the latter's family, who said they were love letters. The one surviving letter, returned since Agostinelli died before he could receive it, does not read like a love letter.[56] If we possess the letter of May 30, it is probably because Anna brought it back with her when she came to stay with Proust after Agostinelli's death. Kolb says that Proust wanted the letters back not only to prevent anyone else from reading them, but in order to leave open the possibility of using them in his novel.[57] If Kolb is right—the fact that Proust preserved this letter may be an important indication of his intention to quote it in the novel—

then the novelist had already decided to use Agostinelli as one of the models for Albertine before the pilot's death. Henri Bonnet, on the other hand, thinks that the only reason Proust quoted the letter to Agostinelli was because the latter was already dead.[58]

The letter of May 30 reveals that Proust had written previously to Agostinelli, asking him to cancel the order for the airplane and another gift—most likely a Rolls-Royce—that Proust intended for him as well.[59] Without explaining why, Proust thinks it indelicate to ask Agostinelli to cancel the order for the first unnamed gift ("je ne trouverais pas cela délicat . . ."). The munificence of the gifts that Proust offered Agostinelli would be surprising if we did not know how dependent he had become upon the young man. His attempts to win back Agostinelli with the gift of an airplane are the direct source for similar episodes involving Albertine in the novel. The details of Proust's letter to Agostinelli are reproduced in the novel almost point by point; the gifts the Narrator offers as bait to lure Albertine back to him are a yacht and a Rolls-Royce.[60] Kolb's investigations have led him to discover that the cost of a Rolls in 1914 was almost exactly the same as the price of an airplane: "*L'Auto* du mardi 9 décembre 1913 annonce . . . sous le titre *La Rolls-Royce/La meilleure voiture du monde*, que le prix du châssis Rolls-Royce 40/50 HP 6 cylindres, est de 26 200 francs, livrable franco, à Paris."[61] In the novel, Proust substituted a yacht for the airplane because at that time a yacht was a more appropriate gift for a woman.[62]

Proust writes to Agostinelli that if he decides to keep the airplane, he will have verses from a Mallarmé poem inscribed on the fuselage:

> je ferai graver sur (je ne sais pas le nom de la pièce et je
> ne veux commettre d'hérésie devant un aviateur) les
> vers de Mallarmé que vous connaissez:

> Un cygne d'autrefois se souvient que c'est lui
> Magnifique, mais sans espoir qui le délivre
> Pour n'avoir pas chanté la région où vivre.
> Toujours il secouera cette triste agonie

Par l'espace infligée à l'oiseau qui le nie
Mais non l'horreur du sol où son plumage est pris.
Fantôme qu'à ce lieu son pur éclat assigne
Il s'immobilise au songe muet de mépris
Que vêt parmi l'exil inutile, le Cygne.

These verses, quoted from memory by Proust from Mallarmé's poem "Sonnet," are appropriate for the aviator, who seeks to defy gravity. The image of the bird whose plumage is held by the ground expresses exactly the tethered condition of the prisoner. It had apparently been Agostinelli's intention to have the word "Cygne" painted on the front of the airplane. Indeed, when Agostinelli signed up for flying lessons, he did so under the name Marcel Swann. The words "Cygne, Marcel Swann" echo the verses about a swan and a prophecy that was being fulfilled even as Proust wrote the lines. The wing of Agostinelli's plane, so briefly aloft, was caught and held by the water. In the novel, as we shall see, Proust denies Albertine any association with the aviator. However, the yacht he buys her is to bear the name "Cygne": "Le yacht était déjà presque prêt, il s'appelle, selon votre désir exprimé à Balbec, *le Cygne*" (III, 455). The continuation of the quotation from Proust's letter to Agostinelli, which is really the beginning of the poem, also contains the image of the tethered bird:

C'est la poésie que vous aimez tout en la trouvant obscure et qui commence par:

Le vierge le vivace et le bel Aujourd'hui
Va-t-il nous déchirer avec un coup d'aile ivre
Ce lac dur oublié, que hante sous le givre
Le transparent glacier des vols qui n'ont pas fui.

Hélas "Aujourd'hui" n'est plus ni "vierge", ni "vivace", ni "beau"![63]

The intention to inscribe verses from Mallarmé's poem on an object was later used by Proust for the Rolls and the yacht that the Narrator promises to buy in order to win back Albertine:

> je ferai graver sur le . . . du yacht (mon Dieu, ne je
> n'ose pas mettre un nom de pièce inexacte et commet-
> tre une hérésie qui vous choquerait) ces vers de Mal-
> larmé que vous aimiez. . . . Vous vous rappelez, c'est la
> poésie qui commence par: *Le Vierge*. . . . Quant à la
> Rolls, elle eût mérité plutôt ces autres vers du même
> poète, que vous disiez ne pas pouvoir comprendre:
>
> Tonnerre et rubis aux moyeux . . .

Proust then quotes from memory the last six lines of Mallarmé's sonnet, which begins with the very Proustian line: "M'introduire dans ton histoire . . ." (III, 455–56).

The letter to Albertine ends with a postscript in which he denies that he sent Saint-Loup to her aunt, Mme Bontemps, in an attempt to bribe the lady and thus assure the girl's return to his apartment: "C'est du Sherlock Holmes. Quelle idée vous faites-vous de moi?" (III, 456). Proust had instructed Nahmias to deny any suggestion that he had been sent on the writer's behalf to arrange Agostinelli's return.[64] Proust was, in fact, as mendacious in his dealings with Agostinelli as the Narrator and Swann are with the women they pursue.

Céleste saw in Agostinelli a vain and presumptuous young man who sought to rise above his station. When we read what she has to say about Alfred, whom she treats as an arriviste, we are reminded of the maid Françoise at Combray, who is jealous of any potential rival: "il était travaillé par le désir d'être autre chose. Il a fini par demander à M. Proust de devenir son secré-taire." About his intention to take flying lessons and have the word *"Swann"* painted on the airplane, she has this to say: "C'était un flatteur. . . . son idée était de convaincre M. Proust de l'aider à acheter un appareil pour son usage personnel, qu'il aurait baptisé 'Swann', disait-il, du nom du personnage principal du livre que M. Proust venait de publier."[65]

The lavish gifts Proust gave Agostinelli nearly ruined him financially. As early as 1912, the year before the Agostinellis moved in with him, Proust had begun speculating wildly on the stock market, a game that would cost him dearly with the onset of the war, at which time Proust found himself ruined in the financial panic of 1914.[66] After Agostinelli's death, in pleading to his friends to help Anna and Emile, Proust points out that he would gladly help them but cannot because he is on the brink of bankruptcy.[67]

In his appeals for help for the Agostinellis, Proust stresses his former secretary's intellectual gifts.[68] If, as Philip Kolb maintains, Proust exaggerates Agostinelli's intelligence in these letters to his friends, he does make Albertine somewhat less intelligent in the novel. But, as we have seen in the pianola episode, although Albertine is clearly more intelligent than Odette, Proust does not allow this faculty to become an important reason for the Narrator's attraction to her: "Il est certain que j'avais connu des personnes d'intelligence plus grande" (III, 495). He ends the passage with a statement about the totally subjective nature of love. In a final touch, Proust employs a spatial analogy wherein the desired woman is again identified with a country or landscape. Here the country becomes generalized space, as befits the aphoristic nature of the statement:

> l'infini de l'amour, ou son égoïsme, fait que les êtres
> que nous aimons sont ceux dont la physionomie intel-
> lectuelle et morale est pour nous le moins objective-
> ment définie . . . ils ne sont qu'un lieu immense et
> vague où extérioriser nos tendresses. (III, 495)

Concerning Agostinelli's intelligence, Proust had observed as early as 1907 (the year they met) that the chauffeur had a verbal facility that went well beyond what one would normally expect of someone from his class and educational background. Proust had noticed this when Agostinelli sent him a letter after the publication of "Impressions de route en automobile." At the time, Proust wrote to Mme Straus: "Imaginez-vous parmi quelques autres lettres que j'ai reçues quelle était la plus jolie: celle d'Agostinelli à qui mon valet de chambre avait envoyé l'article."[69]

In a letter to Gide written not long after Agostinelli's death (June 10 or 11, 1914), Proust speaks of his great love for Agostinelli without actually naming him, describing "la mort d'un jeune homme que j'aimais probablement plus que tous mes amis puisqu'elle me rend si malheureux." He also mentions Agostinelli's humble origins and says that although his friend is very intelligent, it was only after he fell in love with him that he noticed this quality. This letter contains an expression of sincere regret while at the same time stating—as did the quote from the novel—Proust's belief that when we love a person it is not necessarily for that person's good qualities but because of our subjective vision of the beloved:

> C'était un garçon d'une intelligence délicieuse; et ce n'est pas du reste pour cela que je l'aimais. J'ai été longtemps sans m'en apercevoir, moins longtemps que lui d'ailleurs. J'ai découvert en lui ce mérite si merveilleusement incompatible avec tout ce qu'il était, je l'ai découvert avec stupéfaction, mais sans que cela ajoutât rien à ma tendresse.[70]

The details of the amorous relationship between Proust and Agostinelli are likely to remain unknown. Louis Gautier-Vignal, who often saw Proust during the period after Agostinelli's death and observed his poor health and dependence on others—especially Céleste—believes that all of Proust's crushes on young men were platonic, going so far as to say that he thinks Proust was impotent.[71] With no convincing evidence to support his view, George Painter had maintained that Proust was virile. Recent testimony, if it is to be believed, supports Painter's view by refuting the notion of an impotent Proust and shedding new light on his sexual practices. Henri Bonnet has published information he found in a notebook written by the novelist Marcel Jouhandeau.[72] Bonnet does not tell us the origin of the notebook,[73] but according to the account it contains, Jouhandeau had interviewed a man who, when young, was often summoned to Proust's room in

Albert Le Cuziat's brothel.[74] When the young man entered the room, the writer would be in bed with the sheet pulled up to his chin. Proust would smile at the youth, who would then undress and begin masturbating; Proust would do the same. Once Proust had ejaculated, he would smile again and the young man would leave the room without ever having touched his client or seen more of him than his head peering out over the sheet. If Proust were unable to have an orgasm, caged, famished rats would be brought in and Proust, watching the bloody spectacle of the rats clawing and biting each other, would succeed in reaching a climax.

It is likely that we will never know the truth about Proust's sexual habits, but so far as interpreting the novel is concerned, it really makes no difference. Whether his love for Agostinelli was physical in any sense or not, it is evident that Proust fell in love with him and that this young man lent many details, though certainly not all, to the character of Albertine.

The guilt the Narrator feels over Albertine's death is less easy to justify than the guilt Proust felt over Agostinelli's. There is a direct reference in the novel to the guilt the writer felt over the aviator's death in the aftermath of Albertine's death: "de ma prison elle s'était évadée pour aller se tuer sur un cheval que sans moi elle n'eût pas possédé . . ." (III, 500). Had Proust not lavished money on Agostinelli, the young man probably could not have afforded to relocate in Antibes and enroll in the aviation school: "Hélas, j'ai le chagrin aujourd'hui de penser que s'il ne m'avait pas rencontré et n'avait pas gagné tant d'argent par moi, il n'aurait pas eu les moyens d'apprendre l'aviation. . . ." In the beginning, Proust apparently did try to discourage Agostinelli from becoming a pilot ("J'avais tout fait pour l'empêcher de faire de l'aviation. . ."[75]), but later he tried to take advantage of Agostinelli's passion for aviation and win him back by promising him an airplane. According to Gautier-Vignal, "Quand Proust apprit sa mort, il éprouva un vif chagrin auquel s'ajouta, me dit-il, . . . le remords de l'avoir encouragé à apprendre le dangereux métier, en lui promettant un avion."[76]

Although the Narrator cannot be held responsible for either death, he assumes guilt for the deaths of his grandmother and Albertine. This is the guilt we feel toward those whom we have loved: guilt at having survived them; guilt at not having loved them enough while they were alive; in short, guilt over the general failure of love:

> Et j'avais alors . . . la honte de lui survivre. Il me semblait, en effet . . . que je bénéficiais . . . de sa mort, car une femme est d'une plus grande utilité pour notre vie, si elle y est, au lieu d'un élément de bonheur, un instrument de chagrin. . . . Dans ces moments-là, rapprochant la mort de ma grand'mère et celle d'Albertine, il me semblait que ma vie était souillée d'un double assassinat. . . . (III, 496)[77]

Less than a month after Agostinelli's death, the second tragic event of 1914 occurred. This one would have global implications and would alter considerably the novel Proust was writing: the assassination on June 28 of Archduke Franz Ferdinand of Austria, the event that precipitated World War I. In letters written in the closing days of the year, Proust refers to the difficult times as "l'Enfer qu'est l'époque actuelle" and "cette affreuse année."[78] The largest conflict the world had yet seen made the publication of the next projected volume, Le Côté de Guermantes, impossible. After the war broke out, Bernard Grasset, who had published Du côté de chez Swann and was about to publish Le Côté de Guermantes, was drafted, making it necessary to close the publishing house.[79] According to Louis Gautier-Vignal, who saw Proust often during the war, the events of the global conflict saddened him even more than the death of Agostinelli and that of his mother years earlier.[80]

Gautier-Vignal's testimony is supported by the letters that Proust wrote during the period. The loss of Agostinelli; the anguish the writer suffered over Bertrand de Fénelon's disappearance and the sorrow he experienced when the dreaded confirmation of Fénelon's death came; the constant concern about the

safety of his brother, Robert, and that of his lifelong and closest
friend, Reynaldo Hahn, both of whom were in the war zone—all
these became recurrent themes in letter after letter. This letter to
Clément de Maugny is typical:

> Et pourtant [mes peines] sont bien grandes, tu ne le
> sais, tant nos vies sont séparées maintenant, d'un ami
> [Agostinelli] que j'ai perdu il y a un an, et qui avec ma
> mère, mon père, est la personne que j'ai le plus aimée.
> Mais depuis les morts se sont succédé[s] sans interrup-
> tion. Bertrand de Fénelon, qui . . . s'est montré pour
> moi un ami incomparable, Bertrand de Fénelon qui
> n'avait pas à être mobilisé et rendait plus de services où
> il était, a voulu partir et a été tué. Il y avait dix ans que
> je ne l'avais pas vu, mais je le pleurerai toujours.[81]

Proust's intense preoccupation with the war and his concern for the safety of his brother and friends can be seen in his
daily practice of devouring the war reports from seven newspapers: "Nuit et jour on pense à la guerre, peut-être plus doulou-
reusement encore quand comme moi on ne la fait pas."[82] The
newspapers Proust read and his discussions with friends about the
progress of the war served as the source of the Narrator's interest
in military strategy and his conversations with Saint-Loup.
Fénelon's death and his homosexuality, which had been concealed
for some years, were attributed to Saint-Loup.[83]

The only real-life people to whom Proust pays tribute in *la
Recherche* are Bertrand de Fénelon, Céleste Albaret, and some of the
latter's relatives, whose names appear a few times. In *La Prisonnière*,
Proust speaks of Céleste's genius in the context of Albertine's intelligence, a topic that has already been discussed: "Albertine s'était
étonnamment développé. Ce qui m'était entièrement égal. . . . Seul
le curieux génie de Céleste m'eût peut-être plu" (III, 17). Of
Bertrand de Fénelon, Proust writes that he is "l'ami le plus cher
l'être le plus intelligent, bon et brave, inoubliable à tous ceux qui
l'ont connu" (II, 771). It is reasonable to believe that Proust considered such mention in his novel to be the greatest tribute he could

pay to these friends. We can judge the significance of this homage when we think of those who are left out, notably Reynaldo Hahn, Mme Straus, and Agostinelli. Had Proust wanted to pay tribute to Agostinelli, the fact that the chauffeur contributed to the character of Albertine would not have prevented him from doing so. Céleste contributed significantly to the portrait of Françoise, as did Bertrand de Fénelon to that of Saint-Loup and to Albertine, yet Proust mentioned them both by name.

With the coming of the war, Proust had more time to write and additional material to consider; Agostinelli's death lent new life and direction to the novel, leading to the development of Albertine, in whom he would concentrate all that remained for him to say about erotic love, jealousy, death, memory, oblivion, and the relationship of suffering to the creative act.

In a long letter written to Marie Scheikévitch in November 1915, Proust outlines the developments to come in the unpublished portions of his novel. He insists especially upon the importance of a new central character, Albertine: "j'aimerais mieux vous présenter les personnages que vous ne connaissez pas encore, celui surtout qui joue le plus grand rôle et amène la péripétie, Albertine."[84] This letter is remarkable because it shows that in the year following Agostinelli's death Proust had already worked out all the plot details for the new characters, whose presence would greatly alter the original structure, though not the meaning and substance, of his novel. The letter summarizes the Narrator's entire experience with Albertine: the initial attraction, first suspicions, appeasement, and boredom, which always happens to Proustian lovers whenever they feel secure in their possession of the desired woman; his intention of breaking with her; the terrible revelation about Albertine's relationship with Mlle Vinteuil and her friend, which causes a reversal of his feelings and determines him to marry her; her imprisonment in his apartment, flight, and death; and, finally, the process of remembering and forgetting as each of his multiple selves (*les moi successifs*) remembers, grows indifferent to, and ultimately forgets the various Albertines:

Albertine n'aurait rien pu me reprocher. On ne peut
être fidèle qu'à ce dont on se souvient, on ne peut se
souvenir que de ce qu'on a connu. Mon moi nouveau
tandis qu'il grandissait à l'ombre de l'ancien qui
mourait avait souvent entendu celui-ci parler d'Albertine. A travers les récits du moribond, il croyait la connaître, l'aimer. Mais ce n'était qu'une tendresse de seconde main.[85]

In a letter to Reynaldo Hahn written in the fall of 1914,
Proust also talked about grieving and multiple selves in much the
same terms as those used in the letter to Marie Scheikévitch, but
this time he referred directly to Agostinelli. The occasion of the
letter was Proust's desire to explain to Hahn that if he seemed to
have recovered quickly from Agostinelli's death, he nonetheless
had genuinely grieved for him, finding it impossible to sustain
such feelings for very long. Hahn had written to Proust expressing his concern that the first trip Proust made to Cabourg in
September—only a few months after his secretary's fatal accident—might be especially painful for him, given all the associations that the Normandy resort shared with the memory of
Agostinelli. In late October, Proust wrote back, telling Hahn that
in spite of the genuineness of his love, there were times at
Cabourg when he thought little or not at all of his late friend.
The letter merits quotation at length, especially since the second
page was only discovered in 1985 and published for the first time
by Philip Kolb in 1986. (The previously unpublished portion
begins with the line: "Mais j'ai aussi la tristesse. . . .)

Mais enfin à Cabourg sans cesser d'être aussi triste ni
d'autant le regretter, il y a eu des moments, peut-être
des heures, où il avait disparu de ma pensée. . . .
J'aimais vraiment Alfred. Ce n'est pas assez de dire que
je l'aimais, je l'adorais. Et je ne sais pourquoi j'écris cela
au passé car je l'aime toujours. Mais malgré tout, dans
les regrets, il y a une part d'involontaire et une part de
devoir qui fixe l'involontaire et en assure la durée. Or

ce devoir n'existe pas envers Alfred qui avait très mal
agi avec moi, je lui donne les regrets que je ne peux
faire autrement que de lui donner, je ne me sens pas
tenu envers lui à un devoir comme celui qui me lie à
vous, qui me lierait à vous, même si je vous devais
mille fois moins, si je vous aimais mille fois moins. . . .
Mais j'ai aussi la tristesse de sentir que même vives [mes
souffrances] sont pourtant peut-être moins obsédantes
qu'il y a un mois et demi ou deux mois. Ce n'est pas
parce que les autres sont morts que le chagrin diminue,
mais parce qu'on meurt soi-même. Et il faut une bien
grande vitalité pour maintenir et faire vivre intact le
"moi" d'il y a quelques semaines. Son ami ne l'a pas
oublié, le pauvre Alfred. Mais il l'a rejoint dans la mort
et son héritier, le "moi" d'aujourd'hui aime Alfred
mais ne l'a pas connu que par les récits de l'autre. C'est
une tendresse de seconde main. . . . D'ailleurs je n'ai
plus à . . . formuler [de telles idées]. Il y a longtemps
que la vie ne m'offre plus que des événements que j'ai
déjà décrits. Quand vous lirez mon troisième volume
celui qui s'appelle en partie *A l'ombre des jeunes filles en
fleurs,* vous reconnaîtrez l'anticipation et la sûre
prophétie de ce que j'ai éprouvé depuis.[86]

By November 22, Proust had moved on to other consid-
erations and was working on sections of the novel that have nothing to do with Agostinelli and Albertine; he was rereading Joseph
Reinach's book on the Dreyfus affair in order to document passages for *la Recherche* about France's most famous cause célèbre.[87]

The statement in the last paragraph of the letter reveals
that Proust had already worked out the implications of love and
fidelity to the memory of a beloved person in his notes for the
novel *before* such implications were proven to him by the tragedy
of Agostinelli's death. Thus, according to Proust, the theory of
multiple selves concerning love, jealousy, death, guilt, and sorrow
was already established in *A l'ombre des jeunes filles en fleurs,*
which became a case of life confirming art. We know now that

Proust embroidered upon these tenets about love and death, adding details from his experience with Agostinelli to make them more precise, and working them into passages later to be published in *La Fugitive*. The experience with Agostinelli provided new and painful examples to sustain a theory already held by Proust. In addition, the letter states Proust's realization that his attachment to Agostinelli was not as strong as the love and sense of duty that bound him to friends such as Reynaldo Hahn and Bertrand de Fénelon. The latter's death affected him greatly, even though he had not seen Fénelon for over ten years. Although we do not know the details behind Proust's assertion that Agostinelli was unkind to him, Proust obviously resented the way his protégé had treated him. If the time frame in the letter to Hahn is to be taken seriously, Proust's period of intense grief over Agostinelli's death lasted only a few weeks. Philip Kolb points out that when Proust wrote the letter, he was already thinking about the section of *La Fugitive* where he describes the three stages of the Narrator's growing indifference to the memory of Albertine.[88]

Proust ends his letter to Mme Scheikévitch with a maxim-like statement about death and mourning:

> Le regret est bien un mal physique, mais entre les maux physiques, il faut distinguer ceux qui n'agissent sur le corps que par l'intermédiaire de la mémoire. Dans le dernier cas le diagnostic est généralement favorable. Au bout de quelque temps un malade atteint de cancer sera mort. Il est bien rare qu'un veuf inconsolable au bout du même temps ne soit pas guéri.[89]

At one point in *la Recherche*, this belief is expressed as a generalized cynical statement about death and mourning: "toute mort est pour les autres une simplification d'existence, ôte le scrupule de se montrer reconnaissant, l'obligation de faire des visites" (III, 978). In relation to Albertine, Proust had written a passage—later omitted—before her death that shows the Narrator would not grieve over her for long. He confesses his utter lack of sincerity when telling her of the great sorrow he would experience after her death: "sachant qu'Albertine ne pouvait plus que . . . me causer des chagrins, que je ne ferais que gâcher ma vie pour elle . . . je me disais que cette mort m'eût rendu . . . ma liberté d'esprit et d'action."[90]

These remarks reflect the Narrator's attitude before he learns the importance of suffering to the creative act. J. E. Rivers delivers a facile explanation of the role of suffering in relation to the Albertine episode when he misreads the last line in Proust's letter to Mme Scheikévitch: "Hélas Madame le papier me manque au moment où cela allait devenir pas trop mal!" The line does not mean, as Rivers translates it, "Alas, Madame, I'm running out of blank pages just as the suffering was becoming less acute," but "I'm running out of paper just as it was getting good!" Instead of ending on a tragic note, as Rivers suggests, Proust ends with characteristic humor. Rivers then provides the following analysis of Proust's suffering:

> There is a telling ambiguity in the remark, and also a moving statement of one of the relationships Proust establishes in [the novel] between suffering and artistic creation: as long as there are more blank pages to be filled with writing, with analysis, with self-confrontation, the grief can be controlled and the pain understood. The pages of writing are the suffering, but they are also the means of banishing the suffering. They are, to borrow a central paradox from Proust's description of love, the sickness and the cure.[91]

The telling ambiguity in the remark comes from Rivers's mistranslation. The suffering does not result from the writing—which was perhaps in Proust's later life his only source of joy, in spite of the immense labor necessary to create such a work, and certainly his only raison d'être—but from his disappointments in love and society, the evils of war, and at times even the lack of suffering, that is, from our inability to maintain our love and fidelity to loved ones now lost. That writing heals wounds is true in the sense that any act of self-expression releases tension and brings with it the satisfaction of having done something rather than remain passive; but, as we shall see in the chapter on "The Cosmos Builder," there is a more profound relationship between suffering and the creative act than mere therapeutic expression. Furthermore, as the letter to Hahn shows, Proust had essentially recovered from his grief over Agostinelli's death by the time of his trip to Cabourg.

In Rivers's efforts to correct what he feels is vagueness or homophobia on the part of critics who refuse to allow for Agostinelli's metamorphosis into Albertine,[92] Rivers goes too far in the other direction, overstating the case and, on some points, wrongly attributing sources for passages in the novel. Though he admits Agostinelli was not the only model for Albertine, he makes a strong case for Proust's experience with the chauffeur-secretary as having been the determining one in changing the course of the novel and providing the material for Proust's treatise on love and jealousy. This is all true, and yet Rivers clearly exaggerates the importance of the period Proust spent grieving for Agostinelli and working out the implications of their relationship; nor does he make any allowance for World War I as a factor in permitting Proust to expand greatly the scope of his novel after 1914.

> Proust's relationship with Alfred Agostinelli shook the very foundations of his original conception and helped to impart to the novel both its tragedy and its universality. It played a major role in transforming what might have been simply a work into a great work, a grand œuvre in the moral sense, in the structural sense. . . . Proust spent the rest of his life working out the implications of his relationship with Alfred Agostinelli. When Proust died in 1922, he was still revising and adding to *La Prisonnière* and *La Fugitive*.[93]

This last argument is particularly weak. Had Proust died a year or so later, he would have been revising and adding to *Le Temps retrouvé*. In a letter to Paul Souday written in 1919, Proust speaks of the effects of war and ill health on the length of time it took him to write his novel, pointing out that the beginning and concluding sections were written first and the middle section "long ago." He then continues: "La guerre m'a empêché d'avoir des épreuves, la maladie m'empêche, maintenant, de les corriger. Sans cela, il y a beau temps que la critique n'aurait plus à s'occuper de moi."[94] If Proust continued to revise *La Prisonnière* in 1922, it was not because he was working out the implications of his relationship with Agostinelli but because it had been materially and physically impossible for him to publish the novel any sooner.

Proust, of course, made many additions to *la Recherche*, but the evidence we have indicates that thematically and structurally the essential elements of the novel were present in the early notebooks of *la Recherche* and, in some cases, in material from *Les Plaisirs et les jours* and *Jean Santeuil*. If, as Rivers maintains, after 1914 Proust spent the rest of his life working out the implications of his relationship to Agostinelli in order to incorporate them in his novel, then all one can say is that the results are neither very flattering to the model nor encouraging to lovers. In *la Recherche*, Proust orchestrates elaborate variations on the themes of love and jealousy, with the same results that were present in his earliest published works: heterosexual or homosexual lovers who become obsessive waste their lives on illusions. Proust knew this before and after he met Agostinelli. The experience with Albertine shows the Narrator's struggle with and eventual triumph over eros and jealous obsession, vices to which Swann, a heterosexual, and Charlus, a homosexual, succumb. What Proust spent the rest of his life doing was writing, expanding, and revising a literary masterpiece that, after all, goes far beyond the implications of his relationship with Agostinelli, which were very quickly worked out because they ratified previous experiences and confirmed long-held beliefs, as is clearly shown in Proust's letters of 1914 and 1915 to Reynaldo Hahn and Marie Scheikévitch.

There is important evidence that an Albertinelike figure existed in earlier, pre-Agostinelli texts leading up to the creation

of such a character in *la Recherche*. There is no denying the importance of Agostinelli in Proust's life and the plot elements that were
derived directly from Proust's experience with him, but to maintain that without him there would be no such character as Albertine forces us to ignore far too much textual and biographical evidence to the contrary.

Philip Kolb points out that the episode of the refused kiss
belonged to a character named Charlotte in *Jean Santeuil* but was
given to Albertine in *la Recherche* (I, 931-34). He concludes that
"Charlotte doit donc être un modèle d'Albertine bien antérieur à
Agostinelli, que Proust n'a rencontré qu'en 1907."[95] The jealousy
that Proust felt toward Bertrand de Fénelon during their 1902 trip
to Holland—years before he met Agostinelli—is another important source for Albertine and the portrait of the jealous lover.
There is no essential difference between Proust's behavior toward
Fénelon during their trip to Holland and his apparent anguish
over Agostinelli's carefreeness and presumed infidelities. Proust
transposed a scene of jealousy that took place in Amsterdam
between himself and Fénelon, first using it for the character of
Maria and then for Albertine, who ultimately assumed Maria's
role.[96] In *la Recherche*, the paranoia of the jealous lover is such that
the Narrator imagines the banks of the canals are crowded with
people Albertine knows, whose images he sees reflected "dans les
yeux brillants d'Albertine, comme dans les glaces incertaines
d'une rapide voiture, les feux innombrables et fuyants" (III, 385).
This passage contains a link between speed and desire that predates by years Proust's meeting with Agostinelli.

A reading of Proust's letters to his male friends from his
school days through young adulthood reveals the same pattern of
attachment, insecurity, possessiveness, and jealousy. There is no
doubt that Agostinelli was the catalyst for the development of Albertine's role in the novel, but in order to portray her Proust re-
lied on the knowledge of a lifetime and not just on his passion for
Agostinelli. Maurice Bardèche is surely correct when he writes
that in spite of the importance of Agostinelli in Proust's sentimental

life, the author drew upon his experiences with all the young men
he had known in order to depict his emotions toward Albertine:
"il est probable que les sentiments de Proust envers Reynaldo
Hahn, Lucien Daudet, Antoine Bibesco ou Fénelon, ont été, pour
beaucoup de raisons, la source véritable de son expérience, beaucoup plus que ceux qu'il éprouva pour Agostinelli. . . ."[97]

In a conversation with Gide in the spring of 1921, Proust
confided that in order to depict the attractive features of the girls
of the little band, of which Albertine is the most important representative, he drew upon his memories of homosexual experiences.
Ironically, having done so, he felt he had nothing left for his
homosexual portraits but mean and grotesque qualities. His
acknowledgment of this to Gide, whose stance was that of a mili-
tant homosexual—Gide had written but not yet published *Cory-
don*—has the overtones of a confession. Gide recorded the gist of
the conversation in his diary:

> il dit se reprocher cette "indécision" qui l'a fait, pour
> nourrir la partie hétérosexuelle de son livre, transposer
> "à l'ombre des jeunes filles" tout ce que ses souvenirs
> homosexuels lui proposaient de gracieux, de tendre et
> de charmant, de sorte qu'il ne lui reste plus pour
> *Sodome* que du grotesque et de l'abject. Mais il se mon-
> tre très affecté lorsque je lui dis qu'il semble avoir voulu
> stigmatiser l'uranisme; il proteste; et je comprends enfin
> que ce que nous trouvons ignoble, objet de rire ou de
> dégoût, ne lui paraît pas, à lui, si repoussant.[98]

Comparing his novel to a cathedral, Proust referred to the
Montjouvain scene at Combray as the column that supports the
vault of his novel. This episode, which has its origin in Proust's
earliest writings, is also present in the proofs of *Du côté de chez
Swann* and thus predates the period of the writer's infatuation
with Agostinelli. The primary importance of this scene, evident
from the novel itself, was underscored by Proust in a letter casti-
gating critics who generally misunderstood the overall structure of
the work, or who thought there was no structure at all:

J'ai si soigneusement bâti cet ouvrage que cet épisode
du premier volume [la scène du sadisme à Montjou-
vain] est l'explication de la jalousie de mon jeune héros
dans les quatrième et cinquième volumes, de sorte
qu'en arrachant la colonne au chapiteau obscène,
j'aurais fait plus loin tomber la voûte. C'est ce que des
critiques appellent des ouvrages sans composition et
écrits au hasard des souvenirs.[99]

The structural and thematic significance of the Montjouvain scene is so great that from the moment he began writing *la
Recherche,* Proust must have envisaged a female character who
would play the same role as Odette in relation to the Narrator.
The Narrator's ultimate comprehension of Albertine's true role in
his life and the lessons learned from the suffering she caused him
is essential to the conclusion of the novel and the hero's discovery
of a vocation. These plot elements were present at the conceptual
stage of the novel and were not suddenly inspired by Agostinelli
during his brief stay in Proust's apartment.

Given the textual evidence, it is hard to believe that the
Agostinelli episode accounts entirely for the importance of the
prison theme. In his comparison of the Grasset proofs of 1913,
printed shortly after Agostinelli moved into Proust's apartment,
and those of June 1914, which date from just after Agostinelli's
death, Douglas Alden finds compelling evidence that an Albertine existed from the earliest texts and was to have played essentially the same role in relation to the Narrator as she did after
Proust's experience with Agostinelli. Alden points out that the
prisoner motif was, in fact, already in the text at the point where
Odette is held "captive" since "Charlus-Fleurus is appointed to
take her out and in general to report her comings and goings."
This, in fact, is exactly the nature of Albertine's imprisonment;
she is often allowed to go out, escorted by Andrée or by a
trusted chauffeur, who then gives the Narrator an account of her
activities. Alden also quotes an early version of the scene involving the good-night kiss, in which are found traces that prove

"without question that the narrator is to have a mistress and that the leitmotif of their affair will be jealousy."[100] Jealous lovers have always sought to surround the objects of their passion with real and psychological barriers.

Jean Milly, in his recent edition of *La Prisonnière*, points to texts that existed prior to *Du côté de chez Swann* containing the essential elements of Proust's analysis of love. Milly quotes a sentence from *Le Carnet de 1908* that sums up succinctly the experience of all Proustian lovers: "Dans la deuxième partie du roman la jeune fille sera ruinée, je l'entretiendrai sans chercher à la posséder par impuissance du bonheur." In "Avant la nuit" (1893) and "La Fin de la jalousie" (1896) there are descriptions of jealous lovers that alternate between feelings of confidence and suspicion, contain manifestations of homosexuality, and recount the death of the jealous lover in a horseback riding accident.[101] All of Proust's lovers exemplify this "incapacity for happiness," with variations on the theme of obsessive jealousy: Swann/Odette, Saint-Loup/ Rachel, the Narrator/Albertine, and Charlus/Morel. Milly has found that the Albertine cycle had the greatest impact on the structure of the novel rather than on its content:

> l'importance, bien réelle, des éléments biographiques a été surévaluée par la critique, qui tend à voir dans [le cycle d'Albertine] une excroissance contingente de l'œuvre, alors qu'on ne peut le comprendre que dans le cadre d'une restructuration d'ailleurs progressive et accompagnée de fréquentes remises en question, de l'ensemble de *la Recherche* depuis 1913.[102]

George Painter also sees the alternating pattern of love and death present in Proust's writings before the arrival of Agostinelli. In his view, which is somewhat dramatically stated yet essentially true, the chauffeur was caught up in the wheels of love and death and murdered by a masterpiece: "Agostinelli was conducted along the road to his tragic end by the ineluctable mechanism of a work of art; he was killed by *A la Recherche. . . .*"[103]

The sorrows of the lover and of the mourner will play an important role in the creation of art, as the Narrator learns upon discovering the secrets of his vocation, but particular sorrows and regrets are in themselves transitory since we are not capable of sustaining such emotions over protracted periods of time: "il y a dans ce monde où tout s'use, où tout périt, une chose qui tombe en ruine, qui se détruit encore plus complètement, en laissant moins de vestiges que la Beauté: c'est le Chagrin" (III, 695).

From what we know about Proust's philosophical beliefs, it is evident that the concept of multiple selves that Proust elaborated upon in letters to Reynaldo Hahn and Mme Scheikévitch was a long-held belief and did not result from self-analysis as he went through the process of mourning the death of Agostinelli. Philip Kolb has demonstrated that in developing his theory of multiple selves, Proust was influenced by Gabriele d'Annunzio's novel *L'Innocente* (1892), in which Proust found a direct expression of the kind of self-analysis that results in such a formulation. Proust read d'Annunzio's novel in a French translation, *L'Intrus*, in 1893, when he was only twenty-two; he wrote to Daniel Halévy that the first thirty pages enraptured him. Here is part of the excerpt cited by Kolb from the French translation of the novel:

> Selon les temps et selon les lieux, selon le heurt acci-
> dentel des circonstances, d'un fait insignifiant, d'un
> mot, selon des influences internes beaucoup plus
> obscures encore, le fond permanent de son être revê-
> tait les aspects les plus changeants, les plus fugitifs, les
> plus étranges. En lui, un état organique spécial corre-
> spondait à chaque tendance spéciale en la renforçant,
> et cette tendance devenait un centre d'attraction où
> convergeaient les états et les tendances directement
> associés, et l'association se propageait de proche en
> proche. Alors son centre de gravité se trouvait dé-
> placé; sa personnalité devenait une autre personnalité.
> Des ondes silencieuses de sang et d'idées faisaient

fleurir sur le fond permanent de son être, soit gradu-
ellement, soit tout d'un coup, des âmes nouvelles. Il
était *multanime*.[104]

It would be difficult to imagine a more Proustian text;
d'Annunzio's description of his character's "multiple souls" finds a
direct parallel in Proust's multiple selves. In *L'Intrus* such selves are
even summoned into existence in a Proustian way, resulting from
"le heurt accidentel des circonstances," and are "changeants,"
"fugitifs," and "étranges." The fact that these pages thrilled Proust
would seem to indicate that they confirmed or echoed feelings and
thoughts that he was already in the process of developing. The
early date of this text, whose importance he acknowledged, is
additional proof that insofar as the theory of multiple selves is concerned, Proust had worked out his theory of relativity, subjectivity,
and the use of multiple perspectives long before he met Agostinelli.

Those accounts of Agostinelli's role in Proust's life that do
justice to the part he played in the creation of Albertine often
overstate or misinterpret the relationship between the chauffeur-
secretary and the figure of the aviator in the novel. The airplane
is the dominant symbol in Proust's vertical imagery describing the
ascent of the creative person. The association of the aviator with
Agostinelli may have been unavoidable, given what we know of
Proust's personal life, but it is entirely coincidental to the symbolic
intent of the novel.[105] Proust would still have used the airplane as
the dominant symbol of the creative artist had he never met
Agostinelli. Albertine fulfills exactly the same role of handmaiden
in relation to art as did Agostinelli in Proust's life. Albertine cranks
the pianola for the Narrator just as Agostinelli drove the car
through Brittany and Normandy and, most likely, pedaled the
pianola for Proust, but she in no way represents the creative person. The passage where the Narrator sees his first airplane, in fact,
has nothing whatever to do with Agostinelli, contrary to what
George Painter and other critics have maintained. Since this key
passage has so often been misinterpreted, it would be well to
quote it again here:

Tout à coup mon cheval se cabra; il avait entendu un
bruit singulier. . . . Je pleurais aussi . . . à la pensée que
ce que j'allais voir pour la première fois c'était un aéroplane. . . . l'aviateur . . . plana quelques instants au-
dessus de la mer, puis . . . semblant céder à quelque
attraction inverse de celle de la pesanteur . . . d'un léger
mouvement de ses ailes d'or il piqua droit vers le ciel.
(II, 1029)

Painter attributes the Narrator's tearful reaction on sighting his first airplane to grief over Agostinelli's death: "Proust
alludes secretly to the death of Agostinelli, when the Narrator
at Balbec bursts into tears on first seeing an aeroplane. . . ."[106]
J. E. Rivers also links the deaths of Albertine and Agostinelli to
this text: "But Alfred's death and Proust's grief are more clearly
memorialized in another passage, a strange and beautiful interlude
haunted with private symbolism."[107] By overstating the influence
of Agostinelli on Proust's novel, these commentators confuse the
purpose of the episode.

The incident that inspired this passage is in no way related
to Agostinelli, but instead has as its source another young man,
Marcel Plantevignes, in whom Proust had taken an interest during
the summers he spent at Cabourg in 1908-10, where the youth
vacationed with his family. In his memoirs, *Avec Marcel Proust,*
Plantevignes relates two episodes that Proust combined to create
the scene where the Narrator sees his first airplane. This passage,
which was only published in 1966, was unavailable to Painter and
was ignored by Rivers and Margaret Mein, who consequently
mistakenly attributed the source of the incident to Proust's experience with Agostinelli. It is perhaps worth examining at some
length the pertinent passages from Plantevignes's memoirs.[108]

Margaret Mein, strangely enough, quotes the second passage from the memoirs, where Plantevignes recalls bursting into
tears on first seeing an airplane, but not the first episode, where
the horseback rider is frightened by a low-flying airplane. It is this
episode that is clearly the origin of the Narrator's sighting his first

airplane at Balbec; yet Mein persists in interpreting the horse at Balbec as a presage of Albertine's death and as "an autobiographical incursion" relating to Agostinelli. In speaking of Albertine's death, Mein expresses her surprise that, except for the airplane encounter, Proust suppressed even veiled allusions to Agostinelli's death. Th﹐s is because the airplane encounter has nothing to do with Agostinelli's accident, nor does Ag﹐stinelli's death have anything to do with Albertine's.[109]

Plantevignes begins by describing his horseback rides at Cabourg and Houlgate; Proust, so far as Plantevignes knew, had never mounted a horse. Plantevignes believes that the many rides he took with Proust's friend the vicomte d'Alton, which the former either witnessed or had described to him by his friends, were the source for the equestrian rides of Albertine and Andrée.[110] Plantevignes then describes the incident that occurred when he was out riding one of his favorite horses, a steady, reliable mare named Serpolette. As he was ambling peacefully along, suddenly an airplane appeared out of nowhere. It was this incident that Proust developed into the Narrator's sighting of his first airplane. In fact, in one of the notebooks where Albertine's name occurs for the first time, Proust refers to the horseback ride and the encounter of the aviator as "une promenade . . . déjà écrite."[111] Here is the passage from Plantevignes's memoirs:

> Tout à coup un avion surgi de l'horizon des arbres, volant très bas . . . fonçait vers nous avec un bruit d'enfer. . . . Ma jument prise de terreur . . . sursauta sur ses jambes . . . puis faisant un grand bond en avant, partit à travers champs, au triple galop. . . .

All his efforts to calm the panic-stricken horse proved useless since the airplane continued to follow them and, as Plantevignes points out, planes flew very low and very slowly at the time. The machine stayed right above the rider and his frantic horse. Once the plane finally relented and flew off, Plantevignes was obliged to walk the shaken horse back to the stables. As soon as Plantevignes saw Proust that evening, he told the writer of his adventure and narrow escape:

> Proust, frappé en effet par la nouveauté de cette impression de peur tombant du ciel me demanda la permission de s'en approprier la description comme étant arrivé à lui et d'y faire allusion dans ses écrits. . . . Et en effet dans *Sodome et Gomorrhe*, Proust parle de cet incident . . . comme arrivé à lui. . . .

The horse being terrorized by the airplane may have encouraged Proust to have Albertine die as a result of a horse-back riding accident. If he reached this decision after Agostinelli's death, then it is possible to say that subliminally the airplane caused Albertine's death as well as Agostinelli's. Yet we must remember that Honoré, the jealous hero of the story "La Fin de la jalousie," also died as a result of a fall from a horse. But there is no reason to believe that Agostinelli's death determined Albertine's; the girl who was to play a crucial role in the Narrator's life was most likely required by the plot to die anyway, since his obsession with her serves as the main obstacle to the successful completion of his quest to discover his true being and his vocation as a writer. The suffering and guilt that he experiences after her death are key elements in this process of development.[112]

The passage describing how the Narrator burst into tears upon seeing his first airplane was based on another incident described to Proust by Plantevignes:

> C'est également à moi . . . qu'il fait allusion, lorsque dans les lignes suivantes, il décrit qu'il a pleuré en voyant volé [*sic*] . . . un avion . . . durant une promenade en auto avec mes parents. . . . je m'étais soudain pris à pleurer d'émotion en repensant à mon grand'père qui . . . eût été si curieux, si intéressé, et si surpris et saisi par cette merveilleuse et inoubliable nouveauté en voyant soudain apparaître . . . le monoplan de Latham. . . .

> Proust, qui m'avait deviné, dit combien il comprenait cette émotion, et m'en avait même vivement félicité par rapport au souvenir de mon grand'père, me demanda également la permission de relater cette émotion comme arrivée à lui.[113]

This is just the kind of emotion that would have pleased Proust: the memory of a beloved grandparent linked to the young man's astonishment at witnessing a revolutionary technological achievement and his regret that the grandparent did not live to share the sense of elation. This passage may have been the starting point for the identification of the Narrator's grandmother with the church steeple of Saint-Hilaire at Combray and other vertical imagery, including the airplane. Because an earlier version of the aviator episode at Balbec contains an allusion to Homer, Margaret Mein sees the source of the Narrator's tears as coming from Homeric reminiscences. She later observes that "la seule 'sublimité' de ce bruit d'avion serait une explication trop facile des larmes que verse le narrateur. Comme presque toujours chez Proust, nous avons affaire plutôt à un symbolisme multiple. . . ."[114] We may indeed be dealing with multiple symbols, but Mein misses the point again.

The Narrator's tears are not merely the result of his having witnessed an extraordinary human feat for the first time—man in flight—but the fact that the sight of the free-flying aviator reminds him of his own bondage and failure. Rather than having an ancient source, the Narrator's tears are inspired by modern man's achievements. The Futurists, for whom the airplane was the ultimate symbol of modern technology, understood very well the sort of elation that could result from the sight of an airplane:

> Si l'homme cherche la beauté des formes, la souplesse des lignes, et le mystère de la matière elle-même, il doit, selon Marinetti, regarder un avion prêt à décoller. Le vol des avions crée de nouvelles sensations plastiques et remplit l'homme de sentiments nouveaux. Les héros de "L'Ellisse e la Spirale" pleurent de joie et volupté au cours d'un vol.[115]

Jacques-Henri Lartigue described his emotion upon seeing an airplane pass directly overhead in 1909. The text is similar
to Proust's not only in terms of the emotional response of the
observer but in the conception of the aviator as ascendant visionary. Lartigue identifies so strongly with the pilot that he believes
the aviator's eyes have become his own:

> Hier, un aéroplane est passé au-dessus de moi! juste au-
> dessus de moi! J'ai vu d'en dessous l'homme vivant assis
> sur son siège, jambes écartées. . . . Et soudain quelque
> chose de mystérieux s'est produit dans ma tête . . . un
> peu comme un vertige à l'envers! C'était comme si
> j'avais vu passer cet homme avec d'autres yeux que les
> miens, *avec les siens!?!?* Je l'ai regardé s'éloigner, tou-
> jours en l'air. Son moteur faisait un bruit résonnant
> empli d'air. On a quelquefois des premières émotions
> uniques, après lesquelles, ensuite, on court sans jamais
> plus pouvoir les rattraper.
>
> Je me demande comment on peut appeler ce "con-
> traire de la peur" cette "peur joyeuse" qui, d'un coup,
> était entrée dans ma cervelle . . . et que personne (???)
> plus tard ne pourra peut-être plus comprendre.[116]

When the Narrator sees the airplane at Balbec, he is cha-
grined because whenever he is in love, he sees himself as a prisoner, a failure. He is therefore both moved and intimidated by the
sight of the aviator, a symbol of creativity and freedom. However
much Proust may have loved Agostinelli, he clearly did not consider him an artist. The airplane, unlike the bicycle, car, train, and
other machines of speed, has no erotic associations; as was noted
in earlier chapters, the automobile and train are often used in the
context of eroticism and social commentary.

The figure of the aviator is unadulterated in the novel
and is never linked to aspects of the horizontal quest because the
airplane is the symbol of the creator. Since the only symbolic
function the plane serves in the novel is to represent the creative
person, it is contrary to Proust's intention to say that the figure

of the aviator is intended as an homage to Agostinelli. The emotion felt by the Narrator when he sees his first airplane does not imply that a loved one is immortalized through art, as Rivers claims:

> The passage . . . is at once [Agostinelli's] memorial and his apotheosis as an inspiring spirit of Proust's novel. In life Icarus must fall; but in art he can fly on and on. In *A la recherche* Alfred Agostinelli soars, lives, and returns to his native land—the mind and imagination of Marcel Proust.[117]

In fact, there is no connection whatever between Agostinelli and the symbol of the aviator in *la Recherche*. In the novel, the aviator represents the creative person who is able to free himself from habits and obsessions, realize himself fully, and transcend his ordinary being, his social self (*le moi social*), by attaining the artist's vision.

There is one more passage from Plantevignes's memoirs that is worth quoting for two reasons: not only does it demonstrate once again that Proust's interest in aviation was entirely independent of his relationship with Agostinelli, but it also shows the great interest that Proust always took in modern inventions and technological progress:

> d'une façon générale, Proust suivait avec émoi les progrès de l'aviation naissante, et un soir—aux alentours de 1910,— dans sa chambre du Grand-Hôtel de Cabourg, comme nous devisions tranquillement, un avion important tout bruissant d'un bruit apocalyptique, et semblant avoir rasé de près l'hôtel, tant il volait bas, passa avec fracas au-dessus de nous dans le ciel nocturne, nous coupant la parole, et Proust, alerté, s'interrompant soudain de ce à quoi il songeait, et me désignant d'un doigt dramatique le bruit et le ciel, me dit gravement:
> —Ecoutez, Marcel, écoutez, les temps futurs qui sont en marche!

Proust would have been just as fascinated by airplanes if he had never met Alfred Agostinelli. Plantevignes's testimony about Proust's early interest in aviation is supported by various texts and letters. In an unpublished pastiche in the "Lemoine affair" series, Proust described the Wright brothers' flights in 1908-9 above Paris; Philip Kolb dates the composition of this text in 1909.[118] In a posthumously published text entitled "Les Œuvres de M. Reynaldo Hahn," Proust uses the image of an aviator taking off to describe Hahn's music; Philip Kolb, who was the first to publish this text, dates it between June 1, 1909, and July 10, 1914. Hahn began composing at age sixteen; one of his first compositions was inspired by a Victor Hugo poem bearing a title that suggests flight: "Si mes vers avaient des ailes."[119] After alluding to a Hugo poem and the freedom of the artist, Proust says that Hahn's music takes wing as it comes into contact with the text. Given the latest date at which this article could have been written, it is almost certain that Proust wrote it before Agostinelli's death and even more likely that he wrote it much earlier than in the period when he began concentrating on his major novel. There is nothing in the letters of the Agostinelli period to suggest that Proust was writing an article devoted to Hahn.

On December 15, 1909, we find Proust writing a congratulatory letter to his friend Armand de Guiche, who was a pioneer in the field of aerodynamics:

> Un de mes amis (en m'écrivant que votre étude sur les circonstances du mouvement d'un disque dans l'air et la déduction que vous en tirez sur les formules donnant la valeur de la réaction de l'air sur une surface plane en mouvement—est d'un grand intérêt au point de vue de la construction des aéroplanes) me dépeint ainsi sans y songer un Guiche faisant penser à Vinci, cet aviateur qui s'occupait aussi de physique, de peinture, et même disent les Allemands, de sculpture.[120]

The comparison of Guiche to da Vinci may be an example of the kind of hyperbole that Proust often engaged in when

praising friends, but it may also be another indication of the relationship that Proust saw among creative people in all domains—
science as well as art—and a factor in his choice of the aviator as
the perfect symbol for the discoverer, inventor, and artist. Da
Vinci was, after all, the epitome of the Renaissance man who
excelled in all fields as sculptor, painter, architect, physician, engineer, writer, and musician; in addition, as Proust points out in the
comparison of Guiche and Leonardo, he was also passionately
involved in the question of manned flight.

Proust was as interested in the present and future as he was
in the past. This is proven out by the profusion of imagery drawn
from modern inventions that appears in his writings. There is
scarcely an invention, new at the time, that was not put to good
metaphorical use by the writer; obvious examples would include
the telephone, X-ray machine, and camera. Proust's interest in
technology was such that he anticipated inventions that even
today are only in very limited use, such as the voice-print and the
photo-telephone.[121]

The name Marcel Swann, the alias chosen by Agostinelli
when he began pilot training, echoes both the manuscript of
Du côté de chez Swann—parts of which the young aviator had
typed—and the given name of the author. Thus, the tribute
paid was not by Proust to Agostinelli but by Agostinelli to his
benefactor. Agostinelli understood the symbolic use of the aviator as artist and also that in a very real sense Proust's narrator's
name might appropriately be Marcel Swann.[122] Swann, who
had been the young Narrator's rival for his mother's attention
when he dined at Combray—thus making it impossible for the
mother to go upstairs in time to bestow the crucial good-night
kiss ("[Swann,] l'auteur inconscient de mes tristesses" [(I, 43)]—
will later be seen as the "author" of his book ("[Mon livre] me
venait de Swann . . ." [III, 915]). Thus, Swann fulfills the same
function as Albertine in the sense that all those whom the Narrator loves become "authors of his sorrows" and, by extension,
his muses.

Swann is tethered to the horizontal plane by his obsession with Odette and by a genetic disorder that Proust labels "paresse d'esprit" (I, 268). Swann has only two lucid moments in the entire novel: a negative one when he sees that he has wasted his life on a woman who was not his type, and a positive one when he begins to free himself from Odette and happens to hear the Vinteuil sonata at Mme de Saint-Euverte's salon. In a note to himself in *Cahier 57*, Proust indicates that Swann's failure to distinguish between eros (Odette) and art (Vinteuil's music, which is trivialized as "their national anthem") and to follow the path of art is perhaps the most important point in the entire novel. Swann is compared to Moses, who died before reaching the promised land:

> capitalissime, issime, issime, peut-être le plus de toute l'œuvre. . . . quand je parle du plaisir éternel de la cuiller, tasse de thé, etc. = art: était-ce cela ce bonheur proposé par la petite phrase de la sonate à Swann qui s'était trompé en l'assimilant au plaisir de l'amour et n'avait pas su où le trouver (dans l'art). . . . [123]

The Narrator's power of analysis and comprehension also increases, whenever he believes he is about to recover from his obsession with Albertine. In Swann's one lucid meditation on Vinteuil's music, the laws of nature and the beauties of art are represented as divine captives apprehended by such "discoverers" as Vinteuil, Ampère, and Lavoisier. The unknown force in the universe that guides explorers toward such discoveries is represented by horses ("l'attelage invisible") that fly through the ether (I, 351). Meditating on the music, Swann sees what art really is, but, given his nature and character, is unable to sustain and profit from his insight, thus forever remaining a failed artist, one of the many dilettantes who have the desire to fly but who cannot get off the ground (III, 892). The Narrator's most constantly expressed desire throughout the novel is to free himself from habit, sloth, and obsessions in order to become an artist. As we will discover in the next chapter, the dream of conquering gravity is one of man's oldest ambitions.

CHAPTER 7

The Artist and the Aviator

la rencontre quasi mythologique d'un aviateur . . . avait été pour moi comme une image de la liberté. . . . (III, 105)

The image of the artist as aviator occurs in the earliest passages of *la Recherche,* where Proust first defines artistic genius. In an astonishing metaphor, he depicts Bergotte, the successful writer of bourgeois origin, as the pilot[1] of a car that, though modest in appearance and lagging behind the others in such earthbound matters as wit or social refinement, is able to transform itself into an airplane and fly over the society people in their Rolls-Royces: "[Bergotte], de son modeste appareil qui venait enfin de 'décoller', il les survolait" (I, 555).

Proust explains the superiority of the artist in terms of power conversion. In order to take to the skies, that is, to become an artist, it is not necessary to have the most powerful car but one that is "capable de convertir en force ascensionnelle sa vitesse horizontale" (I, 554). As we shall see, other aviation encounters and symbols of elevation prove important indicators to the Narrator of the path he must follow on his quest.

Genius is first described as the ability to reflect or mirror, with the quality of the artist's vision depending not upon the value of the thing reflected but on the reflecting capacity of the mirror, that is, the artist's power to render correctly his chosen subject, "le génie consistant dans le pouvoir réfléchissant et non dans la qualité intrinsèque du spectacle reflété" (I, 555).[2] People, places, and names do not in themselves constitute ideal, integral entities; they can only be endowed with such qualities through the artist's vision. It is not social polish that matters but the brilliance of the artist-mirror. Like Proust, Bergotte attains his supreme triumph as an artist by perfectly mirroring the mediocrity of those who are more socially elevated than he is. To paraphrase a well-known aphorism, Bergotte finds that "writing well is the best revenge." Although the young Narrator is dazzled by the apparent brilliance of the aristocratic world, the mature Narrator, like Bergotte, will eventually see the vanity and inferiority of this milieu.

This key passage combines a number of Proustian images that illustrate the artist's experience in society and hint at the development of others to come. The artist is first presented as a mirror that reflects and then as an aviator who looks down and visually encompasses the lives of others. The artist as a mirror, reflector, or projector of light often leads into another metaphoric image for Proust's artists, namely, that of planets.[3] It is an ideal metaphoric image for the novelist's purposes, combining as it does the essential features of the Proustian artist: planets are integral worlds, giant reflectors of light orbiting the cosmos. Planetary imagery thus embodies two principal elements associated with the Proustian artist—light and flight—and also implies an absolute freedom and an integrated existence.

Later in the novel, the Narrator compares dilettantes, those would-be artists who always fall short, to prototype airplanes that never got off the ground (III, 892).[4] The "artistes manqués" are those who cannot "décoller," although they have the desire to fly; they are presented as an inferior but necessary stage in the perfection of flight. Proust thus combines aerodynamics and natural science in the form of Darwinism to describe metaphorically the development of artistic genius.

Throughout la Recherche, as we have seen, characters who are victims of their obsessions are described as being tied down, tethered by their manias. The Narrator sees his first airplane when, bored with Albertine and desiring to be alone, he goes horseback riding in a forest near Balbec. He is at first thrilled by the experience of first sighting an aviator, but later dismayed when he compares himself, a prisoner of habit, to the flyer who soars overhead and seems to have "ouvertes devant lui . . . toutes les routes de l'espace . . ." (II, 1029). This mythological encounter occurs just before the bleakest period of his existence. This combination of the mythological and the mechanical to illustrate the Narrator's lack of progress on his quest is typical of Proust's metaphorical style. When the symbolic meaning of the airplane takes hold in the Narrator's mind, a transformation of the pilot from aviator to angel occurs with the wings of steel becoming wings of gold. The detail of the golden wings, the means by which the aviator propels himself through space, indicates the nature of his native region: he is a heavenly creature. Before disappearing, the aviator pauses above the sea, the element where earth and sky merge, and then heads back to paradise.[5]

During the war, at a time when the world seems topsy-turvy, the Narrator will remember this encounter during an air raid by German bombers, where the airplane that had seemed to be a winged messenger from paradise temporarily becomes a god of evil.[6] Here the airplane is treated realistically, assuming a value that is the opposite of its earlier symbolic portent. Proust contrasts this experience with the vision of the aviator-god first seen near Balbec. The airplane, usually the symbol of an altruistic creator, becomes a satanic destroyer: "Je ne retrouvais plus mon chemin. Je pensai à ce jour . . . où j'avais rencontré, comme un dieu qui avait fait se cabrer mon cheval, un avion. Je pensais que maintenant la rencontre serait différente et que le dieu du mal me tuerait" (III, 833).

There is a direct link here between the Icarus-Daedalus myth and the Narrator's quest to find a way out of the labyrinth of social ritual. In the woods near Balbec, the noise of the airplane made his horse rear; in wartime Paris, he is lost one night in the dark streets and cannot find his way: "Je ne retrouvais plus mon chemin." At the end of the novel, when he arrives at the princesse de Guermantes's matinée after an "airborne" ride through the streets of Paris and trips on the uneven cobblestones, he has at last "stumbled" upon the right path.

So powerful is the impression of freedom the first airplane made on him that, once back in Paris, the Narrator visits airfields with Albertine in order to witness this display of liberty and defiance of gravity, the triumph over being earthbound and tethered. These outings are, in fact, the only ones that he makes with her. During these excursions, it becomes apparent to him that the freedom of the airplane in flight is in direct contrast to his own shackled existence with Albertine; because of his obsessive jealousy, he is as much her prisoner as she is his. Such passages can be interpreted as additional refutations of the notion that the aviator represents Agostinelli, who is also the chief model for Albertine. The aviator is a liberating force, whereas Albertine is a confining one.

Proust's generation was determined to conquer gravity through manned flight. In 1903, when the Wright brothers made their first successful flight at Kitty Hawk, North Carolina, the distinctions between the horizontal and vertical axes were dramatically demonstrated, as one of mankind's oldest dreams became a reality. Manned flight crystallized metaphorical associations that had long been part of stock imagery. According to Stephen Kern, the directional shift that came about with the advent of the airplane was unique and universal:

> [The airplane's] cultural impact was ultimately defined by deeply rooted values associated with the up-down axis. Low suggests immorality, vulgarity, poverty, and deceit. High is the direction of growth and hope, the source of life, the heavenly abode of angels and gods. From Ovid to Shelley the soaring bird was a symbol of freedom.[7]

But if flight had always been a universal symbol of freedom, a human being could now soar in a flying machine above
the earth. Proust and his contemporaries assigned a moral value to
the conquest of gravity, as is demonstrated in this passage by his
contemporary Paul Souriau:

> de toutes les forces de la nature que l'homme regarde
> comme hostiles et prend plaisir à vaincre, celle qui lui
> inspire le plus d'antipathie et contre laquelle il lutte,
> dans tous ces exercices, avec le plus d'acharnement,
> c'est la force de la gravitation. . . . On a été jusqu'à
> voir dans ce rêve [de voler] comme une réminiscence
> d'une vie antérieure, où la pesanteur n'existait pas pour
> nous. . . . Dans notre lutte contre les puissances de la
> nature . . . c'est déjà quelque chose de protester, de lut-
> ter, comme le prisonnier secoue sa chaîne, ne pouvant
> la briser . . . c'est un effort vers la liberté, et un com-
> mencement d'émancipation morale.[8]

In the passage where the Narrator sees his first airplane,
the aviator-angel's freedom to return to his own realm is represented as a force that is the opposite of gravity, "quelque attraction
inverse de celle de la pesanteur" (II, 1029). If being tethered is the
equivalent of hell—since for Proust's hero failure as an artist is primarily associated with hell ("l'art, c'est le vrai Jugement dernier";
III, 880)—then free flight represents artistic achievement and freedom. In fact, the French word for taking off (décoller) literally
means to become unstuck. When Proust uses the word he puts it
in quotes since the new meaning of becoming airborne had not
been consecrated through repeated use. The first attestation of this
meaning in French occurs in 1907, at about the same time that
Proust began la Recherche; the immediately preceding years were
marked by false starts and discouragement, including the abandoned novel Jean Santeuil and the Ruskin translations, which
Proust felt were not true creative work.[9]

Throughout la Recherche, lack of will and freedom is
expressed by means of images of being tethered or chained. Such

images become central in *La Prisonnière*. In the prison section of the novel, the most urgent question becomes whether or not the Narrator will regain his lost will, since he cannot work nor free himself from his obsession with Albertine. The title *A la recherche du temps perdu* here resonates with an alternate meaning, namely, as wasted time or a lost life.

If Aunt Léonie is representative of the kind of relative the young Narrator fears he may one day resemble—a fear that is later realized (III, 79), there is another character who serves as a model but whom the sickly, dependent boy finds himself incapable of imitating: his grandmother. Like the steeple of Saint-Hilaire with which she is associated, she represents natural distinction and courage: "ma grand'mère trouvait au clocher de Combray ce qui pour elle avait le plus de prix au monde, l'air naturel et l'air distingué" (I, 64). She always argues with the boy's father, who sends him to his room with a book on rainy days instead of letting him go out, and she is annoyed that their garden at Combray is too symmetrical, that straight paths rather than crooked ones run through it (I, 11). If no one is looking, she will remove stakes from some of the rose trees to make them appear more natural (I, 14). This gesture of removing a stake is significant, indicating that she is unlike Aunt Léonie, who is compared to the tethered water lily (I, 168). The grandmother's restless nature, her love of walks even in bad weather, and her admiration for steeples are all signs that she is free in mind and body, as opposed to the obsessed and inert Aunt Léonie.[10] The grandmother is a woman who seeks emancipation and epiphanic experiences in her daily life, just as the Narrator will seek and finally realize the ability to seize and render in art those moments that would otherwise be lost.

On his last excursion with Albertine to an airfield near Paris, the Narrator hears an airplane overhead and remembers both the most important vertical symbol of his childhood days in Combray, namely, the steeple of Saint-Hilaire, and his grandmother, the most important mentor as far as his will and strength are concerned. He thinks of her because it was she, more than anyone, who realized the damage that had been done to him as a boy and who had as her dying ambition the restoration of his will: "Soudain j'éprouvais de nouveau la nostalgie de ma liberté perdue en entendant un bruit que je ne reconnus pas d'abord et que ma grand'mère eût, lui aussi, tant aimé" (III, 406). As has been noted, the Narrator's regret that his grandmother did not live to see the advent of the airplane probably originated in the incident that Marcel Plantevignes related to Proust. This is completely in keeping with the other aspects of her character. It is not Agostinelli/Albertine who is identified with the airplane but the grandmother/artist.

The Narrator's sighting of an airplane in flight and his discouragement when the scene reminds him of his lost will recalls the passage where as a child at Combray, the steeple represented for the Narrator "une existence individuelle et responsable" (I, 64). During the epiphanic section at the end of Le Temps retrouvé, the airplane is one of three things in which reality is contained and is equated with the steeple as the embodiment of grandeur, "la grandeur dans le bruit d'un aéroplane, dans la ligne du clocher de Saint-Hilaire" (III, 895). The primary objective of the Narrator's quest is to rediscover lost time—the church at Combray embodies this element of his quest ("un édifice occupant . . . un espace à quatre dimensions—la quatrième étant celle du Temps" [I, 61])—and capture it in a work of art. As both the steeple and airplane indicate, the recovery of lost time will be achieved through elevated vision. Just as the steeple is an important early signpost of the route the Narrator must take— the steeple is envisioned as the finger of God pointing to heaven (I, 66)—the airplane proves that flight is possible, that the sky can be reached. However, troubling questions still remain about the Narrator's dependency upon Albertine and the materiality of mechanical flight.

In the manuscript of Jean Santeuil, Proust's earlier version of what was to become la Recherche, there is a character who is a county engineer.[11] Jean is astounded one day when he learns that this engineer, who exhibits so many vices and vulgarities, is also an extraordinary musician. In developing this character, Proust attempts to fuse within one personage—a figure who appears to his neighbors to be an ordinary if not an inferior person—the artist and the scientist. In later drafts the naturalist was called Vington.[12] In la Recherche, aspects of this early character are given both to Legrandin (he is an engineer and a man of letters) and Vinteuil, who receives not only the first syllable and the initial consonant sound of the second syllable of his name (the final sound comes from the hero's family name, Santeuil) but also a number of scientific and technological associations. These are present in the passage on Vinteuil and the real-life artist the Narrator identifies most closely with him, namely, Richard Wagner. In the case of Wagner as presented by Proust, the relationship between music and engineering is provided by aerodynamics.[13]

The Narrator's most serious crisis of faith in art occurs in La Prisonnière, when he plays Vinteuil's music and is reminded of the Combray of his childhood and the time when he first knew that he wanted to be an artist. Beset by jealousy, lacking will, and believing that he has no talent, the Narrator comes to doubt the existence of this higher reality. Discouraged and tired, he asks himself if in giving up the ambition to create art he has given up anything real: "y avait-il dans l'art une réalité plus profonde où notre personnalité véritable trouve une expression que ne lui donnent pas les actions de la vie?" (III, 158).

As he plays Vinteuil's sonata, something in it reminds him of Wagner's music. He switches to Tristan and continues to play and meditate. He realizes that Wagner possesses the two essential qualities of a great artist—genius and craftsmanship. The Narrator appreciates Wagner's creative genius, especially his ability to isolate essences and particularize musical motifs for the various characters in his operas. He compares the maestro of Bayreuth to a carpenter who selects wood to make a piece of furniture only after having carefully considered the grain and other properties of the wood in relation to its intended use. As he reflects on the development of Wagner's music while playing parts of *Tristan*, he is struck by what he calls the joy of the fabricator (III, 161), which emerges from the music irrespective of the mood of the composition.[14] He concludes that the poet in Wagner is dominated by the technician. This brings about a crisis of faith in the Narrator, who is now troubled by the cleverness of the craftsman and wonders again if art is perhaps no more real than life. What if music is nothing more than cleverly organized noise?[15] What if art is only the "produit d'un labeur industrieux?" (III, 162). This questioning shows Proust's mystical yearning for an assurance that art and all great human achievements are proof that life is not senseless, that the fruits of our best efforts are not merely the material products of hard work.[16]

The Narrator now focuses on an essential philosophical question: Does art correspond to any reality? If the answer is negative, then art is nothing but a highly complex, sterile game consisting of wonderful mechanics ("mécanique et sublime"; II, 731), but ultimately illusory in nature. If it is this Vulcanlike skill that gives art the illusion of corresponding to a fundamental, irreducible originality, if art is nothing more than a material product, then he should have no regrets about giving it up. As he continues to play, he is struck even more by the technical brilliance of the composition. Contrasting the poet/fabricator, he compares Wagner's music to an airplane that is no longer an idealized vision of artistic soaring but only a mechanical contraption that, though airborne, makes so much noise that it precludes artistic contemplation and exploration: "Peut-être . . . fallait-il de ces appareils vraiment matériels pour explorer l'infini, de ces cent vingt chevaux marque Mystère, ou pourtant, si haut qu'on plane on est un peu empêché de goûter le silence des espaces par le puissant ronflement du moteur!" (III, 162)[17]

He tries to resolve the conflict between the mechanical and the divine by using an airplane named *Mystère* as a metaphor for the unity of opposing forces. In his correspondence, Proust uses an automobile, which he also calls *Mystère*, to make a similar analogy. The occasion was a letter to Georges de Lauris about Maurice Maeterlinck's articles on death, which were published in *Le Figaro* in 1911. Here the mechanical analogy is employed to criticize Maeterlinck's style:

> Et puis la beauté même du style, la lourdeur de sa *carrosserie* ne conviennent pas à ces explorations de l'Impalpable. Je dis carrosserie parce que je crois que c'est ainsi que parlent nos amis qui ont des automobiles et que je me souviens que je me suis permis devant vous de petites irrévérences à l'endroit de Maeterlinck—ma grande admiration du reste—en parlant d'Infini quarante chevaux et de grosse voiture marque Mystère.[18]

In the scene from *la Recherche*, Wagner's music is likened to an airplane in that, although a product of technique and craftsmanship, it does indeed take off and fly. It works as musical art, although the Narrator now sees Wagner's music in less idealized terms. These disturbing doubts about art are soon dispelled when he attends a concert where he hears the Vinteuil septet for the first time. Vinteuil's masterpiece will serve as the great synthesizer for the Narrator's entire experience, although for most of his adult life he will remain a passive witness, like the supine Aunt Léonie at her window in Combray, rather than a dynamic creator, such as Wagner or Vinteuil. Proust's protagonist continues to waste the energy he possesses in the pursuit of Albertine. This pursuit belongs to the horizontal plane of his quest and consists of those false paths whose links to the vertical plane will be discovered only much later. At this point in the narrative, he wonders if the solid reality of the airplane does not detract from its validity as a symbol of art. This lack of understanding about the true nature of art, including its human and divine aspects, reflects his unwillingness to engage in further exploration and to undertake the labor necessary to become a creative artist.

After listening to the septet, he feels he is once again on the threshold of making significant discoveries about the nature of art when he suddenly learns something that leads him to believe Albertine had been seeking to make a lesbian contact the afternoon of the concert. His jealous obsession overwhelms him once more, forcing him to postpone indefinitely his artistic investigations and attempts to write. His constant capitulation to amorous passion is proof of his continued lack of will.

By the middle of *Le Temps retrouvé*, we have witnessed the flaws of the three major figures who possessed the potential to become artists: Swann, Charlus, and the Narrator. Swann, now deceased, eventually realized, in a bitter moment of self-awareness, that he had wasted years of his life on Odette, a woman who was not his type. He was also defeated in his aspirations because he had inherited a "paresse d'esprit" (I, 268) that made it impossible for him to think things through. Because of these shortcomings, he committed a number of errors, the most serious of which was mistaking life for art. Charlus has given himself over entirely to a life of painful and bloody physical gratification. The Narrator lacks will and has apparently taken the wrong paths in his quest for the artist's vision.

The Narrator does exhibit a reserve of will and the beginnings of artistic vision during his meditation on the Vinteuil septet, when he formulates his intention of giving up Albertine, but we must remember that it is she who finally abandons him, and once that happens he does everything possible to get her back. Death alone prevents her return. Nor does his obsession die with Albertine; even after her demise, his efforts to discover the truth about her sexual conduct consume all his energy, leaving none for artistic explorations. But now his health is declining and he is discouraged by his apparent lack of talent and ability to observe, felt keenly when he compares his capacity to that of the Goncourts. In a masterful Proustian trick, we read a parody of the Goncourts (III, 709-17) by Proust, whose alter ego lacks the ability to imitate and thus is profoundly discouraged in his artistic aspirations. Tired and defeated, the Narrator withdraws from society. The final decline of Swann and Charlus and his own withdrawal must take place before he can return to the world and discover his vocation.

Some years after Albertine's death, the Narrator, still unable to write and in ill health, withdraws to a sanatorium outside Paris. Years pass, but he remains uncured and inactive as a writer. Convinced that he lacks talent and cannot become an artist, he decides to return to society and end his self-exile by resuming the sterile, empty life he previously led. Such are his thoughts as he returns to Paris by train.[19] The last train bearing him to Paris stops for repairs in the open countryside. As he waits for the repairs to be concluded, he notices a group of trees[20] near the train. When he fails to respond with genuine emotion, as a poet would to the beauty of sunlight cutting an oblique line across the trees, he becomes totally discouraged about his prospects for becoming a writer: "Si j'ai jamais pu me croire poète, je sais maintenant que je ne le suis pas." The disillusionment he experiences on the train strengthens his decision to return to society, convinced that he will never be able to create anything of value because he is himself "sans valeur" (III, 854-55). This moment of total discouragement is the low point of the horizontal quest, just prior to his ascension as an artist.

The next day, back in Paris, he takes a cab to attend a party at the princesse de Guermantes's. As the car moves through the streets near the Champs-Elysées that were so familiar to him as a child, he suddenly has the feeling that he is becoming airborne. This sensation of taking off marks the true beginning of the novel's climactic scene: "comme un aviateur qui a jusque-là péniblement roulé à terre, 'décollant' brusquement, je m'élevais vers les hauteurs silencieuses du souvenir" (III, 858). Although he had meditated on the "flights" of Bergotte and Wagner, and on the symbol of the aviator, this is *his* first flight. Until now he has been a dilettante, wishing to fly but unable to get off the ground (III, 892). Now he is ready to undergo the transition from prototype to a fully operational aircraft.

In the passage, referred to earlier, when the Narrator and Albertine visit an airfield near Paris, he had witnessed the liberating ascension of an aviator. Here, as elsewhere, Proust insists on the conversion from the horizontal plane (containing things that are mundane, banal, habitual, and vain) to the vertical plane (representing freedom, vision, and will): "tout à coup, [l'avion] s'élevait lentement, dans l'extase raidie, comme immobilisée, d'une vitesse horizontale soudain transformée en majestueuse et verticale ascension" (III, 105-6).

Proust insists on the vertical nature of the event; in fact, the word "verticale" was added by hand to the typescript of the text in what may have been one of the last revisions made by the novelist.[21] Since any ascension is vertical in nature, the inclusion of this word would be redundant were it not for the thematic importance of the aviator's ascension. The phrase "dans l'extase raidie, comme immobilisée" is quintessentially Proustian in that he delights in isolating the moment of transition from one state to another, looking, as it were, into the very heart of the metaphor. This transition from horizontal captive to vertical creator is crucial for the successful completion of the Narrator's quest. Throughout the novel, the Proustian quest is worked out on the horizontal-vertical axes; at the conclusion, vertical imagery predominates.

In the final pages, the Narrator realizes that an artist is part god (desire and the mystery of flight) and part man (machine and matter, technique and craft, as he had sensed during his meditation on the problems posed by his doubts about Wagner's artistic genius). He understands the role of all the human faculties in the creative process: vision, instinct, memory, intelligence, craftsmanship, and suffering. This comprehension is a major aspect of his own initiation as an artist. He is given positive signs that the quest was worth pursuing through a remarkable series of "moments bienheureux," beginning with his arrival at the house of the princesse de Guermantes (III, 866ff.) he willingly accepts the labors of Daedalus, reaffirms his belief in mystery, and sees great achievements in art and science as signs of a higher order and a more perfect realm of existence. The feeling that such a higher order exists is, according to Proust's spokesperson, "ce qui nous émeut le plus dans la vie et dans l'art" (III, 1033).

The airplane is transcendental and makes possible the stereoscopic vision that allows the hero to see the relationship of one thing to another. Prior to this, all his perceptions had been fragmentary or intermittent. The artist's vision provides unity in multiplicity since it is made up of various images viewed simultaneously. The last two hundred pages of the novel, wherein the Narrator continues to explore the nature and purpose of art, amount to an ascension, replete with vertical imagery: airplanes, planets, telescopes, and people on stilts who stand tall, occupying space as they have occupied time.[22] Proust uses vertical imagery and the example of the telescope to show that the Narrator can now see in time. In addition to stating Proust's aesthetics and ethos, this final section illustrates the effects of time on existence. This is done superbly in the famous "bal de têtes" passage (III, 918ff). By tracing imagery of elevation and speed, we can see that according to the ultimate Proustian formula, when our experience is converted into a work of art, time-speed becomes space-art through elevated vision.

Proust's metaphors describing the aviator as visionary anticipated some of the unforeseen results of space photography. A striking parallel exists between the Proustian concept of seeing in time and the revelations resulting from some recent photographs taken in outer space. Proust uses images of telescopes, people on stilts, planets, and geology to show that the past is not merely past but buried and lost.

One of the main purposes of satellite photography is to make scientifically accurate maps by taking radar photographs of the earth from an orbiting satellite. An unexpected bonus of this endeavor has been the ability to take photographs of the past. The radar photographs taken during the second voyage of the space shuttle *Columbia* revealed ancient, unknown river systems as large as the Nile that had been buried for thousands of years. John F.

McCauley of the U.S. Geological Survey has described this discovery: "The radar penetrated through to give us an entirely different view of this area than we ever had before. . . . In the Sahara [we were] able to look through and use radar as a time machine."[23] In other words, geologists were able to use radar to see through the sand of the present and into the riverbeds of the distant past and to photograph them. Such a technique is essentially Proustian in nature, especially if one takes into account the abundant geological imagery used by him.[24] If Proust were writing today, in his continuing search for lost time he might be tempted to employ the analogy of radar photographs, images that converted the sands of the Sahara into a readable palimpsest.

Roger Shattuck has shown how the three basic ways of seeing the world or of recreating it—the cinematographic, montage, and stereoscopic principles—are related to stages and periods of the Narrator's life.[25] The most common level is that of habitual vision, which Proust himself relegated to realism and cinematography (III, 883). For Proust, art is the opposite of habit; hence his rejection of the realist doctrine, since that which anyone can observe does not deserve the distinction of being called art. The Proustian artist is one who refashions the world, or makes a new world, by discovering or unveiling new scientific or artistic laws.[26]

The importance of the vertical imagery at the conclusion of the novel is to provide the artist-to-be with stereoscopic, wide-angle vision in order to take in all his experiences, both on the horizontal and vertical planes. Throughout the novel, Proust employs speed and flight to represent fleeting motion and artistic ascension. Horizontal speed—typified by erotic obsessions and social ambitions that belong to the world of vanity—only leads to frustration and self-imprisonment. By attaining the vertical plane, the Narrator is able to make creative and altruistic use of his past by absorbing it and converting it into the substance of art.

To illustrate the second principle of seeing, Shattuck quotes filmmaker Sergei Eisenstein's observation, "Montage is conflict." He demonstrates that in la Recherche montage corresponds to the period of the Narrator's explorations of love, society, and art. Proust's protagonist routinely contrasts habitual vision, and his own lack of perceptions, with his idealistic expectations of finding absolutes in his encounters. Life as he experiences it ordinarily is fragmented, relativistic, and demoralizing. If, according to Shattuck's interpretation, the contrast is sharp and clear between the Narrator's expectations and his experiences, there is another aspect of vision related to perception that is also important to his quest, namely, blurred vision resulting from speed or fugacity.

At every turn the protagonist notices that those things he wishes to seize and capture, erotically or aesthetically, always escape him. Since desired objects are seen as a grayish blur under these conditions, the observer is unable to name and distinguish what he sees and therefore cannot fulfill his function as an artist. At one point Proust uses a photographic analogy to illustrate this phenomenon: "Le modèle chéri . . . bouge; on n'en a jamais que des photographies manquées" (I, 490). Even if the earliest and consequently the richest visions—because they are still uncontaminated by reality—of desired women, names, and places are recaptured in daydreaming, the whirlwind experience of daily life makes it impossible for the Narrator to seize and hold those impressions: "dans le tourbillon vertigineux de la vie courante . . . les noms ont perdu toute couleur comme une toupie prismatique qui tourne trop vite et qui semble grise . . ." (II, 12). On rare occasions he does succeed in momentarily perceiving the true colors of things, but reality soon forces him to abandon such impressions (II, 13).

The third and highest level of existence is that of the artist who is capable of creating a work containing a unified vision for others to behold. This is the state the Narrator finally attains when he comes into possession of his artistic powers, as did Bergotte when he became a mirror and then an airplane.[27] The hero's works will be superior even to those of Bergotte because he will avoid the major flaw of the latter's works, a flaw that Bergotte became aware of too late, namely, intellectual dryness. This moment of recognition and disappointment comes for Bergotte when he at last sees Vermeer's *View of Delft*: "C'est ainsi que j'aurais dû écrire, disait-il. Mes derniers livres sont trop secs, il aurait fallu passer plusieurs couches de couleur, rendre ma phrase en elle-même précieuse, comme ce petit pan de mur jaune" (III, 187).

The warning against spiritual aridity becomes a leitmotif in the novel. The Narrator reminds us that his grandmother's nature is the opposite of his own, which is totally egocentric (I, 852).[28] A warning to avoid the mistake of spiritual desiccation was given to him by those twin mentors of his childhood, his grandmother and the steeple of Saint-Hilaire. His grandmother makes this connection: "Mes enfants, moquez-vous de moi si vous voulez, [le clocher] n'est peut-être pas beau dans les règles, mais sa vieille figure bizarre me plaît. Je suis sûre que s'il jouait du piano, il ne jouerait pas *sec*" (I, 64; Proust's emphasis).

This remark is illustrative of the grandmother's importance as a moral and artistic mentor. Her observation about the steeple illustrates a major Proustian aesthetic tenet: it is the task of each new artist to find something unique, something that is beautiful, but not according to preconceived rules ("pas beau dans les règles"). It is precisely because of the singular, surprising beauty of new, genuine works of art that they are at first disconcerting to the viewer.

The dynamic speed of the creator is vertical, ascèndant, and exhilarating, making possible the true perception of things. The elevated perspective created through the use of such imagery as telescopes, planets, and old people who have become giants on stilts is not only stereoscopic—bringing different epochs into sharp focus in the same field of vision—but panoramic—juxtaposing different epochs (past, present, and future) within the same horizon—thereby utilizing the artist's vision to solve the problem of the disconnected, fragmented world perceived through the multiple perspectives of multiple egos ("les moi multiples"). The exhilarating but puzzling epiphanies of the steeples of Martinville, the madeleine, and the three trees of Hudimesnil will now be permanently cast in the cathedral-novel, along with all other aspects of the Narrator's experience. All of the previous doubts that had plagued him concerning the reality of art have disappeared: "Ceux qui m'assaillaient tout à l'heure au sujet de la réalité de mes dons littéraires, et même de la réalité de la littérature, se trouvaient levés comme par enchantement" (III, 866-67).

Proust's original plan was for a tripartite novel consisting of *Du côté de chez Swann*, *Le Côté de Guermantes*, and *Le Temps retrouvé*. Given such a structure and the analogies used by Proust, it seems possible that he intended the last section to be devoted to the air. Such a conception is not only strongly indicated by all the vertical imagery but was suggested in a letter he wrote to Jacques Rivière: "Je comptais vous donner quelques passages marins (contrastant avec les paysages terriens du premier volume) de Balbec. . . ."[29] Taking into account Proust's cosmological outlook and the abundant vertical and planetary imagery in the last section, it is probable that he envisaged three stages for the evolution and progress of the Narrator's quest: land (Combray), sea (Balbec), and air (the artist ascends to his native region): "d'un léger mouvement de ses ailes d'or [l'aviateur] piqua droit vers le ciel" (II, 1029).

In the closing pages of the novel, the Narrator's entire experience, both past and future, is seen from the elevated perspective of the artist's vision. As in the automobile-airplane metaphor illustrating Bergotte's superiority as an artist, the horizontal motion of the Narrator's life has been converted into vertical lift. The blurred distinction between sea and land was a major feature of Impressionist painting, as it is in Elstir's works, especially *The Port of Carquethuit*. As J. M. Cocking points out, it is likely that while reading Ruskin's works Proust learned about Turner's refusal to distinguish between the two elements after he had beheld the sea for the first time. Here is how Ruskin described the importance of Turner's discovery:

> The sea up to that time had been generally regarded by painters as a liquidly composed, level-seeking thing, with a smooth surface, rising to a water-mark on sides of

ships. . . . But Turner found . . . that the sea was *not* this: it was, on the contrary, a very incalculable and unhorizontal thing, setting its "water-mark" sometimes on the highest of heavens, as well as on sides of ships. . . .[30]

Cocking points out that the water lilies at Combray have the function of blurring distinctions between sea and sky:

> The sea is the point where the horizontal meets the vertical and loses its distinction, where land joins the sky. Water is the transitional element between the earth and sky, the great metaphor. Monet's water lilies described in the novel as those of the Vivonne at Combray have the same function. . . .[31]

Recalling that the water lilies at Combray are said to be "un parterre céleste," we find the same movement from the horizontal to the vertical: "[ce parterre] semblait les [les nymphéas] avoir fait fleurir en plein ciel" (I, 170).

It is only when the Narrator is ultimately capable of vertical ascension that everything becomes still and visible and hence translatable into literature. Now he can truly enter into possession of his past and transmute it into a durable form, a work of art. Thus, elevation is important not only in representing freedom and transcendence but in providing the necessary condition for the creation of art. Until now the Narrator's field of vision has been limited by his own lack of talent, will, and energy. He has misunderstood the nature of his experience and has squandered on social and erotic pursuits the little will and energy he was able to muster. The dilettantish voyeur who could not get off the ground becomes the airborne seer and attains artistic vision. Thus, the metaphor of the artist as aviator—prefigured in the meditation on Wagner's music and its comparison to an airplane—represents not only the Narrator's attainment of the artist's vision but the restoration of his will and the mastering of a craft.[32] The sickly, irresolute, insecure protagonist, his energy and will restored, has become the mighty Daedalus, ready to refashion his cosmos.

CHAPTER 8

The Cosmos Builder

Heat Becomes Light

The day of revelations begins when the Narrator, on his way to a reception at the Guermantes's town house, enters the courtyard and literally stumbles upon the key to his quest in the form of an uneven paving stone similar to the one he had tripped over in Venice. Suddenly images of the Italian city well up before him and alternate with the view of his actual surroundings. This time he is determined to find out what lies behind the phenomenon of involuntary memory. He continues to rock back and forth on the stone, concentrating and trying to understand this mystery. The Narrator, as resolute as Jacob wrestling with the angel, will not release the stone until he has solved the riddle of this experience. Remembering that he experienced the same feeling of felicity from the madeleine episode, he asks himself: "Mais pourquoi les images de Combray et de Venise m'avaient-elles, à l'un et à l'autre moment, donné une joie pareille à une certitude, et suffisante, sans autres preuves, à me rendre la mort indifférente?" (III, 867). At such moments he is freed from the present and exists outside of time: "Seul [l'être extra-temporel] avait le pouvoir de me faire retrouver les jours anciens, le temps perdu, devant quoi les efforts de ma mémoire et de mon intelligence échouaient toujours" (III, 871). The revelations he is about to receive and the reassertion of his will empower him to write. This is the ultimate goal of his quest, the moment when the sickly, nervous, insecure, and inept Narrator is about to become, at last, the cosmos builder.[1]

The artist's ability to recapture the past and cast it in a work of art was foreshadowed in the madeleine episode as well as other experiences involving involuntary memory. These epiphanies occur fortuitously throughout the novel, but in the last multiple series occurring near the end of his quest they create a crescendo effect, heralding the moment when he comes into full possession of his artistic powers. These "moments bienheureux," which release the permanent but normally hidden essence of things, are characterized by a sensation of joy caused by the feeling that death has been vanquished. After experiencing the depths of despair, the Narrator-Lazarus is brought back to life as a creator through the celestial nourishment[2] provided by these epiphanies: "notre vrai moi qui, parfois depuis longtemps, semblait mort, mais qui ne l'était pas entièrement, s'éveille, s'anime en recevant la céleste nourriture qui lui est apportée" (III, 873). He will interpret these epiphanies as proof of laws and ideas he must convert into a work of art (III, 879), realizing that literature is the sole means of regaining lost time. The Narrator now sees that the experience of his life is the subject of his future work: "Ainsi toute ma vie jusqu'à ce jour aurait pu et n'aurait pas pu être résumée sous ce titre: Une vocation" (III, 899).[3]

Among the significant discoveries he makes in the concluding section is that Albertine's role, which he had thought negative, is essential to his becoming an artist. Now he sees the usefulness of suffering in providing him with subjects and a will to work.[4] The Narrator has progressed from the fire[5] of pain to the light of understanding, reason, and art. In order to complete his quest and save himself by bringing forth the work he bears within him, the fire that burns and consumes becomes the light that illumines and gives birth to new worlds. Each sorrow creates a visible, permanent image that will become the substance of his work:

> puisque l'ardeur qui dure devient lumière et que l'électricité de la foudre peut photographier, puisque notre

sourde douleur au cœur peut élever au-dessus d'elle,
comme un pavillon, la permanence visible d'une image
à chaque nouveau chagrin, acceptons le mal physique
qu'il nous donne pour la connaissance spirituelle qu'il
nous apporte. . . . (III, 906)[6]

He now sees that, contrary to his grandmother's wishes,
he was right to neglect Elstir at Balbec in order to pursue Albertine. The tortures he suffered because of his jealous obsession with
the elusive Albertine are more important to his future work than
the lessons he learned from Elstir because the girl is the instrument[7] by which grief becomes knowledge and sorrow is converted to joy: "Chaque personne qui nous fait souffrir peut être
rattachée par nous à une divinité . . . (Idée) dont la contemplation
nous donne aussitôt de la joie au lieu de la peine que nous
avions" (III, 899*).

The apparently destructive aspects of his relationship with
Albertine are converted into a great, positive force when he discovers his vocation as an artist and sees how these "fragments"
from his past, the erosion of time and memory,[8] and those parts of
his own being destroyed by suffering will become the material for
his book. The wasted elements of his body are converted into useful particles, luminous and legible for the construction of his work:
"Le chagrin finit par tuer. . . . laissons se désagréger notre corps,
puisque chaque nouvelle parcelle qui s'en détache vient, cette fois
lumineuse et lisible . . . s'ajouter à notre œuvre" (III, 906).[9]

The Narrator's thorough exploration of subjective love
allows him to see beyond it. Writing will be the purpose of his
life and his one true passion, "la vraie vie" (III, 895). Paradise lost
can only be regained at the price of suffering and hard work.
Whereas the Eden of his childhood had not been earned, the
mature artist sees that he must make a universe of his own design.
Thus, suffering, which he had sought to avoid, is one of the keys
to artistic creativity. The *via dolorosa* leads to salvation. His work is
altruistic because his life experience will be offered to others in
the only assimilable form possible—a work of art.[10]

The Narrator earlier acknowledged a sterile form of ego-
tism and said that his nature was the opposite of his grandmother's
(I, 852). Edmund Wilson sees the grandmother as the golden
mean of *la Recherche:* "Perhaps the narrator's grandmother may be
taken as playing for Proust the same rôle that the speed of light
does for Einstein: the single constant value which makes the rest
of the system possible."[11] At the end of the novel, the protagonist's
nature has evolved from a selfish, subjective nervousness that prevented him from finding time lost to an enlargement of the soul
wherein the past is made present: "le bonheur que j'éprouvais ne
venait pas d'une tension purement subjective des nerfs qui nous
isole du passé, mais au contraire d'un élargissement de mon esprit
en qui se reformait, s'actualisait ce passé" (III, 1036).

The hero, now representative of the utopian figure of the
artist, of men and women of great achievement, is able not only
to save himself from aridity and aimlessness but also to benefit
others by transcribing for them the experience of his love for
Gilberte and Albertine. The egotist becomes the altruist: "[cet
amour] doit . . . se détacher des êtres pour en restituer la généra-
lité et donner . . . la compréhension de cet amour, à tous, à
l'esprit universel . . ." (III, 897).[12] All creativity becomes part of
the cosmic stock of beauty, knowledge, and laws, just as all living
creatures contain in miniature the species's entire genetic inheritance. The negative elements of suffering resulting from his vain
pursuits in society and love are also converted into the positive
value of art, thereby making "un égotisme utilisable pour autrui."
Proust goes on to explain that the necessary withdrawal of the
artist from society in order to create will appear egocentric, "car
tous les altruismes féconds de la nature se développent selon un
mode égoïste" (III, 1036).[13]

The point of view of the Proustian narrator is egocentric
in the literal sense of the word; so far as sensory perceptions are
concerned, each of us necessarily occupies the center of a universe—our own sentient being. Through his frequent analogies
comparing individuals to planets, Proust, like Pascal, underscores

the solitude of human existence. But an artist, like a planet, absorbs light in order to project it outward by means of creative vision, thus making his experience useful to others. It is only through this projected light—we recall the analogy of the artist to a magic lantern—that we can enter into the world expressed by the vision of each creative person. Bergotte, the writer admired by the young Narrator, is compared to a slowly cooling planet as he nears death (III, 184). Swann, ill with terminal cancer, is seen as a declining moon (II, 690); a failed artist, he generates no light of his own but only reflects light, whereas Bergotte, a genuine creator, does generate—for a time at least—the light of his work.

After a long tour of hell, the Narrator has finally come to understand the true nature of his quest, realizing that the sum total of his experience will be useful to him in building his own art-cosmos. By sharing his knowledge with the reader and pointing to the dangers he now knows how to avoid, the Narrator will serve as a role model for the reader. Such vain pursuits as social prestige and profane love, to which Swann and Charlus fall victim, should not make us abandon higher goals. The Narrator reclaims lost time through the acceptance of his vocation as a writer and soars above the crowd, as did Bergotte, in his car-airplane (I, 555).

We recall that genius, as represented by Bergotte, is the power to convert one's experience into a mirror that reflects the truth (I, 555). Bergotte's works were first identified as mirrors of truth (I, 96), and his example is repeated toward the end of the Narrator's quest: "ce n'est pas le plus spirituel, le plus instruit, le mieux relationné des hommes, mais celui qui sait devenir miroir et peut refléter ainsi sa vie, fût-elle médiocre, qui devient un Bergotte . . ." (III, 722). The positive moral influence of an artist who may be a bad person is expressed in the passage on Bergotte's genius: "souvent les grands artistes, tout en étant mauvais, se servent de leurs vices pour arriver à concevoir la règle morale de tous" (I, 558). Just as Bergotte's elevation was explained in terms of power conversion, so the Narrator's errors on his quest—yielding to jealous, base passions and to the superficial distractions of society—are translated into artistic ascension. The years of his past that he thought were wasted and lost ("temps perdu") will be transformed into a work of art. As we have seen, the contrast between profanation and art is paralleled by the imagery describing horizontal and vertical planes of the search. The horizontal is represented by excursions into the vain worlds of love and society,[14] a movement that never allows the Narrator to get off the ground, whereas the soaring achievement of the artist who attains an elevated vision is symbolized by the aviator and the steeple of Combray.

Vinteuil's music is associated with both the dystopic theme of sadism and the utopian theme of art. These intertwined themes of profanation and art, of heaven and hell, run throughout the novel and are intimately linked with the Proustian quest. The resurrection of Vinteuil's music by the very women who humiliated him and hastened the end of his mortal life is matched by the trial of the Narrator, who has also suffered because of his frustrated efforts to possess Albertine and his jealousy over her alleged sexual misconduct. His erotic longings for an unknown woman—usually a mysterious girl in motion—is transposed into the aesthetic domain of music when he discovers Vinteuil's septet, "la seule Inconnue qu'il m'ait jamais été donné de rencontrer" (III, 260). This discovery was promised to Swann by the little phrase of the sonata, but he was only capable of trivializing it in his love for Odette. Swann reduced art to eros, but the Narrator will elevate eros and suffering to the level of art.

Proust's linkage of the sacred and profane through the Vinteuil family—their lives contain elements of bourgeois mediocrity and sadism, but the music Vinteuil creates is a masterful thematic and structural composition releasing pure joy—recalls Wagner's use of the "Pilgrim's Chorus" and the Venusberg music in *Tannhäuser* as opposing themes only resolved at the end of the opera when the sacred triumphs. In *la Recherche*, the minor theme of sadism is a voluptuous, subterranean motif in counterpoint to the elevated symbolism of Vinteuil's music, which expresses light, joy, and the intimation of eternal life. All of *la Recherche* is built on the contrast between the sacred and the profane. The two extremes are reconciled when the profane elements are converted to the positive in a timeless vision of art.

Voyager

le fauteuil magique le fera voyager à toute vitesse dans le temps et dans l'espace. . . . (I, 5)

The concept of an artist as a creator of new worlds is stated explicitly in the first notebook of *la Recherche:* "Quand la pluie battait j'aurais pu enfanter des mondes. Voyageur!"[15] The Proustian cosmogony is the real story of *la Recherche*. Throughout the novel, the artists the Narrator hopes to emulate are seen as cosmos builders, as interplanetary voyagers who discover new worlds: "Le seul véritable voyage . . . ce ne serait pas d'aller vers de nouveaux paysages, mais d'avoir d'autres yeux, de voir l'univers avec les yeux d'un autre . . . de voir les cent univers que chacun d'eux [un Elstir, un Vinteuil] voit . . . avec leurs pareils, nous volons vraiment d'étoiles en étoiles" (III, 258).[16]

Never in fiction has there been a more unpromising hero than the Narrator of *la Recherche*. The suspense of the novel results from whether or not this unlikely candidate for greatness—a modern, nervous Ulysses who cannot find his way back home, does not know how to observe, lacks will, energy, and talent—can become an artist. Can he create something comparable to what Bergotte, Elstir, and Vinteuil have done in literature, painting, and music?

On a number of occasions, the Narrator is discouraged by his lack of will and inability to observe. When he tries to concentrate, his mind shuts down and he finds nothing: "mon esprit s'arrêtait de fonctionner, je ne voyais plus que le vide en face de mon attention, je sentais que je n'avais pas de génie ou peut-être une maladie cérébrale l'empêchait de naître" (I, 173). At such times he is so discouraged by his lack of talent and prospects that he renounces literature forever. This mental malfunction reminds us of Swann's congenital inability to concentrate when faced with a difficult problem.

Proust's frequent comparisons of characters, such as Swann and Albertine, to figures in paintings endow them with prestige and a plastic beauty. But when he compares the Narrator to a minor figure (I, 393), a person barely visible in the corner of a painting or photograph,[17] the analogy serves a different purpose, namely, to cast the protagonist as a person of little importance who is weak, nervous, and lacking will. The Narrator frequently engages in self-denigration. For example, he seems helpless when his idealistic dreams are confronted with the reality that lies behind the names he finds so magical, especially those of Balbec and Guermantes. If the Narrator is to evolve from a minuscule figure of little worth to become an artist, a great explorer, and a creator of new universes, he must discover that this heroic past no longer exists in order to forge his own.[18] He now realizes that the assumptions and ideas of others are of no use to him; the artist does not confirm but disturbs and recasts the material of his experience, molding it into an original vision. In order to carry out the enormous task he has accepted, he must retreat to the darkroom of his inner self.

"An Urgent Appointment with Myself"

To describe the Narrator's descent into his inner being, Proust uses two primary sets of images: enclosed, private spaces and geological strata. To experience wholeness the hero must withdraw from the world and resolve to live in solitude in order to create his book: "L'art véritable n'a que faire de tant de proclamations et s'accomplit dans le silence" (III, 881).[19] The inner darkroom is where experience becomes thought and art: "Ce sont nos passions qui esquissent nos livres, le repos d'intervalle qui les écrit" (III, 907*). The quest turns inward since it is the interior book of unknown signs that he must decipher while "explorant mon inconscient" (III, 879).[20] Herein lies the true source of the book he intends to write: "Ne vient de nous-même que ce que nous tirons de l'obscurité qui est en nous et que ne connaissent pas les autres" (III, 880).[21] The awareness of approaching old age and death makes his decision urgent: "j'avais . . . un rendez-vous urgent, capital, avec moi-même" (III, 986).

Friendship, society, and conversation are distractions that the artist must avoid, but he no longer fears society because he has extinguished within himself the desire for social glory: "ce qui était dangereux dans le monde c'était les dispositions mondaines qu'on y apporte" (III, 918-19). He will continue to make forays into society in order to gather material for his book, since he is determined to create his great work (III, 932). As for deriving the laws of human experience, society people are as good a source as any: "les grandes lois morales, aussi bien que celles de la circulation du sang ou de l'élimination rénale, différant peu selon la valeur intellectuelle des individus" (III, 882*).[22]

The Narrator had been puzzled about the role of intelligence in artistic creation and was worried that his writings, like Bergotte's, might be too dry. He now realizes that although Bergotte's books are accomplished in many ways, he can avoid the aridity evident in the elder writer's works by always assigning the primary role to sense impressions and the elucidation of his subconscious to the intellect. It will be recalled that on his last visit to a museum to see Vermeer's *View of Delft*, Bergotte discovers that, compared to the painting, his own works were too dry and lacked color (III, 187). The aging writer is profoundly discouraged by the realization that, despite his popularity and reputation as an artist, he has failed the ultimate test by allowing himself to become spiritually desiccated. This terrible moment of recognition is Bergotte's last judgment, for he discovers that he has been banished to the circle of inferior artists because he did not trust his inner being. This error is one that the Narrator is determined to avoid: "à tout moment l'artiste doit écouter son instinct, ce qui fait que l'art est ce qu'il y a de plus réel, la plus austère école de la vie, et le vrai Jugement dernier" (III, 880).

Because Proust believes that intellectual endeavors are basically sterile, he presents them as belonging to the horizontal plane. If his hero were capable only of such activity, he would not be interested in pursuing it: "le Destin m'eût-il accordé cent ans de vie de plus, et sans infirmités, il n'eût fait qu'ajouter des *rallonges* successives à une existence toute en *longueur*, dont on ne voyait même pas l'intérêt qu'elle *se prolongeât* davantage . . ." (III, 866; emphasis added). In keeping with the Symbolist and Impressionist tenets of his day, Proust casts intelligence in an essential but subordinate role.[23]

In order to explain his conception of the function of intelligence in artistic creation, he employs a photographic analogy. In each of us the impression, or negative exposure, is made, followed by the intellect's conscious development of the many frames of exposed film into a work of art. According to Proust, we all have the capacity to undertake this development process, but most are unwilling to perform the labor necessary to convert impression into expression (III, 882). The artist is capable of processing the exposed film so that others can see it: "La vraie vie . . . enfin découverte et éclaircie . . . c'est la littérature . . . qui . . . habite à chaque instant chez tous les hommes. . . . [leur passé] est encombré d'innombrables clichés qui restent inutiles parce que l'intelligence ne les a pas 'développés' " (III, 895).[24] The Narrator's withdrawal to his lodgings—his inner darkroom—is similar to the transformation of Proust's own sickroom into a workroom where a masterpiece could be created. Louis Gautier-Vignal has described Proust's occasional reluctance to hurry back to his cork-lined cell after an evening together at the Ritz: "Proust n'était point pressé de regagner la triste chambre de son appartement, sa 'geôle' comme il l'appelait et où il était, en effet, retenu par sa mauvaise santé et son dur labeur."[25]

In the preface to *Les Plaisirs et les jours*, Proust writes of his solitude in a sickbed at an earlier period in his life. Solitude at first has a negative value; the total isolation reminds him of Noah in his ark: "aucun personnage de l'histoire sainte ne me semblait aussi misérable que celui de Noé." Then he realizes how clearly one sees the world from the dark chamber: "Je compris . . . que jamais Noé ne put si bien voir le monde que de l'arche, malgré qu'elle fût close et qu'il fît nuit sur la terre" (IV, 6).

Writing to Lionel Hauser, his friend and financial adviser, about the latter's interest in art, Proust uses a similar analogy, borrowed from Montaigne. Proust hails his friend as a *homo duplex*, since he does not limit himself to his profession but maintains "ce que Montaigne appelait trop modestement l'arrière boutique puisqu'elle donne sur l'infini."[26] In the back room of our being we are alone and free to contemplate our true nature. Proust knew that his own freedom was never so great, nor his vision so vast, as when he withdrew into his inner darkroom, with its window on the universe.

Once the Narrator has understood this and experienced the pain of rejection and isolation, he is ready to explore his inner world, the rich mineral field of his own being. Proust compares the infinite ephemerality of Albertine to a stone containing the salinity *(salure)* of oceans and the light beam of a star: "je sentais que je touchais seulement l'enveloppe close d'un être qui par l'intérieur accédait à l'infini" (III, 386).[27] Solitude is cosmic (III, 450), but if the other being remains unattainable, the inner room, like Noah's ark, has a window that opens onto the cosmos. The Narrator sees but one remedy for his fundamental isolation: the creation of his own world.

"Un riche bassin minier"

Proust's geological analogies are related to his planetary imagery in the sense that geology is the science that studies the present features and the processes occurring in a given region of a celestial body. In a geological sense, each person—especially the artist— has developed his individuality to such a degree that he becomes a separate planet offering us a new vision of life: "Tel est l'univers nouveau et périssable qui vient d'être créé. Il durera jusqu'à la prochaine catastrophe géologique que déchaîneront un nouveau peintre ou un nouvel écrivain originaux" (II, 327). New worlds will form and old ones will disintegrate, his own artistic works among them.

These geological images applied to the artist function on a vertical axis, which, for Proust, always indicates creativity. Upward movement gives the artist a larger view of society and the world, allowing him to gauge accurately the spectacle of human folly and vanity and explore vistas of time and space. A descent along the vertical axis into one's inner self makes possible the discovery of truths about emotions, memory, art, and the laws of the universe. This is the region of the "moi profond," which the artist must mine in order to bring its treasures to light for others to behold: "Je savais très bien que mon cerveau était un riche bassin minier, où il y avait une étendue immense et fort diverse de gisements précieux" (III, 1037).[28]

When lost moments of the past are discovered within us, we experience a feeling of exhilaration. The incident involving the madeleine and other episodes of involuntary memory occur when such a moment unexpectedly surfaces from deep within the Narrator's being and enters his consciousness. In the madeleine passage (I, 46) the rush of a lost moment of the past to the surface is described as something vast that becomes unanchored (*désancré*)—an image that again underscores the fact that our ordinary senses and disposition are tethered and bound. The artist must gain access to the deepest regions of his being in order to fathom his entire experience. The depth of this experience may be determined by the degree to which one has suffered: "on peut presque dire que les œuvres, comme dans les puits artésiens, montent d'autant plus haut que la souffrance a plus profondément creusé le cœur" (III, 908). The descent into the depths of his inner being will result in lucidity, but it will require great courage, since he must find and acknowledge the truth and abandon cherished illusions about love: "au lieu de se bercer une centième fois de ces mots: 'Elle était bien gentille', lire au travers: 'J'avais du plaisir à l'embrasser' " (III, 896).

The geology of a planet consists of many different layers, from the surface to the core. In terms of Proustian imagery, these layers correspond to different epochs (memory and forgetting), different aspects of the personality, areas of consciousness (such as the descent into the world of sleep or that of the inner being, "le moi profond"), or to sociobiological entities such as race, heredity, and culture.[29] Here is an example of a character almost pulverized by the immense pressure exerted on him by the geological strata of race and history:

> Bloch était mal élevé, névropathe, snob et, appartenant à une famille peu estimée, supportait comme au fond des mers les incalculables pressions que faisaient peser sur lui non seulement les chrétiens de la surface, mais les couches superposées des castes juives supérieures à la sienne. . . . (I, 744)

In this passage Proust utilizes the action of intense geological pressure to illustrate the individual's struggle to overcome or deny (as Bloch eventually denies his Jewishness by changing his name to Jacques du Rozier), the nearly overwhelming force exerted by inherited genetic and social layers. On a broader scale, Proust argues that social and natural history, represented as geological ages, are essential elements of literary art. He says that Victor Hugo's poem "Booz endormi," is the most beautiful of all nineteenth-century verse because it depicts an entire age of history and geology.[30] Historical truths and observations about society are among the elements that comprise the building materials of the Narrator's cosmos. Such materials, although essential, are made of baser stuff than the loftier parts of his edifice: memory, art, and things beyond time. To convey intellectual truths and observations about society, Proust uses images of jewelry-making ("enchâsser d'une matière moins pure" [III, 898]; "sertir" [III, 932]) and masonry: "De changements produits dans la société je pouvais d'autant plus extraire des vérités importantes et dignes de cimenter une partie de mon œuvre qu'ils n'étaient nullement . . .

particuliers à notre époque" (III, 967). Proust's Narrator sees fashion, culture, biology, and our personalities as part of the same cosmic stock reserves, which he compares to geological phenomena:

> en écoutant parler Cottard, Brichot, tant d'autres,
> j'avais senti que, par la culture et la mode, une seule
> ondulation propage dans toute l'étendue de l'espace les
> mêmes manières de dire, de penser, de même dans
> toute la durée du temps de grandes lames de fond
> soulèvent, des profondeurs des âges, les mêmes colères,
> les mêmes tristesses, les mêmes bravoures, les mêmes
> manies à travers les générations. . . . (III, 944)

After particularizing his characters, the Narrator places them all in the evolutionary sweep of the universe. This concept of the cosmic stock reserves of materials is expressed elsewhere in Proust's writings. We must listen to our heart and instinct in choosing our vocation because what pleases us will certainly please others, for underneath it all we are very much alike: "c'est dans une trame universelle que nos individualités sont taillées. . . . il entre dans la composition de ce que nous croyons être notre personnalité, des substances fort communes et qui se retrouvent un peu partout dans l'Univers."[31]

History repeats itself, but with variations, like the glass chips in a kaleidoscope. The sociological aspects of the Proustian novel are truly "baser" elements in that they form the foundation, the cement, that supports the more elevated parts, the laws and vision of art associated with images of elevation and the interplanetary voyager. Above all, the revelation provided by the Narrator's final view of society—in the famous scene known as the masked ball, or "le bal de têtes" (III, 920-55)—is the manifestation of the evolutionary force of time on his social group. Time becomes tangible in the ravaged faces of the Narrator's friends, inspiring geological analogies of people as planets embodying their entire past:

> On était effrayé, en pensant aux périodes qui avaient
> dû s'écouler avant que s'accomplit une pareille révolu-

tion dans la géologie d'un visage, de voir quelles éro-
sions s'étaient faites le long du nez, quelles énormes
alluvions au bord des joues entouraient toute la figure
de leurs masses opaques et réfractaires. (III, 946)

The geological stratification of epochs manifested in the
"masks" of his friends is the concretization of time. The Narrator
first witnessed the embodiment of time as a visible entity in the
form of the church of Combray (I, 61). Now, at the end of his
quest, he links this new and troubling manifestation of time to
that moment of awareness in his childhood, "la forme que j'avais
pressentie . . . habituellement invisible, celle du Temps" (III,
1045). He determines that the discovery of the nature of time in
its various manifestations, including the geological and archaeological, will be a key to the book he is now ready to write. He
will mark his characters with the seal of time and depict each of
them as occupying a larger place in time than in space: "du moins
ne manquerais-je pas d'y décrire l'homme comme ayant la longueur non de son corps mais de ses années . . ." (III, 1046).[32]

The conceits of the river of time and the masked ball
scene may have been nurtured, in part, by a number of Homeric
associations in the early stages of la Recherche. In the later versions,
these have become merely allusive, but they were explicit in the
early sketches for the scene: "je dirais: Toute cette foule se pressait
autour de moi comme les morts de l'Odyssée venant dire à Ulysse
leur nom et lui rappelant le passé. . . ."[33] In another passage based
upon a performance of Parsifal Proust attended, where he saw so
many once-familiar faces made unrecognizable by the work of
time, the author understands that only by restoring their names
can he save them from the destructive forces of time. But rescuing
them will be difficult, for they beckon to him from the other side
of "un grand fleuve qui mettait entre nous de l'espace et élevait
des brumes . . . c'était le fleuve du Temps."[34]

The masked ball scene may have an additional biographical source. In a letter to Reynaldo Hahn dated April 11, 1907,
Proust described a musical soirée he had just attended at the

princesse de Polignac's: "Que tous les gens que j'ai connus ont vieilli. . . . Ce sont des portraits de monstres du temps où on ne savait pas dessiner."[35] Years earlier, in December 1902, Proust expressed his desire to abandon the Ruskin translations in favor of an original work. The novelist, discouraged about creating anything of his own, wrote to Antoine Bibesco: "je sens tout le néant de ma vie, cent personnages de romans, mille idées me demandent de leur donner un corps comme ces ombres qui demandent dans *L'Odyssée* à Ulysse de leur faire boire un peu de sang pour les mener à la vie. . . ."[36] Perhaps without realizing it, Proust had at this early date—some five or six years before beginning *la Recherche* in earnest—already stumbled upon the main story line of his novel: the Narrator's journey through time in search of his true vocation.

Epaisseur

The technique of layering (*épaisseur*) results from Proust's determination to depict the totality of experience by capturing characters, events, and impressions in all their multiplicity and complexity. The unusually rich text resulting from this and other narrative devices is one of the most striking features of Proust's novel. Many aspects of *la Recherche,* such as Proust's theory of multiple selves and multiple perspectives, contribute to the impression of narrative layers, all this reinforced by the abundant geological and planetary imagery. This accumulation of narrative perspectives makes it possible for Proust to create a complex, unified vision out of everyday impressions that would otherwise appear fragmentary and meaningless.

Ramon Fernandez and Brian Rogers have described Proust's method of layering as it relates to narrative voices. Fernandez traces the Narrator's development by identifying three stages of his quest: youth, experience, and the formulation of laws. Youth reflects the age of idealism, a period when the Narrator still believes in absolutes and is hopeful that he will find in the real world the equivalent of his dreams. The second stage is the result of experience, wherein the Narrator's disappointments leave him skeptical and discouraged. The third stage is that of laws, where creative relations are established between the mind and reality. It is the careful elaboration and orchestration of these three stages that create the psychic, poetic, and pseudoscientific layers of the novel.[37]

In his study of Proust's narrative techniques, Brian Rogers has shown that the novelist's elaboration of the three stages of the quest is highly complex because he often presents simultaneously different moments of narrative time.[38] Rogers speaks of the ambiguous double vision caused by sudden, unannounced shifts in the narrative point of view that make it difficult to determine whether the reader is encountering an experience for the first time with the young, inexperienced Narrator or reliving it with the mature Narrator who is telling the story. Often, after recounting an experience, the Narrator provides a commentary that shifts the apparent time line ("As I would learn later"; "Had I known then what I would discover so many years later"; "I thought at the time but have since learned"). Such a technique creates layers of narrative points of view that endow the reader with stereoscopic vision as past, present, and future are brought into the same focal plane, into one moment of being.

A major factor in the creation of layers of impressions is Proust's choice of the metaphor as a key stylistic element:

> Une heure n'est pas qu'une heure, c'est un vase rempli de parfums, de sons, de projets et de climats. Ce que nous appelons la réalité est un certain rapport entre ces sensations et ces souvenirs qui nous entourent simultanément . . . la vérité ne commencera qu'au moment où l'écrivain prendra deux objets différents, posera leur rapport . . . [et] dégagera leur essence commune en les réunissant l'une et l'autre pour les soustraire aux contingences du temps, dans une métaphore. (III, 889)[39]

The beauty of one thing is revealed only in that of another: "Le rapport peut être peu intéressant, les objets médiocres, le style mauvais, mais tant qu'il n'y a pas eu cela, il n'y a rien" (III, 890). Noonday at Combray is revealed in the sound of church bells, the totality of Combray in a cup of tea, and mornings at Doncières are recalled in the noises from the heater. The example of the heater is interesting because it presents a unique case in the novel. During the time the Narrator is consciously recalling his days at Doncières, the newly installed central heating makes an unaccustomed and disagreeable noise. Henceforth this noise will be capable of recalling to him the mornings at Doncières (II, 347). This is the only time in the novel when we witness the actual storing up of memories in the presence of the object-sensation that will revive them in his mind.

In the course of the Narrator's quest, a number of key sites vacillate between what they really are and past or unknown places that seem to beckon to him. When he finally makes the long-awaited trip to Venice, he finds reminiscences of Combray in the Italian city: "j'y goûtais des impressions analogues à celles que j'avais si souvent ressenties autrefois à Combray, mais transposées selon un mode entièrement différent et plus riche" (III, 623). When Elstir glimpses nature poetically and suppresses the cognitive demarcation of land and sea, he succeeds in introducing "cette multiforme et puissante unité, cause . . . de l'enthousiasme qu'excitait chez certains amateurs la peinture d'Elstir" (I, 836). The true sign of an original artist is the ability to fashion a multiple and powerful unified vision from all the fragments and impressions of experience.

Proust delights in giving us examples of multiple impressions, of simultaneous awareness. In his depiction of the young Narrator reading in the garden at Combray, the author makes us aware of the complex perceptions experienced while reading (I, 84).[40] Sitting in a real garden, the youth is absorbed by the story and finds the landscape described in the book more real than the actual landscape, which is only partially rendered because it is not fully perceived. The boy is also conscious of the emotions aroused by the characters and their actions, which are registered in another area of his perception. As the book is read over a period of days, memories and associations from the surroundings, circumstances, and his own emotional state cling to the book, which, like other objects from his past, contains layers of past impressions.

This is the case with George Sand's *François le Champi*. Though not an extraordinary book in and of itself, the aged Narrator unexpectedly encounters a copy of the novel in a binding similar to one he owned as a child and this encounter resurrects his childhood when his mother read the story to him: "et voici que mille riens de Combray, et que je n'apercevais plus depuis longtemps, sautaient légèrement d'eux-mêmes et venaient à la queue leu leu se suspendre au bec aimanté, en une chaîne interminable et tremblante de souvenirs" (III, 884).

Literature that fails to take into account the importance of memory and associations between the past and the present, being content to describe mere lines and surfaces, is the farthest removed from reality, as Proust's narrator defines it in the passage on metaphor: "Ce que nous appelons la réalité est un certain rapport entre ces sensations et ces souvenirs qui nous entourent simultanément. . . ." So-called realist literature impoverishes us by cutting off "toute communication de notre moi présent avec le passé, dont les choses gardaient l'essence, et l'avenir, où elles nous incitent à la goûter de nouveau" (III, 885). Proust refuses to give a flat, one-dimensional, photographic view of things and hence rejects realism; his aesthetics requires him to render the rich multiplicity of the human experience in perception, memory, and time.

A person is as multilayered in a psychological and genetic sense as is a planet in a geological sense. The events of our lives are not static, isolated, one-dimensional episodes; they form a time-space continuum in our own being.[41] We each contain many accumulated layers of experience, memory, and time. To reveal the rich complexity of our lives, so often unperceived by us, is one of the prime functions of art. Proust's conception of the diversity of our own experience through time also explains why he thought people should be depicted as occupying as large a position in space as they do in time. Such a view transforms each of us into a being of superhuman proportions. In the wonderful but brief portrait of the princesse de Nassau, Proust shows how her eyes reflect her entire life history: "ses maris, les hommes qui l'avaient entretenue, deux guerres, et ses yeux stellaires, semblables à une horloge astronomique . . . marquèrent successivement toutes ces heures solennelles du passé si lointain" (III, 979).[42] In the comparison of her eyes to an astronomical clock, Proust joins together human and cosmic time.

Odette is the best example of the layering technique applied to a character in the novel. We see her in many different guises and situations: as the lady in pink, Odette de Crécy, Madame Swann, Odette de Forcheville, Miss Sacripant, and finally as Saint-Loup's mother-in-law and mistress to the aging duc de Guermantes. Through Swann's aesthetic game of matching real people with portraits by the great masters, she becomes a Botticelli woman and a lady in a Rembrandt hat. For the Narrator, who has followed her life's story, she embodies not only her own personality and past but an entire historical period (III, 948, 950).[43]

Most novelists are generally content when they posit one convincing motivation to explain a character's behavior, but Proust often provides us with a number of motivations that are plausible. Many such passages might be cited. For example, when the Narrator discovers that Bloch has been meddling in the delicate negotiations to secure Albertine's return to her prison, the culprit can only laugh. The Narrator gives three possible reasons for Bloch's laughter (III, 443). Similarly, he provides three motivations for Charlus's effusive greeting of Mme de Saint-Euverte, a woman he especially despises and has spent a lifetime persecuting (III, 860). Lastly, when the Narrator refuses to present Bloch to the prince de Guermantes, Proust proposes four different reasons for the inconsiderate act (III, 953-54).

Has any other author delineated more fully the richness of personality within a given individual and demonstrated how self-contradictory human behavior often is, how we are influenced by heredity, society, culture, and time?[44] Possessing multiple person-alties within one body, we react at any given moment to a variety of stimuli and motivations. We are different according to place, circumstance, mood, health, and even the weather: "un change-ment de temps suffit à recréer le monde et nous-mêmes" (II, 345). Proust delves beneath the facade of the social personality, seeking psychological truths about human behavior. He depicts his protagonist as an X-ray machine in his ambition to disclose hidden motivations rather than remaining on the surface like the Goncourt brothers (III, 718-19).[45] Proust's formulation of the laws of human behavior carries on the grand French moralist tra-dition exemplified by such writers as Montaigne, Pascal, and La Rochefoucauld.[46]

We have seen the Narrator's frustrating and vain pursuit of many different Albertines, suspected most often of betrayal. His endless investigations lead him to conclude that a desired creature is too complex, too fugitive ever to be seized and known. Alber-tine is the proof writ large of Proust's theory of multiple selves. At the end of the quest, the Narrator sees that he must present his characters as having the same complexity as real people: "pour chaque caractère [faire] apparaître les faces opposées pour montrer son volume . . ." (III, 1032).[47] By creating layers of perception, presenting characters who are multifaceted, and refusing to be omniscient and didactic, Proust invents a universe that is open-ended and dynamic.

La Recherche fulfills Proust's basic aesthetic tenet concern-ing reading—a tenet that also partially explains his ultimate rejec-tion of Ruskin's beliefs concerning reading and the acquisition of knowledge. For Proust, reading is the threshold of knowledge and not its culmination, as Ruskin would have it: "La lecture est au seuil de la vie spirituelle; elle peut nous y introduire: elle ne la constitue pas."[48] At the end of the Narrator's quest, Proust leaves us at the door with a splendid guidebook called *A la recherche du temps perdu*. We must decide whether or not to cross over and enter our own "arrière boutique," with its view on the infinite.

All of the layers of the Narrator's past, both geographical and personal, are brought into sharp metaphorical focus in the figure of Mlle de Saint-Loup, who suddenly stands before him at the Guermantes' matinée. He describes her features and then states: "Je la trouvais bien belle: pleine encore d'espérances, riante, formée des années mêmes que j'avais perdues, elle ressemblait à ma Jeunesse" (III, 1032). Time manifests itself in the girl as the intersecting lines of his past join to form the radiating trajectories of a star ("l'étoile carrefour"). The two ways (Swann's and the Guermantes), the people, and the geography (Combray, Paris, and Balbec) of his past are united in the person of this ultimate girl in flower (III, 1029-31).

The family lines and bloodlines of his characters—even those he thought forever separated by an impenetrable wall of social distinctions—are joined in the end: "Et pour mieux fondre tous mes passés, Mme Verdurin tout comme Gilberte avait épousé un Guermantes" (III, 1031). The insistence on "all my pasts" reminds us of the multiple nature of Proust's conception of memory. This is the ultimate incarnation of the theme first sounded in the opening pages of the book, suggesting the rich nexus of memories that lie buried within each of us: "Un homme qui dort tient en cercle autour de lui le fil des heures, l'ordre des années et des mondes" (I, 5). The final images of the novel bring together his entire past, with which he will construct a new world.[49] In Mlle de Saint-Loup, he sees how the threads from the divergent paths of his entire life are woven together: "entre le moindre point de notre passé et tous les autres un riche réseau de souvenirs ne laisse que le choix de communications" (III, 1030).

Proust's *Recherche* is an open-ended novel built on the model of the universe. In fact, its open-endedness is one of the work's most modern aspects. Writing in 1931, Edmund Wilson went so far as to declare that Proust's novel was the literary equivalent of Einstein's theory of relativity: "He has recreated the world of the novel from the point of view of relativity: he has supplied for the first time in literature an equivalent on the full scale for the new theory of physics."[50] Proust seeks not merely to tell a story but to capture a world in motion; his novel is dynamic, freed from the effects of entropy, of winding down to a conclusion. The Proustian universe, like the real one, is constantly expanding. Proust saw *la Recherche* not as a static, frozen text but as a dynamic entity "en perpétuel devenir" (III, 1041). One is reminded again of a primary characteristic of Proust's concept of art, namely, the wedding of stasis and kinesis.

The form of the work, like that of the universe, is circular. Indeed, its circularity is such that the end marks the beginning, the birth of the "real" novel, in the Proustian sense, in time regained. Joan Rosasco has described the utopic nature of the circular topography of Combray as seen by the young Narrator: "Le Combray diurne est présenté comme un paradis printanier dont la forme circulaire est celle de toutes les utopies."[51] This characteristic will be greatly accentuated when Gilberte reveals to him that the two paths of his youth are not, as he had thought, separate, leading off into different directions, but the same circular way. The linking of the two *côtés* represents the symbolic unification of his entire experience—as does Mlle de Saint-Loup, who incarnates the point where all the paths of his life intersect.

This desire to capture an entire universe explains why, for Proust, revision always meant the addition of new texts and multiple views. The apparently shapeless nature of *la Recherche* has troubled critics since the publication of the first volumes. However, many commentators understand the organic necessity for Proust to extend constantly the circumference of *la Recherche*. Chantal Robin, for example, states:

> Proust aurait pu sans cesse grossir son œuvre, remanier son texte, sans que l'unité profonde en soit touchée. . . . Nier l'existence d'une unité créatrice dans la *Recherche*

c'est nier l'évolution spirituelle inscrite dans l'œuvre:
celle-même du narrateur qui va vers l'unification du
réel et l'expérience, qui passe de la séparation au lien.[52]

Robin's interpretation of Proust's quest for unity and the
"poetic" shape of his novel seems closer to the mark than that of
critics who accuse Proust of losing control of his material.[53]
Proust's unity lies in the relationship of the parts to the whole as
seen through the unique vision of the artist. The unity of *la
Recherche* is not a rigid structural order but one of vision, of poetic
truth of the kind the Narrator finds in Elstir's paintings and Vinteuil's music. Proust speaks of such unifying vision in a letter:

> si on cherche ce qui fait la beauté absolue de certaines
> choses, on voit que ce n'est pas la profondeur, ou telle
> autre vertu qui semble éminente. Non, c'est une espèce
> de fondu, d'unité transparente, où toutes choses, per-
> dant leur aspect de choses, sont venues se ranger les
> unes à côté des autres dans une espèce d'ordre,
> pénétrées de la même lumière. . . .[54]

According to Proust, each work of art or scientific discovery represents a new world, a small mirror reflecting the infinite,
and thus is profoundly emblematic and unifying. Proust's vision is
cosmic in the sense that he believes all works of art and science
are manifestations of universal harmony. The duty of the artist is
to capture the vision of this unity and create its aesthetic or scientific equivalent. Proust's statements to this effect imply a belief
in the idea of progress and perfectibility, of the gradual creation by
artists and scientists past, present, and future of a fundamental
unity consisting of all the fragments of true discoveries and corresponding to the ideal universe, a harmonious unity of all that
exists. In her study of mythology in *la Recherche*, Marie Miguet-
Ollagnier points out that the figure of the unicorn—to which
Proust's narrator compares Swann as he listens to Vinteuil's music
(I, 237)—was the symbol of mystical unity in medieval mythology, represented by the unicorn's single horn. Proust, who was

well versed in medieval mythology through his translations of Ruskin's writings and his reading of Emile Mâle's studies of medieval art, knew the symbolic relationship between the unicorn and mystical unity and chose to utilize the fabulous beast in this passage, where Swann comes closest to attaining the artist's vision of the fundamental unity of the universe.[55]

The Proustian cosmos is holographic, that is, its totality can be recreated from any single part: "tout se tient." Wallace Fowlie has seen this clearly: "The miracle of Proust's novel is the relationship established between every character, every scene, every theme, within the entire work."[56] The holographic nature of Proust's work is created, in large measure, by means of thematic orchestration and a layering technique, based on Proust's conception of the novel as a mirror of the universe.

Explorers of the Invisible

In a letter to Jacques Rivière, Proust speaks about his concept of working on several levels at the same time in order to avoid "plane" or flat psychology. The author goes on to explain that if the Cottards are mentioned in a certain passage, it is not merely to add variety to the characters evoked but to provide "un aperçu des substructions et des étagements divers."[57] To describe the creation of the Narrator's future novel, Proust chiefly uses images of structuring drawn from both the natural world (geology and astronomy) and from man-made edifices (architecture). In the closing pages, the Narrator's vow to create a cosmic novel is identical to Proust's own, as quotes from the letters and novel show:

> Bientôt je pus montrer quelques esquisses. Personne n'y comprit rien. Même ceux qui furent favorables à ma perception des vérités que je voulais ensuite graver dans le temple, me félicitèrent de les avoir découvertes au "microscope", quand je m'étais au contraire servi d'un télescope pour apercevoir des choses, très petites en effet, mais parce qu'elles étaient situées à une grande distance, et qui étaient chacune un monde. (III, 1041)

The cosmos builder is primarily a discoverer of truths, of the laws that govern nature, human behavior, and aesthetics. Although Proust is capable of observing and appreciating the limitlessness of the microcosm, he rejects the comparison of his examination of the human experience to that of a scientist looking through a microscope because his principal point of view is macrocosmic.[58] The challenge taken up by the Narrator is not the examination of minutiae but the discovery of the great laws that govern the universe: "Là où je cherchais les grandes lois, on m'appelait fouilleur de détails" (III, 1041).[59] This vision of creative people as explorers of the unknown and fashioners of new laws, is briefly comprehended by Swann while listening to the Vinteuil sonata; it is now assumed by the Narrator as his chief artistic function.

For Proust the role of the artist and scientist in society is the same. The only difference between the way in which scientists and artists create is procedural rather than substantive: "L'impression est pour l'écrivain ce qu'est l'expérimentation pour le savant, avec cette différence que chez le savant le travail de l'intelligence précède et chez l'écrivain vient après" (III, 880). As far as vision and imagination are concerned, Proust does not distinguish between artists and scientists; their common duty is to decode, to make clear what was obscure. Vinteuil is compared to Ampère, Lavoisier, and other pioneers in art and science whose mission is to reveal the laws that govern the universe (I, 351). The truths derived from these laws are as precise in art as in science: "La vérité, même littéraire, n'est pas le fruit du hasard. . . . Je crois que la vérité (littéraire) se découvre à chaque fois, comme une *loi* physique. On la trouve ou on ne la trouve pas."[60]

"Rendre visible" is, as we have seen, the watchword of the Proustian artist, a watchword that he extends to his fellow scientific explorers. Vinteuil is the ideal representative of this bond between art and science in that music, with its ancient links to mathematics, makes the connection between art and science more evident. Vinteuil's musical instruments are more than just equipment capable of producing sound; they become tools with which to explore the unknown (III, 256). In his ambition to become a writer, the Narrator refers to himself as an experimenter (I, 948).[61] Some years after Vinteuil's death, the Narrator establishes another link between Vinteuil's music and science by comparing the unpublished notebooks containing the composer's greatest music to the illegible notebooks of a chemist of genius, "les illisibles carnets où un chimiste de génie, qui ne sait pas la mort si proche, a noté des découvertes . . ." (III, 262).

Northrop Frye has classified Proust's book as an encyclopedic novel. In many ways, la Recherche represents the summation of the Western historical and artistic tradition. But this novel is not only encyclopedic in the sense of accumulating and encapsulating the past of a given culture; it must also be described as cosmic in its presentation of new laws and visions of the human experience and even in the anticipation of its own oblivion.[62] Based on the experience of his lifelong quest, the Narrator formulates the sociology, psychology, sexuality, topography, biology, botany, geology, and archaeology of the Proustian cosmos. His quest provides an ethos and an aesthetics, during the course of which many of our tenets, tastes, and mores are exposed and minutely examined. In so doing, Proust creates new ways of looking at the world, making his novel one of the most complex and stimulating optics that we have for viewing our own lives. Through its dynamic use of shifting perspectives as the Narrator journeys toward his goal, la Recherche offers the reader a kaleidoscopic view of a world in motion. Few writers have given us so many ways of looking at the world and our own experience. By making us aware of these unplumbed layers within ourselves, la Recherche celebrates and expands the multiplicity and range of human perception.

"Celui qui pourrait écrire un tel livre serait heureux"

Art, Proust tells us, is the ultimate refuge. It is a paradise, albeit a dynamic one that constantly changes through the labors of the artist. Thus, through a combination of events, luck, involuntary memory, hard work, craft, and will, the Narrator, possessing the supreme vantage point won by age and experience, is at last able to ascend to the heights of the artist's panoramic, stereoscopic vision *and* to plumb the depths of his being. In the Proustian schema of movement in space, the creative person alone is capable of progress along the vertical axis. The past, now that it is understood, may be reconstructed, interpreted, and transposed into literature. The images of the artist as airplane pilot and as a strong miner represent the exploration and exploitation of the inner and outer worlds. The Narrator is now able to construct his vision of the cosmos, although he sees clearly that the range, scope, and depth of his undertaking are immense.[63]

If the writer, as conceived by Proust, cannot render exactly a person or object as seen in a particular light or as relived in memory, that moment or memory is lost and the fear of passing time and death grows more intense. The Narrator's quest is to find a way to rescue life from the destructive forces of time: waste, habit, insensitivity, and other vices embodied in the false gods of snobbery and eroticism. To complete his task he must create a complex, multilayered style to describe not only the many variations of light, form, and memory but also the twistings and loopings of the Narrator's mind as he becomes aware of multiple perspectives and seeks to cast them in a work of art.

The concluding section of *Le Temps retrouvé* shows the Narrator rising above his entire experience, able to see in the past, present, and future as he accepts the responsibility of the Herculean labors that await him. As his hero is initiated into the requirements of his craft, Proust builds up the passage through an accumulation of infinitives.[64] The artist must labor to save the past from the destructive forces of Time, yet ultimately life and art are joined together in mutual intimations of immortality.

> quel labeur devant lui! . . . car cet écrivain . . . devrait préparer son livre minutieusement, avec de perpétuels regroupements de forces, comme une offensive, le

supporter comme une fatigue, l'accepter comme une
règle, le construire comme une église, le suivre comme
un régime, le vaincre comme un obstacle, le conquérir
comme une amitié, le suralimenter comme un enfant,
le créer comme un monde. . . . (III, 1032)

Like a religious quest the artist's search is transcendent.
"Religious" is used here in the classic, universal, and literary sense
as a "sentiment de respect, d'obéissance exacte et scrupuleuse
envers ce que l'on considère comme une obligation morale"
(*Grand Larousse de la Langue française*). At the end of his quest the
Narrator recognizes and accepts the moral duty of the artist and
speaks of it as a religious obligation ("l'accepter comme une règle,
le construire comme une église"). He has taken on nothing less
than the challenge to create a cosmos, "la transcription d'un
univers qui était à redessiner tout entier . . ." (III, 1046).

This challenge will be taken up by a writer who, in his
creative persona, is an androgynous creature. The theme of the
androgyne is sounded in the opening pages of the novel when the
slumbering Narrator recalls the places and rooms he has occupied
in the past. These are recalled through body positions he has
assumed in bed. Sometimes, he says, a woman is born from his
body as Eve was born from Adam's (I, 4). The androgynous birth
of Eve results in the separation of the sexes, which will become—
especially in its homosexual manifestations—one of the major
themes of the novel.[65] During the quest, the protagonist seeks to
recapture his lost will and become a productive creator; Proust's
analogies for this process are primarily those of a genetrix.
Miguet-Ollagnier writes of this aspect of *la Recherche*:

La quête a pris chez lui une forme particulière: celle de
la réunification du masculin et du féminin. Surtout elle
n'est pas restée une théorie. La structure événemen-
tielle du récit, les paysages, les œuvres d'art imaginaires,
nous ont installés au cœur de ce paradis retrouvé où
règne un Adam androgyne et fécond.[66]

Elstir, one will recall, is viewed as a new Adam when he produces paintings that are androgynous in their mingling of land and sea (I, 834-35).[67] At the end of the novel the Narrator, endowed with creative ability, rediscovers the fundamental unity represented by Adam, the androgynous creator.[68] The writer describes himself as impregnated by Albertine and bearing within himself the future work.[69] It is the sorrow caused by his recognition of the extreme distance between himself and Albertine—a distance as vast as that between the sexes—that impregnates him: "c'est . . . parce qu'elle était si différente de moi, qu'elle m'avait fécondé par le chagrin . . . (III, 915*). What was destroyed by pain and sorrow becomes the embryo of the future work, represented by images of gestation and delivery: "je me sentais accru de cette œuvre que je portais en moi" (III, 1036).

In the early notes for *Le Temps retrouvé*, images of feminine creativity predominate: the Narrator's future book will be constructed with the same care Françoise takes in making her "bœuf mode" or a seamstress lavishes on a new dress.[70] In the final version, Proust frequently employs images associated with a female giving birth to describe the Narrator's creative attempts. Proust describes the hero's first—and, for many years, only—literary creation in a feminine, reproductive analogy; having written several pages describing the steeples of Martinville, the young man feels like a hen that has just laid an egg and begins to crow at the top of its voice (I, 182). Writing about the androgynous aspects of his endeavor, Miguet-Ollagnier quotes from the *Carnet de 1908:* "Le travail nous rend un peu mères. . . . Parfois me sentant près de ma fin je me disais, sentant l'enfant qui se formait dans mes flancs, et ne sachant pas si je réunirais les forces qu'il faut pour enfanter, je lui disais avec un triste et doux sourire: 'Te verrais-je jamais'."[71] In *la Recherche* the Narrator sees his work in terms of a mother and son: "[Mon œuvre] était pour moi comme un fils dont la mère mourante doit encore s'imposer la fatigue de s'occuper sans cesse" (III, 1041-42).[72] As a storyteller engaged in a nightly battle against death, the protagonist compares himself to Scheherazade (III, 131, 1043).[73]

By presenting the androgynous characteristics of the creative process, Proust continues an ancient tradition. Bisexuality was a recurring theme in ancient mythology, where a number of creation myths have an androgynous birth as the source of divine and human races.[74] Many mythologies endow bisexuality, which is associated with gods and fertility cults, with a positive symbolic value. According to a medieval concept, the inner being was also androgynous in nature.[75] The soul and mind were divided into two parts, "a feminine sensory part on one hand and masculine reason and will on the other."[76] This is a belief that still has great currency today.

Current belief in the bisexual nature of people, in the sense that an individual possesses both male and female characteristics, was also commonplace in late-nineteenth-century France, especially in artistic and scientific circles. However, according to Françoise Cachin, by the turn of the century "le rêve androgyne 'fin du siècle' paraît ressortir plus de la négation du sexe que de ses ressources de redoublement."[77] With Proust, it is clearly the opposite that prevails; he sees the coexistence of masculine and feminine traits within an individual as a positive, enriching value. Proust explained to Gide that Charlus's ability to understand and appreciate art is due to his sexual nature: "je suis convaincu que c'est à son homosexualité que M. de Charlus doit de comprendre tant de choses qui sont fermées à son frère . . . d'être tellement plus fin, plus sensible."[78] The richness of the double nature of the androgyne appeals to Proust as a symbol for the integral nature of the artist as beholder, interpreter, and creator of new worlds. The sexes that were sundered as a result of the division of the androgyne in two are reunited in the integrated being of the cosmos builder.

Proust's hero is the creative person, the tireless seeker of new laws. The novel ends in a crescendo of joy and the promise of great efforts on the part of the writer. But the Narrator, whose earlier trials were centered on the lack of will and vision, now faces a new and equally formidable obstacle in that he must win the race against death: "Cette idée de la mort s'installa définitivement en moi comme fait un amour. Non que j'aimasse la mort, je la détestais. . . . l'idée de la mort me tenait une compagnie aussi incessante que l'idée du moi" (III, 1042). Like the cathedral builders, he is an architect engaged in a race against time; once the edifice is built, he will close forever the door of his tomb (III, 1041).

   La Recherche is a vast sermon on vanity, a "mise en garde" against love, friendship, snobbery, social prestige, and fame. If we listen carefully, we see that all human pursuits—even art, the most exalted, according to Proust—are dealt with as mercilessly as in Shelley's "Ozymandias." There is a heroic quality in the Narrator's determination to build something monumental and altruistic in the face of apparent oblivion: "Sans doute mes livres eux aussi, comme mon être de chair, finiraient un jour par mourir. Mais il faut se résigner à mourir. . . . La durée éternelle n'est pas plus promise aux œuvres qu'aux hommes" (III, 1043*).

   The true artist is one who knows how to see and to make his vision accessible to others by taking the bitter lessons of wasted time and making of them a durable work of art. Proust casts the artist in the role of a Promethean craftsman able to fashion machinery and convert power into an ascendant force. The work of art—in the Narrator's case, the ideal book he will now write—may contain base elements, but it will be awe-inspiring, encyclopedic in scope, and transcendent, just like a cathedral. It is precisely because he attempted to create the aesthetic equivalent of cosmic unity that Proust repeatedly compares his book to a cathedral. Following his lead, critics have pointed out a number of analogies between the structure of *la Recherche* and that of a Gothic cathedral. A cathedral is an encyclopedia in stone of the real and ideal worlds, enclosing in the same structure the universe in miniature: "L'image de l'église et celle de la cathédrale soulignent l'intention de donner à l'œuvre un caractère pantaculaire, au sens vrai du terme, c'est-à-dire d'en faire comme une sorte d'abrégé de l'Univers."[79] In a letter to François Mauriac, Proust refers to the scene at Montjouvain as the obscene capital of his cathedral-novel.[80] Although the tympanum and other areas of the cathedral may represent the Last Judgment, with its sinister views of victims trapped in hell, the overall effect of flying buttresses, stained-glass windows, and spires is one of elevation and exultation.

Once Proust understood that the subject of his book lay within himself, he withdrew to his own darkroom, accepting a voluntary sentence of twelve years of hard labor, writing in a corklined room with no heat (he believed the fumes from the fireplace irritated his lungs). The book he produced is one of the longest, most complex, and richest in the history of Western culture. Despite its length and the amount of time needed to read it, Proust's novel continues to live in the minds of readers all over the world. It has never been out of print. As of this writing, new editions and translations proliferate. There is no doubt that the creation and publication of *A la recherche du temps perdu* is one of the most sustained creative efforts in the history of literature.[81] At the end of *la Recherche*, the Narrator's ambition and determination to be a writer are finally joined with Proust's own. At last he will be able to engrave on his monument: *Hoc Fecit Marcellus*.

Notes

1. The Age of Speed

1. Unless otherwise stated, all page references are to the Gallimard (Pléiade) editions of Proust's works: *A la recherche du temps perdu,* vols. I, II, and III, edited by Pierre Clarac and André Ferré (Paris, 1954); *Jean Santeuil* and *Les Plaisirs et les jours* (vol. IV), and *Contre Sainte-Beuve, Pastiches et mélanges, Essais et articles* (vol. V), both edited by Pierre Clarac and Yves Sandré (Paris, 1971). References to *la Recherche* give volume and page numbers only. A reference followed by an asterisk indicates a passage that was omitted from the original edition of *la Recherche* but was included in the Pléiade edition. In references to works from the other volumes, the title of the work is given, followed by the volume and page number. All translations, unless otherwise stated, are my own.

    Proust, who followed with great interest the developments of machine technology, referred to his era more than once as "locomotive" and "une époque de hâte." See *Contre Sainte-Beuve* (V, 202), and *A la recherche du temps perdu,* II, 815: "On disait qu'à une époque de hâte convenait un art rapide, absolument comme on aurait dit que la guerre future ne pouvait pas durer plus de quinze jours, ou qu'avec les chemins de fer seraient délaissés les petits coins chers aux diligences et que l'auto pourtant devait remettre en honneur." (There is another version of this same statement at III, 888-89.) In "Mondanité et mélomanie de Bouvard et Pécuchet," Proust characterized the century as that of steam, universal suffrage, and the bicycle. See *Jean Santeuil* (IV, 63-64).

2. This information is provided in Jacques Nathan, *La Littérature du métal, de la vitesse, et du chèque de 1880 à 1930* (Paris: Didier, 1971), p. 12. What is surprising about this otherwise excellent

book is that Nathan, a Proust scholar with two prior books on the writer, makes only one brief mention of him in this study. No French writer of the epoch discussed in Nathan's book was more influenced by the advancements in modern technology or made better narrative and metaphorical use of the material than Proust.

3. See the article by Eugène Nicole, "Les Inventions modernes dans *La Recherche du temps perdu*," *Bulletin de la Société des Amis de Marcel Proust et de Combray* 36 (1986): 528-42.

4. Charles Baudoin, quoted by Pär Bergman in *"Modernolatria" et "Simultaneità": Recherches sur deux tendances dans l'avant-garde littéraire en Italie et en France à la veille de la première guerre mondiale*, Studia Litterarum Upsaliensia, 2 (Bonniers: Svenska Bokförlaget, 1965), p. 8.

5. Quoted by Eugen Weber in *France: Fin de Siècle* (Cambridge, Mass.: Harvard University Press, 1986), p. 236. In the chapter entitled "The Cosmos Builder," I discuss the similarities between Proust's and Einstein's views of the universe.

6. Quoted by Bergman, *"Modernolatria,"* p. 16.

7. See *Correspondance de Marcel Proust*, edited by Philip Kolb (Paris: Plon, 1981), 1912, 11: 292. Unless otherwise stated, all references are to this edition, of which twenty volumes have appeared to date. Each reference will be given as follows: *Correspondance*, year, volume number, and page number.

8. Weber, *France: Fin de Siècle*, p. 54.

9. Ibid., p. 68.

10. See A. D. Trottenberg's introduction to *Eugène Atget, A Vision of Paris* (New York: Macmillan, 1963), pp. 11-28.

11. Quoted by Weber, *France: Fin de Siècle*, pp. 70-71. "No more rank, titles, or race. . . . All is mixed, confused, blurred, and reshuffled in a kaleidoscopic vision," wrote editor François Mainguy in the first issue (1890) of *Le Fin de Siècle*, (p. 10). Proust, too, utilizes the kaleidoscope as one of his principal metaphors to describe social evolution.

12. Ibid., p. 73.

13. Nathan, *Littérature du métal*, p. 18.

14. Ibid., p. 41.

15. Elstir, Proust's fictional painter, gives the Narrator (who is something of a classical idealist when he arrives at Balbec) his first lesson in what Baudelaire called "la beauté moderne." See Baudelaire's essay in his *Salon de 1846* entitled "De l'héroïsme de la vie moderne," in *Œuvres complètes*, edited by Y.-G. Le Dantec and

Claude Pichois, Bibliothèque de la Pléiade (Paris: Gallimard, 1961), p. 952. Claude Monet painted the metal carcass of the Saint-Lazare train station with the same care and style one finds in his pictures of the Rouen cathedral. Many artists and writers were inspired by the new technology. The belief that it is the artist's vision and not the subject of the painting that determines its value is expressed by Elstir, who influences the Narrator's aesthetic ideas: "Il n'y a pas de gothique, il n'y a pas de chef-d'œuvre, l'hôpital sans style vaut le glorieux portail. . . . Tout le prix est dans les regards du peintre" (II, 421).

16. For the influence of the bicycle on social mores, fashion, and the liberation of women, see Weber, *France: Fin de Siècle*, pp. 102, 201, 203.

17. See Bernard Straus's article "Achille-Adrien Proust, M.D.: Doctor to River Basins," *Bulletin of the New York Academy of Medicine* 50 (1974): 833–38.

18. See *L'Hygiène du neurasthénique* (Paris: Masson, 1897), p. 75.

19. In *la Recherche* traces of anglomania can be seen in the fad for the monocle, which gives rise to one of the most amusing passages in Proust's novel, and in Odette's habit of sprinkling her sentences with English words.

20. Quoted in Weber, *France: Fin de Siècle*, p. 58.

21. See Stephen Kern, *The Culture of Time and Space, 1880-1918* (Cambridge, Mass.: Harvard University Press, 1983), p. 113.

22. See Weber, *France: Fin de Siècle*, pp. 69–70.

23. See II, 996–97.

24. Paul Souriau, *L'Esthétique du mouvement* (Paris: Félix Arcan, 1889), p. 23.

25. See Nathan, *Littérature du métal*, p. 13.

26. Quoted by Kern, *The Culture of Time and Space*, p. 118.

27. Ibid., p. 111.

28. Bergman, "*Modernolatria*," p. 11.

29. *Correspondance*, 1907, 7: 263.

30. "En mémoire des églises assassinées," (V, 67).

31. See Robert Cantwell's "Bright Threads in His Tapestry," *Sports Illustrated*, December 17, 1973, pp. 82-96.

32. See the chapter entitled "Speed and Desire" for a detailed discussion of this subject.

33. See the chapter entitled "Death of an Aviator" for an analysis of Agostinelli's character.

34. The word made its entry in Larousse in 1906.

35. See Lucien Métivet's illustrations for Michel Leblanc's novel *Voici des ailes!* (Paris: Paul Ollendorff, 1898). This novel chronicles the liberating effect of a cycling tour on two young couples.
36. Quoted by Kern, *The Culture of Time and Space*, p. 113.
37. Fernand Léger, "A propos du cinéma," quoted in Marcel L'Herbier's *Intelligence du cinématographe* (Paris: Corrêa, 1946), p. 337.
38. Kern, *The Culture of Time and Space*, p. 118.
39. Fernand Léger, "The Origins of Painting and Its Representational Value." Quoted in Kern, *The Culture of Time and Space*, p. 118.
40. See Nathan, *Littérature du métal*, p. 58.
41. Apollinaire, *Les Peintres cubistes*, edited by L. C. Breunig and J.-Cl. Chevalier (Paris: Collection Savoir Hermann, 1980), pp. 55-56.
42. This experience is discussed at length in the chapter entitled "The Cosmos Builder."
43. *Marcel Proust et Jacques Rivière: Correspondance, 1914-1922*, edited by Philip Kolb (Paris: Plon, 1955), p. 264. Rivière's emphasis.
44. Kern, *The Culture of Time and Space*, p. 147.
45. Ibid., p. 22.
46. Bergman, "*Modernolatria*," p. 32.
47. See the chapters entitled "Death of an Aviator" and "The Artist and the Aviator."
48. Man Ray, who would photograph Proust on his deathbed, expressed his preference for photography and aviation in a statement that reminds us of the Narrator's first sighting of an aviator: "A photograph is to a painting what an automobile is to a horse. A rider on his horse is a beautiful thing, but I prefer a man in an airplane." Quoted by Claude Nori, *French Photography: From Its Origins to the Present* (New York: Pantheon, 1979), p. 34. The translation is by Lydia Davis.
49. Quoted by Bergman, "*Modernolatria*," p. 5.
50. Ibid., p. 134.
51. *Matinée chez la Princesse de Guermantes*, edited by Henri Bonnet in collaboration with Bernard Brun (Paris: Gallimard, 1982), p. 403. This passage is an example of an airplane perceived as an airborne automobile.
52. In another passage Françoise is described as an individual "qu'une timidité et une mélancolie ancestrales, appliquées à un objet inconnu de ses pères, empêchaient de s'approcher du récepteur . . ." (III, 155).

53. For a discussion of this subject, see Weber, *France: Fin de Siècle*, p. 4.
54. The scandal caused upheaval in the sporting world as well. In 1900 discussion about the guilt or innocence of Dreyfus became so heated among members of the editorial board at the major sports paper *Le Vélo* that a schism occurred. The anti-Dreyfusards walked out and created a paper of their own, *l'Auto-Vélo*, which soon dropped the biking component and became *l'Auto*. See Weber, *France: Fin de Siècle*, p. 122.
55. In another passage Proust describes the effect of time on the salon of the princesse de Guermantes: "Le temps n'y avait pas seulement défait d'anciennes créatures, il y avait rendu possibles, il y avait créé des associations nouvelles" (III, 949).
56. Terry Eagleton, *Literary Theory: An Introduction* (Minneapolis: University of Minnesota Press, 1983), p. 185.
57. Joseph Campbell, *The Hero with a Thousand Faces*, Bollingen Series 17 (Princeton, N.J.: Princeton University Press, 1949), p. 30. Campbell's emphasis.
58. "Encyclopedic" is Northrop Frye's description of *la Recherche*. See his *Anatomy of Criticism* (Princeton, N.J.: Princeton University Press, 1957), p. 61.

2. Women as Landscapes

1. In Gilberte's case, most of the mobility was transferred to her name: "Ainsi passa-t-il [ce nom de Gilberte], proféré au-dessus des jasmins et des giroflées, . . . imprégnant, irisant la zone d'air pur qu'il avait traversée . . ." (I, 142).
2. Proust uses flowers throughout *la Recherche* as a metaphor for sexuality: Swann and Odette's private term for lovemaking is "faire catleya"; the *filles-fleurs* of *A l'ombre des jeunes filles en fleurs* are erotic creatures; the fertilization of the duchesse de Guermantes's rare plant serves as an analogy for the Charlus-Jupien homosexual encounter. For more on Proustian flowers, see the chapter entitled "The Prison."
3. Stephen Kern has pointed out that "the great historicist systems of the nineteenth century as well as the work of Dilthey, Bergson, Proust and Freud celebrated the historical or genetic approach. . . ." For a discussion of this point, see his book *The Culture of Time and Space, 1880-1918* (Cambridge, Mass.: Harvard University Press, 1983), p. 51.

4. In *la Recherche* Proust compares the physical characteristics of Céleste's face and her at times tempestuous nature to the rivers of her native region, the Massif Central (II, 849-50). Françoise's character is compared to a rough country road: "le chemin rustique et familier qu'était le caractère de Françoise devenait impraticable . . ." (I, 897). Oriane's voice contains "l'or gras et paresseux d'un soleil de province" (II, 205). Mlle de Stermaria embodies the poetry and charm of Brittany, "cette vie si poétique qu'elle menait en Bretagne . . . [qu'elle] contenait enclose en son corps" (I, 689).

5. One is reminded of Emma Bovary, who, when frustrated in her desire to live in a great city, attempts to "possess" Paris through a map. See Gustave Flaubert's *Madame Bovary* (Paris: Garnier-Flammarion, 1986), p. 118.

6. Like his narrator, Proust went to no end of trouble to obtain photographs of those whom he worshiped. He wrote to Mlle Simone de Caillavet: "Quand j'étais amoureux de votre maman, j'ai fait pour avoir sa photographie des choses prodigieuses. Mais cela n'a servi à rien. Je reçois encore au jour de l'an des cartes de Périgourdins avec qui je ne m'étais lié que pour tâcher d'avoir cette photographie!" *Correspondance*, 1910-1911, 10: 40. Cf. *la Recherche*, I, 503.

7. Cf. the Narrator's puerile wish to break with Albertine as a pedal point for the same reason—a smooth, painless diminuendo—providing another link between the pedals of Albertine's bicycle and the pedals of the organ: "de peur que, par une parole nouvelle . . . elle [Albertine] vînt blesser d'une dissonance le silence sensitif où, comme grâce à quelque pédale, aurait pu survivre longtemps en moi la tonalité du bonheur" (II, 835). On another occasion the Narrator muses: "je m'imaginais que le souvenir que je garderais d'elle [Albertine] serait comme une sorte de vibration prolongée par une pédale, de la minute de notre séparation. Aussi je tenais à choisir une minute douce, afin que ce fût elle qui continuât à vibrer en moi" (III, 393). Cf. the closing of a letter that Madame Proust wrote to her son in 1890: "Adieu mon chéri je t'embrasse tendrement avec un point d'orgue à prolonger jusqu'au prochain baiser" (*Correspondance*, 1880-1895, 1: 137). The pedal point separation is a subtle link between maman and Albertine.

8. When Gaston Gallimard, who would eventually publish *la Recherche*, first met Proust at Cabourg in 1908, he was awed by the writer's phenomenal memory. At dinner someone mentioned

Constantinople, whereupon Proust recited a full page on the city from one of Pierre Loti's novels. When the publisher remarked about Proust's extraordinary memory, the author advised him, "Read the Chaix train schedules; it's even better!" Proust then recited whole sections of the schedules one would need to know to take the train from Paris to various cities. See Gaston Gallimard's recollection of meeting Proust entitled "Première Rencontre," in "Hommage à Marcel Proust: 1871-1922," *La Nouvelle Revue Française*, n.s. 112, vol. 20 (January 1923): 65. This incident is also recounted in Gallimard's biography by Pierre Assouline, *Gaston Gallimard: Un demi-siècle d'édition française* (Paris: Balland, 1984), p. 38.

9. When Albertine first arouses his desire on the beach at Balbec, he compares the desired girl to the flag of an unknown country: "je la voyais flotter et claquer brillante et souple devant moi comme un drapeau d'un pays inconnu . . ." (I, 874, n. 1). This metaphor was not retained in the definitive text. The flag of an unknown country is ambiguous as is Albertine. Does it represent a haven or danger? Cf. the following lines from Baudelaire's poem "Femmes damnées": "Et le vent furibond de la concupiscence / Fait claquer votre chair ainsi qu'un vieux drapeau." Charles Baudelaire, *Œuvres complètes*, edited by Y.-G. Le Dantec and Claude Pichois, Bibliothèque de la Pléiade (Paris: Gallimard, 1961), p. 139.

10. The Narrator, as he often demonstrates, shares Baudelaire's "goût de l'infini." Cf. the closing lines of Baudelaire's "Le Voyage": "Nous voulons, tant ce feu nous brûle le cerveau, / Plonger au fond du gouffre, Enfer ou Ciel, qu'importe? / Au fond de l'Inconnu pour trouver du *nouveau!*" Baudelaire's emphasis. Baudelaire, *Œuvres complètes*, p. 127. As we shall see in the chapter entitled "The Prison," the Proustian lover who allows his jealous desire to become obsessive creates his own hell. The solution to the dilemma will be an aesthetic one.

11. André Ferré, *La Géographie de Marcel Proust* (Paris: Sagittaire, 1939), p. 29.

12. Gilberte, who is seen for the first time at Tansonville, evokes the sea only once in an unflattering way. When she and the Narrator are at odds with each other, her face is said to be like "ces plages ennuyeuses où la mer, retirée très loin, vous fatigue d'un reflet toujours pareil que cerne un horizon immuable et borné" (I, 584).

13. For a discussion of the Fortuny material and the peacock as a symbol of resurrection, see Peter Collier's book *Proust and Venice* (Cambridge: Cambridge University Press, 1989).

14. The details of Agostinelli's letter are described in the chapter entitled "The Death of an Aviator."

15. Cf. the following passage, which shows that the Narrator is at times aware of the reason for his attraction to the seaside band of girls: "quand, même ne le sachant pas, je pensais à elles. . . . c'était la mer que j'espérais retrouver. . . . L'amour le plus exclusif pour une personne est toujours l'amour d'autre chose" (I, 833). Cf. also this passage: "Mon désir d'elles, je pouvais maintenant le mettre au repos . . . des figures dans un tableau ayant pour fond la mer . . ." (I, 865).

16. Cf. Proust's description of the princesse de Nassau, whose eyes are compared to an astronomical clock because they contain the entire history of her life (III, 979-80).

17. For the impressions of circling and "capturing" a city, see the steeples of Martinville passage (I, 180-82).

18. Kolb dates this letter September 8 or 9, 1903. See *Correspondance, 1902-1903*, 3: 418.

3. Girls in Motion

1. See Jacques-Henri Lartigue, *Boyhood Photos of J.-H. Lartigue: The Family Album of a Gilded Age*, edited by Jean Fondin (Lausanne: Ami Guichard, 1966), and his *Instants de ma vie* (Paris: Chêne, 1970), n. p.

2. See Claude Nori, *French Photography* (New York: Pantheon, 1979), p. 28.

3. Cf. Andrée's (or Gisèle's) startling leap over the elderly gentleman sitting in a beach chair at Balbec (I, 792).

4. Jacques-Henri Lartigue, *Mémoires sans mémoire* (Paris: Robert Laffont, 1975), p. 80. See also his *Instants de ma vie* under the heading *Mars 1910*.

5. Lucien Daudet, *Autour de soixante lettres de Marcel Proust*, Les Cahiers Marcel Proust, 5 (Paris: Gallimard, 1929), p. 15.

6. Cf. his efforts to seize the true elements of Berma's greatness as an actress: "J'aurais voulu . . . arrêter, immobiliser longtemps devant moi chaque intonation de l'artiste, chaque expression de sa physionomie . . . mais déjà l'actrice avait changé de place et le tableau que j'aurais voulu étudier n'existait plus" (I, 449).

7. Proust, like his artist figure Elstir, also fuses elements of land and sea. The fluid motion of the sea, wind, and water are transferred to stationary land elements. Cf. the mobility of the ivy-covered church of Carqueville: "alors un peu de vent soufflait, faisait frémir le porche mobile que parcouraient des remous propagés et tremblants comme une clarté; les feuilles déferlaient les unes contre les autres; et, frissonnante, la façade végétale entraînait avec elle les piliers onduleux, carressés et fuyants" (I, 715). In another passage the band of girls is described as a hedge of roses wafting in the breeze as the wind caresses the water, "la ligne du flot de leur haie légère, pareille à un bosquet de roses de Pennsylvanie, ornement d'un jardin sur la falaise . . ." (I, 798). The church of Saint-Hilaire is said to have sailed like a ship through the ages of time, from the distant past to the present (I, 61). Most of the major art movements of the time and Einstein's theory of Relativity present us with a universe that is in constant flux. See the chapter entitled "The Cosmos Builder."

8. Although the theme of Vinteuil's music as sacred and profane art began with the Swann-Odette relationship, it will continue and reach its resolution in the love affair between the Narrator and Albertine.

9. See I, 130, 132, 383.

10. Cf. also the following passage: "Ainsi s'était dissipée toute la gracieuse mythologie océanique que j'avais composée les premiers jours" (I, 949).

11. Cf. Proust's technique of presenting a human figure in motion as "un torse féminin, mutilé comme un marbre antique par la vitesse qui nous entraîne . . . une passante fragmentaire et fugitive . . ." (I, 713). Elsewhere Proust writes: "Le visage humain est vraiment comme celui du Dieu d'une théogonie orientale, toute une grappe de visages juxtaposés dans des plans différents et qu'on ne voit pas à la fois" (I, 916-17). Many passages could be cited where a figure in motion is seen as fragmented.

12. Cf. the following passage, in which the Narrator explains the attraction of girls in motion and then goes on to say that "les femmes que nous fréquentons finissent par dévoiler leurs tares . . ." (I, 796). For more on stigmatization, see the chapter entitled "The Prison."

13. Proust explained his preference for young girls in a letter to Georges de Lauris: "Moi je n'aime guère . . . que les jeunes filles comme si la vie n'était pas déjà assez compliquée comme cela.

Vous me direz qu'on a inventé pour cela le mariage mais ce n'est plus une jeune fille, on [n']a jamais une jeune fille qu'une fois. Je comprends Barbe-Bleue, c'était un homme qui aimait les jeunes filles." *Correspondance*, 1908, 8: 326.

14. Proust utilizes the statuary of the church of Saint-André-des-Champs to represent the biological and aesthetic continuation of the classes of French society through the ages (II, 409).

15. In the same passage the girls are compared to Chopin's music wherever "la phrase la plus mélancolique [est semée] de gracieux détours où le caprice se mêle à la virtuosité" (III, 791). The Narrator's inability to distinguish their voices is given a classical Greek musical analogy: "leurs paroles [comme les] strophes des temps antiques où la poésie encore peu différenciée de la musique . . ." (I, 909). For other passages where the girls are compared to music, see: I, 874, n. 1; I, 877-78; I, 918.

16. See I, 638. The source for this analogy is likely the little figure high on the cathedral of Rouen that Ruskin wrote about in *The Seven Lamps of Architecture*. See "En mémoire des églises assassinées" (V, 124ff.). See the article by J. Theodore Johnson, Jr., entitled "Proust, Ruskin, et la petite figure au portail des libraires à la cathédrale de Rouen," *Bulletin de la Société des Amis de Marcel Proust et de Combray* 23 (1973): 1721-36.

17. In one passage three girls seated by their bicycles at an outdoor cafe are compared to winged goddesses: "trois jeunes filles étaient assises à côté de l'arc immense de leurs bicyclettes posées à côté d'elles, comme trois immortelles accoudées au nuage ou au coursier fabuleux sur lesquels elles accomplissent leurs voyages mythologiques" (III, 170). Elsewhere telephone operators are compared to goddesses of the invisible and various other mythological figures. See, e. g., II, 136.

18. See I, 665, for an earlier version of this experience during the Narrator's first elevator ride.

19. Cf. Apollinaire: "les moyens de locomotion, le mouvement pour tout dire, ont modifié notre façon de sentir. . . ." *Anecdotiques* (Paris: Gallimard, 1955), pp. 218-20.

20. In 1883, when Proust was only twelve, Dr. Adrien Proust wrote an article opposing the complicated and cumbersome clothing worn by women, insisting that for purposes of hygiene he favored simpler, more athletic attire. Dr. Proust noted that fashions then in style would not be suitable for depiction on a frieze: "On conviendra qu'aujourd'hui les mouvements impétueux de

Démosthène et l'harmonie des périodes cicéroniennes jureraient avec nos vêtements étriqués, et qu'une frise où figurerait une panathénée de femmes parisiennes avec leurs volants et leur système compliqué de retroussis n'aurait rien de séduisant pour les yeux de l'artiste et du connaisseur" (*Eléments d'hygiène*), quoted by Claude Francis and Fernande Gontier in *Marcel Proust et les siens* (Paris: Plon, 1981), p. 110. Here we see that Dr. Proust condemns the cumbersome female attire for aesthetic as well as hygienic reasons. Could Proust's use of such an analogy be a reminiscence of his father's articles?

21. A recent manuscript discovery indicates that Proust's ultimate choice for the title of the next to last volume of *la Recherche* was *Albertine disparue*. See *Albertine disparue,* edited by Nathalie Mauriac and Etienne Wolff (Paris: Grasset, 1987).

22. Lartigue tells us that the slang term used by aviators for making their first flight was "to lose your virginity": "1er novembre [1916]. Aujourd'hui, j'ai volé! C'était mon 'dépucelage'. C'est le mot pour les futurs élèves pilotes qui montent pour la première fois en aéroplane. . . ." See Lartigue, *Mémoires*, p. 233. This usage is another example of the association between motion and sexuality. The experiences of kinesis made possible by the new modes of transportation were so powerful that the novice making his first flight was transformed, and the transformation was given a sexual analogy.

23. Throughout the novel, the Narrator will be strongly attracted by working-class girls who share Albertine's enthusiasm for biking. At Combray, when very young, he had the same desire for beautiful, young *paysannes*. We know the great attraction that Proust felt for at least one member of the working class, namely, his chauffeur Agostinelli. Similarly, Morel, the son of the Narrator's uncle's valet, who becomes Charlus's great love; the latter is constantly in pursuit of cabdrivers and conductors. Proust recruited young men from among the waiters at the Hôtel Ritz to be his secretaries or to come visit him. See the interview with Camille Wixler, a former waiter at the Ritz, in "Proust au Ritz: souvenirs d'un maître d'hôtel," *Adam International Review* 394-96 (1976): 14–21. In 1918, Proust recruited Henri Rochat from the Ritz to become his secretary. See *Correspondance,* 1918, 17: viii.

24. For the role of Albertine's polo hat, see Diana Festa-McCormick's book *Proustian Optics of Clothes: Mirrors, Masks, Mores,* Stanford French and Italian Studies 29 (Saratoga: Anma

Libri, 1984). She writes: "When Marcel reflects that the only way he can 'possess' the young cyclist . . . is by getting hold of 'what was in her eyes,' he means . . . that only by devoiding her of all mystery can he be free from her. The polo hat has become a symbol of the screen that Albertine interposes between them, of that segment of herself that she will always deny him. It is a symbol, too, of that which keeps Marcel's love obsessively alive" (p. 44).

25. See Eugen Weber, *France: Fin de Siècle* (Cambridge, Mass.: Harvard University Press, 1986), pp. 37, 201.

26. Weber remarks: "Even commentators who appreciated 'the new wheels of the chariot of progress' could not help noticing that, in their velvet breeches, women were beginning to look like men" (p. 201). See Proust's essay "Impressions de route en automobile," where Agostinelli is compared to a "nun of speed" because his motoring attire, consisting of a long coat and hood, makes him look like a woman. See the Lartigue photograph of a chauffeur standing on the sidewalk, p. 55. The Narrator once mistakes a chauffeur in motoring attire for a woman (III, 137). See also the chapters "Death of an Aviator" and "The Artist and the Aviator." For more on clothes and androgyny, see Festa-McCormick, *Proustian Optics of Clothes*, pp. 42, 97.

27. See, among other passages, the following: "Albertine aimait tant faire de l'auto et du yachting" (II, 1123); "Albertine, passionnée pour tous les sports" (III, 105); and "[Albertine] aimant plus que tout les sports" (III, 529). Agostinelli's love of sports and physical danger may have contributed to this aspect of Albertine's character. The Narrator often insists upon his own sedentary role: "couché entre ces jeunes filles, la plénitude de ce que j'éprouvais . . . débordait de mon immobilité et de mon silence..." (I, 910).

28. Lartigue, *Instants de ma vie*. See also his *Mémoires,* pp. 129-30. Here is another notation from the diary that Lartigue kept of his photographs: "Une 'aviette', c'est une bicyclette volante, grâce à laquelle on essaye, sans moteur, sans vent, sans se lancer dans le vide, sans faire tirer l'appareil par une automobile, de 'voler comme un oiseau', par ses propres moyens!" See Pierre Borhan and Martine d'Astier, *Les Envols de Jacques-Henri Lartigue et les débuts de l'aviation* (Paris: Philippe Sers, 1989), p. 60. This work was published on the occasion of an exhibition of Lartigue photographs held at the Grand Palais in Paris in June 1989. The dream of human-powered flight became a reality in 1979, when Bryan Allen pedaled the *Gossamer Albatross* twenty-

two and a half miles across the English Channel. On April 24, 1988, Greek cycling champion Kanellos Kanellopoulos pedaled the *Daedalus* seventy-four miles across the Aegean Sea in a flight that realized the ancient myth of Daedalus.

29. Maurice Leblanc, in his novel about the bicycle, stresses the fervor of cycling enthusiasts by calling his opening chapter "La Nouvelle Religion." See *Voici des ailes!* (Paris: Paul Ollendorff, 1898).

30. Quoted by Jacques Nathan, *La Littérature du métal, de la vitesse et du chèque de 1880 à 1930* (Paris: Didier, 1971), p. 119. For the use of "ange/péri" see I, 793-94. Cf. also Agostinelli at the wheel of the car, where he is described as a "nun of speed" and likened to Saint Cecilia at the organ (V, 67). See the chapter entitled "Death of an Aviator."

31. See the chapter entitled "Death of an Aviator." Albertine will always be associated with sports that involve speed and will die as a result of a horseback-riding accident.

32. Filippo Marinetti, "Premier Manifeste du Futurisme," *Le Figaro*, February 20, 1909, p. 1.

33. See the chapter on "The Prison." Proust often presents characters who suffer from obsessions as being enmeshed in gears; tragedies, with their strict rules of construction, are often seen as wheels or time-keeping mechanisms that crush the characters caught beneath or within them. Albertine, who becomes the Narrator's great goddess of time (III, 387), may also represent for him a wheel of fortune in that his experiences with her plunge him into the depths of despair before he learns how to reinterpret their shared experience and thus rise to creative heights. The theme of verticalization is discussed in the chapter entitled "The Artist and the Aviator."

34. In the same passage, the Narrator expresses the guilt he feels over Albertine's death since he presented her with the means of killing herself: "de ma prison elle s'était évadée pour aller se tuer sur un cheval que sans moi elle n'eût pas possédé. . . ." Although Proust tried to dissuade Agostinelli from taking flying lessons, it was the writer's money that made the lessons possible. See the chapter entitled "Death of an Aviator."

4. Speed and Desire

1. Wallace Fowlie, "Epiphanies in Proust and Dante," in *The Art of the Proustian Novel Reconsidered*, edited by Lawrence D. Joiner,

Winthrop Studies on Major Modern Writers 1 (Rock Hill, S.C.: Winthrop College, 1979), p. 3.

2. Marcel Proust, *La Prisonnière*, edited by Jean Milly (Paris: Garnier-Flammarion, 1984), p. 529, n. 12.

3. This aspect of Proust's characterization will be discussed in the next chapter.

4. For revelations about Fénelon's sexuality, see Henri Bonnet's chapter "L'Amour de Proust pour Bertrand de Fénelon" in his book *Les Amours et la Sexualité de Marcel Proust* (Paris: Librairie A.-G. Nizet, 1985), pp. 45-55.

5. See George D. Painter, *Proust: The Later Years* (Boston: Little, Brown, 1965), p. 225.

6. See my article "Homosexuality in Fiction: Marcel Proust's *A la recherche du temps perdu*," *Adam International Review* 413-15 (1979): 56-62.

7. A related passage describes "le perpétuel élancé de son monocle" (II, 93).

8. See George D. Painter, *Proust: The Early Years* (Boston: Little, Brown, 1959), pp. 366-67. Cocteau, inspired by Nijinsky and the Ballets russes, repeated the feat in 1911, an event that was celebrated by Proust in doggerel verse: "Afin de me couvrir de fourrure et de moire / Sans de ses larges yeux renverser l'encre noire. / Tel un sylphe au plafond, tel sur la neige un ski / Jean sauta sur la table auprès de Nijinsky." See *Le Côté de Guermantes,* edited by Elyane Dezon-Jones, 2 vols. (Paris: Garnier-Flammarion, 1987), 2: 15-16.

9. Albertine's legs on the bicycle and at the pianola are discussed in the chapter entitled "Death of an Aviator." If the passage about "les belles jambes" and the past they contain has a real-life source, it is Fénelon and not Agostinelli. The kinship between Albertine and Saint-Loup is another reason for choosing Bertrand de Fénelon as one of the prime models for the girl.

10. For the questionnaires, see "Questionnaire: Sur un album d'Antoinette Faure" (V, 335), and "Marcel Proust par lui-même" (V, 336). For more on androgyny, see the chapter on "The Cosmos Builder."

11. Cf. the passages describing the church of Saint-Hilaire moving through the ages (I, 61) and the vine-covered church swaying in the wind (III, 715). Cf. also the passage depicting the church at Lisieux and the children who crowd around Proust's

car (V, 66); the latter will be discussed in the chapter entitled "Death of an Aviator."

12. Marey produced a number of studies of the cholera epidemic of 1845-49. In 1884, he wrote a paper on "Les Eaux contaminées et le choléra" (See *Comptes rendus des séances de l'Académie des Sciences,* Octobre 27, 1884, pp. 667-83). For a chronology and an idea of the range of Marey's genius, see Michel Frizot's illustrated book *Etienne-Jules Marey* (Paris: Centre National de la Photographie, 1983).

13. For a good summary of Muybridge's pioneering work, which led to the invention of motion pictures, see the article by Julian "Bud" Lesser, "1879—The Moving Image Is Born," *American Cinematographer* 69 (March 1988): 34-40.

14. See Louis Bolle, *Marcel Proust ou le complexe d'Argus* (Paris: Grasset, 1967), p. 141.

15. See Pierre Cabanne, *Entretiens avec Marcel Duchamp* (Paris: Pierre Belfond, 1967), p. 57. The Italian Futurists knew Marey's work and were influenced by it through the intermediary of Anton Bragaglia and Giacomo Balla.

16. See Freud's article "Mechanical Excitation" in the chapter entitled "Infantile Sexuality" in *The Basic Writings of Sigmund Freud,* translated and edited, with an introduction, by Dr. A. B. Brill, The Modern Library (New York: Random House, 1938), p. 600.

17. In the chapter "Death of an Aviator" we will explore the erotic associations of Albertine's legs with the bicycle and the pianola.

18. Quoted in Eugen Weber, *France: Fin de Siècle* (Cambridge, Mass.: Harvard University Press, 1986), p. 201. Such beliefs, of which Proust certainly must have been aware—we have seen his father writing about the desirability for women to wear more athletic clothing—serve to heighten the epithet he chose for Albertine: *la bacchante à bicyclette.*

19. Bloch, in his usual boastful manner, insists upon the frequency of their lovemaking in relation to distance covered: "une professionnelle [Odette] qui s'est donnée à moi trois fois de suite et de la manière la plus raffinée, entre Paris et le Point-du-Jour" (I, 778).

20. Milton Miller, *Nostalgia: A Psychoanalytic Study of Marcel Proust* (Boston: Houghton Mifflin, 1956), p. 217.

21. See the interview with Germaine Brée, "What Interests Me Is Eroticism," in *Homosexualities and French Literature,* edited with an

introduction by George Stambolian and Elaine Marks (Ithaca,
N.Y.: Cornell University Press, 1979), pp. 88–89.

22. Gustave Flaubert, *Madame Bovary* (Paris: Garnier-Flammarion,
1986), pp. 316–18.

23. See the passage describing Charlus's pursuit of the conductor (II,
610–11). See Irvin Ehrenpreis's review of Justin Kaplan's biography *Walt Whitman: A Life,* in *The New York Review of Books,*
April 2, 1981, pp. 10–14.

24. Henri Bergson, *Matter and Memory,* translated by Nancy Margaret Paul and W. Scott Palmer (New York: Zone Books,
1988), p. 208.

25. This technique is defined and described in the chapter entitled
"The Cosmos Builder."

26. Marcel Proust, *Matinée chez la princesse de Guermantes,* edited by
Henri Bonnet in collaboration with Bernard Brun (Paris: Gallimard, 1982), p. 288; emphasis added.

27. For a commentary on this passage and a discussion of angels, see
Marie Miguet-Ollagnier's *La Mythologie de Marcel Proust* (Paris:
Les Belles-Lettres, 1982), p. 284.

28. Bonnet, *Matinée,* pp. 174–75.

29. According to Bernard Brun and Anne Herschberg-Pierrot,
"Dans un fragment du Cahier 1 . . . le jet d'eau peint par
Hubert Robert est . . . associé à l'onanisme du narrateur: 'Enfin
s'éleva un jet d'opale, par élans successifs, comme au moment
où s'élance le jet d'eau de Saint-Cloud. . . .'" See *Du côté de
chez Swann,* edited by Bernard Brun and Anne Herschberg-
Pierrot (Paris: Garnier-Flammarion, 1987), p. 582, n. 39.

30. Philippe Lejeune, "Ecriture et Sexualité," *Europe* 49 (1971): 141.

31. Ibid., p. 142. To support his notion of the central place occupied
by masturbation and orgasm in the "secret architecture of the
work," Lejeune quotes a conversation that Gide had with Proust,
related in *Ainsi soit-il,* during which Proust explained "sa préoc-
cupation de réunir en faisceau, à la faveur de l'orgasme, les sensations et les émotions les plus hétéroclites." The Narrator's discovery of creative time, time shaping the universe, will be discussed
in the concluding chapter of this study.

32. Proust later compares books to artesian wells: "On peut presque
dire que les œuvres, comme dans les puits artésiens, montent
d'autant plus haut que la souffrance a profondément creusé le
cœur" (III, 908). Cf. Proust's letter of July-August 1902 to Henri
de Saussine, thanking him for his book *Le Voile de Tanit: dialogues*

contemporains: "Le moindre bout de dialogue s'élève à la hauteur de l'esprit d'où il est sorti comme dans les puits artésiens." *Correspondance*, 1902-1903, 3: 80.

33. Proust's fascination with Pompeii doubtlessly derives in part from the fact that the lava permanently froze people in the course of their daily activities, thus turning living creatures into instant statues. Cf. the passage on Saint-André-des-Champs (II, 409).

34. Since the invention of the handheld camera made it possible for anyone to take photographs, thereby democratizing portraiture, the possession of a camera may reflect Saint-Loup's liberal social philosophy and his intolerance of hierarchies.

35. For the passages on the grandmother's photograph, see I, 786-87, and II, 775-82.

36. "Une Cathédrale juive," *Bulletin des informations proustiennes* 2 (Autumn 1975): 47; emphasis in original.

37. We recall Balzac's famous summary in *Le Père Goriot* of the person and character of Mme Vauquer: "toute sa personne explique la pension, comme la pension implique sa personne." *La Comédie Humaine*, 11 vols., edited by Marcel Bouteron, Bibliothèque de la Pléiade (Paris: Gallimard, 1951), vol. 2, 852.

38. See Louis Bolle, *Marcel Proust ou le Complexe d'Argus* (Paris: Grasset, 1967), pp. 141, 207.

5. The Prison

1. "je croyais encore que l'Amour existait réellement en dehors de nous" (1, 401). Cf. the following passage: "en ce temps-là tout ce qui n'était pas moi, la terre et les êtres, me paraissait plus précieux, plus important, doué d'une existence plus réelle que cela ne paraît aux hommes faits. Et la terre et les êtres, je ne les séparais pas. . . . j'étais pour longtemps encore à l'âge où l'on n'a pas encore abstrait ce plaisir de la possession des femmes différentes avec lesquelles on l'a goûté, où on ne l'a pas réduit à une notion générale qui les fait considérer dès lors comme les instruments interchangeables d'un plaisir toujours identique" (I, 157).

2. Quoted by Jean-Yves Tadié in *Proust et le roman* (Paris: Gallimard, 1971), p. 274.

3. Cf. Baudelaire's formula, "transformer ma volupté en connaissance"—expressed by the poet in his article on Richard Wagner—with Proust's description of the Narrator's early, frustrating

attempts to write: "je sentis que mon devoir eût été de ne pas tenir à ces mots opaques et de tâcher de voir plus clair dans mon ravissement" (I, 155). See Charles Baudelaire, "Richard Wagner et *Tannhäuser* à Paris," in *Œuvres complètes,* edited by Y.-G. Le Dantec and Claude Pichois, Bibliothèque de la Pléiade (Paris: Gallimard, 1961), p. 1215.

4. Listing Proust's own manias and disorders has long been a favorite pastime of Proust admirers and detractors. In his book, Bernard Straus, a doctor of medicine, provides such a list. According to Straus, Proust had no less than thirty disorders and at least ten phobias! See his *Maladies of Marcel Proust: Doctors and Diseases in His Life and Work* (New York: Holmes & Meier, 1980), table 1, p. 163. Louis Gautier-Vignal, who saw Proust often from 1914 until the writer's death, was convinced that Proust suffered only from hay fever; all his other health problems were brought on by his diet and odd schedule, a schedule that required soporifics to go to sleep and enormous amounts of caffeine to wake up: "Loin de considérer Proust comme un être maladif, on peut s'étonner, au contraire, qu'il ait pu résister aussi longtemps à un mode d'existence aussi déraisonnable que le sien." *Proust: Connu et inconnu* (Paris: Robert Laffont, 1976), p. 44. See the chapter in Gautier-Vignal's book entitled "La Funeste Alternance," pp. 34–57.

5. Marie Miguet-Ollagnier has this to say about prison beds in *la Recherche:* "Le lit de Léonie est plus encore que la chambre un résumé du monde; il est à la fois tourné vers l'intérieur du sanctuaire . . . et vers le monde extérieur. . . . Le lit du narrateur: 'Une fois dans ma chambre, il fallut boucher toutes les issues, fermer les volets, creuser mon propre tombeau, en défaisant mes couvertures, revêtir le suaire de ma chemise de nuit.' Ce lit tragique peut annoncer le lit-rocher où est enchaîné M. de Charlus-Prométhée. Nous sommes passés par degrés d'un centre heureux du monde, d'un omphalos, à une extrémité mythique de l'univers, lieu des réprouvés." *La Mythologie de Marcel Proust* (Paris: Les Belles-Lettres, 1982), pp. 345–46; see also p. 327, n. 15.

6. At one point the Narrator equates jealousy and hell, the depths of which he must sound, (III, 616). Note Proust's use of the vertical axis to indicate creativity or the lack thereof; examples of this are his earlier comparison of dilettantes to the first prototypes

of airplanes that could not fly and his frequent use of verticalization to indicate creativity. Cf. Gaston Bachelard's description
of Dante as "le plus verticalisant des poètes, le poète qui
explore les deux verticales du Paradis et de l'Enfer." Gaston
Bachelard, *L'Air et les Songes: Essai sur l'imagination du mouvement*
(Paris: Librairie José Corti, 1943), pp. 50-51. See the chapters
entitled "Death of an Aviator," "The Artist and the Aviator,"
and "The Cosmos Builder."

7.   Gautier-Vignal, *Proust: Connu et inconnu*, p. 243.

8.   Cf. Serge Doubrovsky, *La Place de la Madeleine* (Paris: Mercure de
     France, 1974), p. 94: "La manie clinique est l'ultime et subtil
     refuge de la déraison. C'est bien pourquoi la partie de l'œuvre où
     culmine l'obsession logique du discours théorisant (*la Prisonnière*
     et *la Fugitive*) est justement celle où, tante Léonie enfin 'transmi-
     grée' en lui, ayant enfin installé en lui son 'système', le narrateur,
     alité et reclus, atteint à l'apogée de son délire."

9.   Cf. the following, where the Narrator praises "La nature de ma
     grand'mère, nature qui était juste l'opposé de mon total
     égoïsme . . ." (I, 852). In another passage he describes her as
     "ma grand'mère, *si* parfaite" (III, 109; emphasis added).

10. Charlus was "très adonné aux exercices physiques, surtout aux
     longues marches . . ." (I, 748).

11. Miguet-Ollagnier quotes a passage from *Jean Santeuil* where the
     mother's good-night kiss is related in a positive manner to the
     funeral theme: "le baiser de la mère était pour l'enfant qui allait
     s'endormir 'la douce offrande de gâteaux que les Grecs atta-
     chaient au cou de l'épouse ou de l'ami défunt en le couchant
     dans sa tombe, pour qu'il accomplît sans terreur le voyage souter-
     rain, traversât rassasié les royaumes sombres.'" *Mythologie*, p. 205.

12. Cf. the following passages: "ce défaut de volonté que ma grand-
     mère et ma mère avaient redouté pour moi, à Combray . . ." (III,
     343); "la nuit peut-être la plus douce et la plus triste de ma vie
     où j'avais, hélas! . . . obtenu de mes parents une première abdica-
     tion d'où je pouvais faire dater le déclin de ma santé et de mon
     vouloir, mon renoncement chaque jour aggravé à une tâche dif-
     ficile . . ." (III, 886-87); and "C'était de cette soirée, où ma mère
     avait abdiqué, que datait, avec la mort lente de ma grand'mère, le
     déclin de ma volonté, de ma santé" (III, 1044).

13. On the questionnaires, see "Questionnaire. Sur un album
     d'Antoinette Faure," (V, 335), and "Marcel Proust par lui-
     même," (V, 336).

14. Victor Brombert, *The Romantic Prison* (Princeton, N.J: Princeton University Press, 1978), p. 138.

15. *Correspondance,* 1904, 4: 234.

16. Miguet-Ollagnier, *Mythologie,* p. 294.

17. The Champs-Elysées are used both as a mythical reference (fields of paradise) and as a Paris neighborhood. The carriage in which the Narrator and his stricken grandmother return home moves against a landscape that suggests death and destruction by fire: "Le soleil déclinait; il enflammait un interminable mur . . . mur sur lequel l'ombre, projetée par le couchant, du cheval et de la voiture, se détachait en noir sur le fond rougeâtre, comme un char funèbre dans une terre cuite de Pompéi" (II, 318). In earlier versions of this scene, the grandmother's attack was linked to the Narrator's erotic experiments, about which Kazuyoshi Yoshikawa has commented: "Le contraste voulu par l'écrivain nous paraît évident entre la maladie de la grand'mère et les préoccupations mondaines et sensuelles du héros." Quoted by Miguet-Ollagnier, *Mythologie,* p. 113. For a thorough discussion of the theme of sexuality and punishment, see her chapter entitled "Mythes de la faute et du châtiment, violence sacrificielle," pp. 109–49.

18. *Sodome et Gomorrhe,* edited by Emily Eells-Ogée, 2 vols. (Paris: Garnier-Flammarion, 1987), 2: 322–23, n. 46.

19. *Correspondance,* 1907, 7: 265.

20. Vladimir Nabokov, *Lectures on Literature* (New York: Harcourt Brace Jovanovich, 1980), pp. 210–11; page 139 contains his remark about *la Recherche* being the greatest novel of the century. For Serge Doubrovsky's commentary on the book-within-the book idea and his comparison of Proust to Beckett, see *La Place de la Madeleine,* p. 109, where he observes that "la naissance (du livre), c'est la mort (de son auteur)."

21. This same passage contains a wonderful pendant to the conclusion of *Un amour de Swann,* where Swann realizes that he has wasted his life on Odette, who was not his type. At the matinée of the princesse de Guermantes, Odette tells the Narrator that Swann was just her type: "Pauvre Charles, il était si intelligent, si séduisant, exactement le genre d'hommes que j'aimais" (III, 1021).

22. Proust told Louis de Robert that the profanation scene was suggested by an anecdote then current about Dr. Albert Robin and his mistress, the courtesan Liane de Pougy: "L'idée de cette scène m'a été suggéré par différentes choses, mais surtout par

ceci: un homme de grande valeur et fort connu était l'amant d'une courtisane, quoiqu'il fût marié et père de famille. Or, pour avoir le plaisir complet, il fallait qu'il dise à cette courtisane 'le petit monstre' en parlant de son propre fils. Rentré chez lui, il était d'ailleurs très bon père." But in Elisabeth de Clermont-Tonnerre's account, it was Liane de Pougy who forced the doctor to refer to his wife and son as "le monstre et le petit monstre." See Louis de Robert, *Comment débuta Marcel Proust* (Paris: Gallimard, 1969), pp. 105-6; Elisabeth de Clermont-Tonnerre, *Robert de Montesquiou et Marcel Proust* (Paris: Flammarion, 1925), p. 146. For Proust's notation "le petit monstre Gabardine de Robin," see Philip Kolb's edition of *Le Carnet de 1908* (Paris: Gallimard, 1976), p. 54.

23.   Proust's response on the questionnaire, cited earlier, was that what he hated most was whatever evil he harbored: "*Ce que je déteste par-dessus tout. — Ce qu'il y a de mal en moi*" (V, 337).

24.   See George D. Painter, *Proust: The Later Years* (Boston: Little, Brown, 1965), pp. 268-69. Painter gives the wrong month for Sachs's reminiscence, *Historiette,* which appeared under the rubric "L'Air du mois." It was in the May 1938 issue (pp. 863-64)—not July—of *La Nouvelle Revue Française.*

25.   Maurice Sachs, *Le Sabbat* (Paris: Gallimard, 1960), pp. 285, 287. Sachs's book, which reads like memoirs, bears the disclaiming subtitle *roman.* Sachs is not generally considered the most reliable of witnesses. He was for a time a protégé of Cocteau and Gide, who influenced Gallimard to hire Sachs in 1933. Sachs thought nothing of stealing original drawings and manuscripts from his friends, selling them, and keeping the money for himself. Among the books sold by Sachs were autographed editions of works by Proust and Apollinaire. When he was caught at such thievery, he forged a letter in Cocteau's hand authorizing him to sell rare papers and editions. It was not long before the furious Gaston Gallimard fired Sachs. See Pierre Assouline's *Gaston Gallimard: un demi-siècle d'édition française* (Paris: Balland, 1984), pp. 175-77. For more on Sachs's escapades and misadventures, see Henri Raczymow's recent biography entitled *Maurice Sachs ou Les travaux forcés de la frivolité* (Paris: Gallimard, 1988).

26.   In his introduction, Kolb traces this theme for us: "[Le titre] serait à rapprocher de l'épisode de sadisme où le narrateur remarque une ressemblance entre Mlle Vinteuil et son père (I, 264). . . . dans *La Prisonnière,* c'est le narrateur qui commence à

ressembler, non par son visage mais par son langage et ses habitudes, à ses parents (III, 78–79). Saint-Loup ressemblera de plus en plus à sa mère (III, 703). Et M. de Charlus, entrant dans le salon de Mme Verdurin, a 'l'âme d'une parente du sexe féminin' (II, 907), faisant remarquer que les fils comme lui 'consomment dans leur visage la profanation de leur mère' (II, 908)." Kolb, *Le Carnet de 1908*, p. 15.

27. See III, 159. Long before he began writing *la Recherche*, Proust compared his early work to a photograph of himself in a letter to the Comte de Maugny dated July 13, 1899: "Souvent on montre à un ami qui ne vous a connu que tard, une photographie où l'on est enfant. Il en est ainsi de ce livre, *Les Plaisirs et les jours*, qui vous présente un Marcel que vous n'avez pas connu" (*Correspondance*, 1896–1901, 2: 291).

28. See III, 208–9*, where the Narrator talks about the writer in Charlus that has been lost to the world.

29. See also III, 376. Jacques-Henri Lartigue mentions a singer, Chenal, who was asked on auspicious occasions to sing the "Marseillaise," earning her the nickname "notre Marseillaise nationale." See the entry under January 12, 1916, in Lartigue's *Mémoires sans mémoire* (Paris: Robert Laffont, 1975), p. 227. In *la Recherche*, Odette is often representative of precise spans of time: "Mme Swann, n'est-ce pas, c'est toute une époque?" (I, 619). At the end of the novel, she is said to embody the World's Fair of 1878 for those of her own generation and the allée des Acacias of 1892 for the Narrator (III, 950).

30. After her death, she appears to him in a dream as a stranger (II, 761). Following Albertine's death, he feels guilty of a double murder (III, 496). Elyane Dezon-Jones reminds us that in the scene following his telephone call to his grandmother from Doncières—during which her disembodied voice reveals to him the previously unnoticed fact that she has grown old—he rushes home to find before him a stranger (II, 141). Dezon-Jones comments: "Il faut que la grand'mère meure pour que naisse le texte qui fera du narrateur un écrivain." See her edition of *Le Côté de Guermantes*, 2 vols. (Paris, Garnier-Flammarion, 1987) 1: 52–53.

31. The Narrator had earlier received a prophetic warning about jealousy from Swann, which, like all such warnings, went unheeded: "le danger de ce genre d'amours est que la sujétion de la femme calme un moment la jalousie de l'homme mais la rend aussi plus exigeante. Il arrive à faire vivre sa maîtresse comme ces

prisonniers qui sont jour et nuit éclairés pour être mieux gardés. Et cela finit généralement par des drames" (I, 563).

32. Rather than ending their affair on a pedal point that will prolong a moment of calm contentment (cf. III, 393), he experiences the endless anguish of the prison cell: "l'horreur de ces amours que l'inquiétude seule a enfantées vient de ce que nous tournons et retournons sans cesse dans notre cage des propos insignifiants. . . . ce n'est pas notre goût délibéré, mais le hasard d'une minute d'angoisse (minute indéfiniment prolongée par notre faiblesse de caractère, laquelle refait chaque soir des expériences et s'abaisse à des calmants) qui a choisi pour nous" (III, 95).

33. Cf. the following passage: "Qui m'eût dit à Combray, quand j'attendais le bonsoir de ma mère avec tant de tristesse, que ces anxiétés guériraient, puis renaîtraient un jour non pour ma mère, mais pour une jeune fille qui ne serait d'abord, sur l'horizon de la mer, qu'une fleur . . .'' (III, 501). See also III, 394.

34. Obsessions are often given comic touches that serve to lighten the prison theme: Aunt Léonie's curiosity about the world, although she refuses to leave her bed; the scene where the Narrator kisses Albertine the first time; and the scenes of buffoonery in the Verdurin salon.

35. The Oceanides and their airy music are mentioned twice in la Recherche. Both times the Narrator is described as being bound and unable to answer the call of the music: "Enchaîné à mon strapontin comme Prométhée sur son rocher, j'écoutais mes Océanides" (I, 720). Nor can he take flight and free himself when he listens to them beside Albertine, who imprisons him in her embrace: "A côté d'Albertine, enchaîné par ses bras au fond de la voiture, j'écoutais ces Océanides" (II, 994). Cf. Miguet-Ollagnier's comments on the Oceanides and the Prometheus myth in la Recherche: "A chaque fois sont nettement opposés des mythes de salut et de dégradation, de grâce et de pesanteur." Mythologie, p. 296.

36. Chantal Robin, L'Imaginaire du "Temps retrouvé": Hermétisme et écriture chez Proust, Topologie de l'Imaginaire 7 (Paris: Lettres Modernes, 1977), p. 32. Charlus and Saint-Loup both manifest satanic qualities. Charlus mingles the sacred and profane in his fidelity to his patron saint, Saint Michel, and his infatuation with the violinist Morel. He, like the Narrator, sees the object of his obsession as an angelic musician (II, 957). In another passage Saint-Loup, standing on the staircase, recites "un rôle de Satan" (III, 471).

37. Céleste Albaret, *Monsieur Proust* (Paris: Robert Laffont, 1973), p. 240.

38. Even the detestable Verdurins are the donors of anonymous gifts (III, 325, 327).

39. Claude Vallée links this profanation to that of Vinteuil: "[Charlus] se flatte d'avoir demandé à un enfant de chœur son adresse, le jour de l'enterrement de sa femme dont, ainsi, il profane la mémoire, comme Mlle Vinteuil le portrait de son père sur lequel crache une de ses amies au cours d'une scène indécente." See his *Entretiens sur Marcel Proust,* edited by Françoise Fabre-Luce de Gruson (Paris: Mouton, 1966), p. 172.

40. See the conclusion of *Un amour de Swann* (I, 382) for a description of Swann's moment of recognition.

41. In "Avant la nuit," Proust uses aesthetics to justify homosexual behavior (IV, 169-70). See III, 910, on the subjective nature of love and homosexuality. See also III, 205-6, where Proust makes the case that homosexuals are more sensitive and therefore more inclined to be artistic. These passages provide additional examples of Proust's use of flowers in sexual analogies. The passage from "Avant la nuit" contains a botanical reference: "Ainsi les aptitudes physiques, plaisir de contact, gourmandise, plaisir des sens, reviennent se greffer là où notre goût du beau a pris racine" (IV, 170). This floral metaphor is echoed in the obscene doggerel sung by Françoise in *la Recherche:* "Qui du cul d'un chien s'amourose / Il lui paraît une rose" (I, 123). The example of the jellyfish is used in "Avant la nuit" and in *Sodome et Gomorrhe* to represent something that most people find repulsive but which can be visually pleasing. The jellyfish becomes a flower and is named together with the orchid to represent what Proust describes as the strange beauty of the encounter between Charlus and Jupien: "Méduse! Orchidée! Quand je ne suivais que mon instinct, la méduse me répugnait à Balbec; mais si je savais la regarder, comme Michelet, du point de vue de l'histoire naturelle et de l'esthétique, je voyais une délicieuse girandole d'azur. Ne sont-elles pas, avec le velours transparent de leurs pétales, comme les mauves orchidées de la mer?" (II, 626-27). We recall that "faire catleya" becomes Swann and Odette's private expression for lovemaking. The initiation of their lovemaking is subtly linked to the Adamic fall, and Swann, like the first Adam, must find a name for this new pleasure (I, 233-34). Consider Vallée's comments: "Le mal qui revient toujours est celui qui s'est une

fois présenté Swann et Odette, dans cette première partie de la
Bible de Proust, figurent Adam et Eve, et, pour marquer le caractère original de ce premier amour, Proust crée l'expression
mythologique *faire catleya*. Nommer les choses est un attribut de
la puissance divine qui jette les bases d'un monde en même
temps que les fondements d'une religion, à laquelle se rattache
dans le livre de Proust, comme dans la Bible, l'idée d'une faute"
(*Entretiens*, p. 174). In an early letter to a friend, Proust urged
him to accept his own homosexual advances, comparing his sexual urges to a flower that must be plucked before it withers: "je
trouve toujours triste de ne pas cueillir [la] fleur délicieuse, que
bientôt nous ne pourrons plus cueillir. Car ce serait déjà le
fruit . . . défendu. Maintenant c'est vrai que tu la trouves empoi-
sonnée. . . ." (*Correspondance*, 1880–1895, 1: 102; Proust's ellipses).
In *Sodome et Gomorrhe*, Proust quotes a passage from Racine's
Esther where the daughters of Zion are called "tender flowers"
(II, 665). In Wagner's *Parsifal*, the hero in search of the holy grail
"se retrouve dans une prairie au milieu des filles fleurs qui sont
envoyées par le diable comme autant de tentatrices pour lui faire
perdre sa pureté." Dezon-Jones, *Le Côté de Guermantes*, 2: 378, n.
81. In early versions of the novel, Charlus bore the name Fleurus.

42.   For the themes of night, hell, and the underground labyrinth, see
       Robin, *L'Imaginaire du "Temps retrouvé,"* p. 23.

43.   La Rochefoucauld, *Œuvres complètes*, edited by Louis Martin-
       Chauffier, Bibliothèque de la Pléiade (Paris: Gallimard, 1964),
       p. 412.

44.   The following is Doubrovsky's formulation of Proustian hell:
       "L'enfer proustien tient en une brève formule: besoin de
       l'amour de l'autre, qu'on est incapable d'aimer, par quoi ce qui
       remplit le moi, c'est cela même qui l'expulse." *La Place de la
       Madeleine*, p. 44.

45.   Cf. Albertine as "une grande déesse du Temps" III, 387.

46.   Maurice Bardèche acknowledges that such scenes as the flag-
       ellation of Charlus are journalistic reportings rather than lived
       experiences, but he attributes to the Narrator Proust's psy-
       chological makeup regarding jealousy. See his *Marcel Proust:
       Romancier*, 2 vols. (Paris: Les Sept Couleurs, 1971), 2: 303.
       This attribution seems unnecessary, since jealous love as a des-
       tructive force is the dominant theme of Racine's *Phèdre*, the
       literary work most often alluded to in *la Recherche*.

47. It is only in the Narrator's dreams that the two sexes are reunited: "La race qui l'habite [l'appartement du sommeil], comme celle des premiers humains, est androgyne" (II, 981).

48. It will be recalled that it was because of conversations with Swann and Legrandin that the young Narrator was so eager to go to Balbec and see the architecture of the church (I, 384–85). Cf. also the following passage: "cette église . . . presque persane [avait orienté] mes désirs vers le normand byzantin. . . ." (III, 500). These pages contain a summary of his expectations regarding Balbec. Proust's choice of the name Balbec for his Norman seaside resort most likely has a Persian-Arabian source, based on his reading of *The Arabian Nights*. The Narrator, who is to become the chronicler of Balbec, compares himself to Scheherazade, the teller of tales in *The Arabian Nights* (III, 1043–44). According to John Porter Houston, the oriental crescent moon usually appears in the Paris sky, often as an annunciatory motif prior to homosexual encounters. See his "Theme and Structure in *A la recherche du temps perdu*," *Kentucky Romance Quarterly* 17 (1970): 220. Such a moon appears after the Charlus-Jupien encounter (II, 633). Cf. also the following phrase: ". . . le ciel parisien sous le signe oriental du croissant" (III, 809). Baalbeck and Chilminar were, according to legend, two cities built by the Genii as places to hide. Baal, (pl. Baalim) also has a biblical source; it was the name of the Moabite god, a Bacchic divinity of fields and vineyards to whom the Israelites became attached in Shittim (Num. 25:3) and who was associated with licentious orgies (Hos, 9:10). See *Brewer's Dictionary of Phrase & Fable*, revised and edited by Ivor H. Evans (New York: Harper & Row, 1981), pp. 66, 228. We recall the Narrator's epithets for Albertine: "la bacchante à bicyclette" and "la muse orgiaque du golf."

49. It will be recalled from the scenes where the Narrator seduces the slumbering Albertine that it is only when she is asleep that he can imagine her as an angel from paradise: "[son] haleine tirée plutôt d'un roseau creusé que d'un être humain, vraiment paradisiaque pour moi qui dans ces moments-là sentais Albertine soustraite à tout, non pas seulement matériellement, mais moralement, était le pur chant des Anges (III, 113–14). See also the passage at III, 384, where the impression that he possesses in her an angel musician is short-lived. Cf. Albertine at the pianola.

50. Doubrovsky, *La Place de la Madeleine*, p. 42.

51. Cf. the Dantesque water lily, discussed earlier, that was intended as a warning: "le tourment . . . qui se répète . . . pendant l'éternité . . ." (I, 169).
52. Cf. Mlle Vinteuil as the artist of evil.
53. Cf. the Narrator's awareness, after his visits to see Gilberte and Mme Swann, that his conversations with them continue to run through his mind, depriving him of his own thoughts and causing him to live "une vie de salon mentale" (I, 579). Cf. the following: "je n'avais plus besoin de vivre à la surface de moi-même . . ." (III, 70).
54. Elstir plays an essential role as mentor and initiator for the hero by showing him what to look for in ancient architecture, exemplified by Balbec's church, and in modern paintings. Miguet-Ollagnier points out that he also serves as a creator of myths: "à propos des motifs de l'église de Balbec, il insiste à plusieurs reprises sur la faute du toucher sacrilège et sur la punition (autre version du voyeurisme, péché qui reparaît de volume en volume tout au long de la Recherche), cependant que l'éloge de la Vierge, l'évocation de 'tous les cercles du ciel' (I, 831), est le pendant triomphant des cercles d'enfer qu'a traversés Swann, que traversera Marcel dans les livres suivants. . . ." Mythologie, pp. 294-95.
55. Cf. her behavior at the deaths of her favorite pianist, Dechambre (II, 896), and the princesse Sherbatoff (III, 238-39).
56. Cf. the passage at I, 190, where Dr. and Mme Cottard announce their intention to spend the Easter holidays in Auvergne. On another occasion, Mme Verdurin does everything possible to talk Charlus into letting her group accompany him on his pilgrimage to Mont Saint-Michel (I, 957).
57. The following passages provide examples where the women the Narrator pursues have facial blemishes: Oriane (I, 175; II, 61); his mother, who has a blemish under her eye (I, 185); Albertine (I, 874); Swann notices that his "Zephora" has imperfect skin (I, 225); Rachel has pimples and a pockmarked face (II, 174-75). Robin connects facial blemishes to the experience of hell ("les visages rongés"). See L'Imaginaire du "Temps retrouve," p. 70.
58. Cf. this reaction to the guilt later felt by the Narrator in relation to his grandmother's death and that of Albertine, who becomes a mother figure.
59. This mistaking of the profane for the divine is a variation on the Odette/Botticelli error.
60. In a letter to the comtesse de Maugny, Proust described the train

he used to take while vacationing in Savoy: "A Thonon, long arrêt, on serrait la main d'un tel qui était venu accompagner ses invités . . . une forme de vie mondaine comme une autre que cet arrêt à Thonon." This letter is quoted in the Garnier-Flammarion edition of *Sodome et Gomorrhe,* 1: 317, n. 1.

61.   Cf. Bernard Guyon's remark: "La vanité est pour lui [Proust] le péché mortel par excellence . . ." *Entretiens,* p. 189.

62.   There are momentary exceptions to this state, as we shall see in the next chapter. When she plays the pianola, which allows him to discover the hidden secrets of the musical selections, she becomes a muse, "Sainte-Cécile," or an "ange musicien" with divine rather than infernal associations.

6. Death of an Aviator

1.   The literary theme of Œdipus and patricide was also being exploited by Sigmund Freud in Vienna during this period; Proust was unaware of this coincidence. See Jean-Yves Tadié, *Proust* (Paris: Pierre Belfond, 1983), p. 258.

2.   Robert Proust was among the first to own an automobile. According to Robert Soupault, "Robert, féru de sport, richement marié, acheta une automobile dès 1903. Sur une photo à Illiers, aux côtés de l'oncle Jules, il est coiffé d'une large casquette à visière, coiffure à la mode des automobilistes, encore très peu nombreux." See his book *Marcel Proust du côté de la médecine* (Paris: Plon, 1967), p. 77.

3.   Jacques Bizet was apparently one of the founders of the company that built Unic automobiles. See Henri Bonnet, *Marcel Proust de 1907 à 1914* (Paris: Nizet, 1971), p. 47, n. 29; see also the letter to Madame Straus dated by Philip Kolb October 8, 1907, in *Correspondance,* 7: 286, 290, n. 10. According to Céleste Albaret, the automobile-rental company was created by the Rothschilds, who were related to Emile Straus, and was managed by Straus's stepson, Jacques Bizet. See her *Monsieur Proust* (Paris: Robert Laffont, 1973), pp. 131-32. Jacques Bizet committed suicide in 1922, shortly before Proust's death.

4.   Proust also met the driver Jossien, whose name may have contributed to that of Jupien.

5.   The earliest detailed account of Agostinelli's relationship to Proust's novel is the one Robert Vigneron wrote in 1937; see his "Genèse de Swann," *Revue d'Histoire de la Philosophie et d'Histoire*

Générale de la Civilisation 5 (1937): 67-115. A more recent account is given in Henri Bonnet's book *Les Amours et la sexualité de Marcel Proust* (Paris: Nizet, 1985). See also *Correspondance,* 1913-14, vols. 12 and 13.

6.   *Correspondance,* 1907, 4: 259.

7.   Ibid., pp. 62, 160, and 263.

8.   See *Le Carnet de 1908,* edited by Philip Kolb (Paris: Gallimard), 1976; idem; "Historique du premier roman de Proust," *Saggi e ricerche di letteratura francese* 4 (1963): 217-77.

9.   *Correspondance,* 1907, 7: 264-65. In this excerpt from a letter to Georges de Lauris, quoted in the chapter entitled "The Prison" as a source for the emotion felt by the Narrator in the "Intermittences du cœur" episode, Proust expresses his regret that his mother died thinking he would remain an invalid and a failure: "Encore vos succès votre mère pouvait-elle les prévoir. La mienne est morte en croyant que je ne me relèverais jamais."

10.   Ibid., p. 296.

11.   For an account of one such visit, see Elisabeth de Clermont-Tonnerre, *Robert de Montesquiou et Marcel Proust* (Paris: Flammarion, 1925), pp. 101-2. See also Kolb, *Le Carnet de 1908,* p. 138, n. 39.

12.   *Correspondance,* 1907, 7: 248-50. After Mâle replied to his letter, Proust wrote again to thank him and asked if he could suggest "une vieille ville provinciale, balzacienne, intacte . . ." (p. 256).

13.   Ibid., pp. 263, 295.

14.   There is a passage in "Impressions de route en automobile" that Proust would subsequently interpret as an omen of Agostinelli's accidental death seven years later in an airplane crash: "puisse le volant de direction du jeune mécanicien qui me conduit rester toujours le symbole de son talent plutôt que d'être la préfiguration de son supplice!" (V, 67).

15.   The article was later used by Proust as the first chapter of *Mélanges,* which he entitled "En mémoire des églises assassinées I. Les églises sauvées. Les clochers de Caen. La cathédrale de Lisieux" (V, 63-69). The automobile excursions with Agostinelli were also used in *la Recherche,* where they became those the Narrator makes with Albertine in *Sodome et Gomorrhe* (II, 995ff.).

16.   A slightly different version of this section first appeared as "Albertine au pianola: sources biographiques (La Synesthésie dans l'univers proustien)," *Bulletin de la Société des Amis de Marcel Proust et de Combray* 36 (1986): 517-24.

17. Proust had talked about purchasing a piano as early as 1906. See *Correspondance*, 1906, 6: 291, 294, n. 3.
18. *Correspondance*, 1914, 13: 31-32.
19. Jacques-Henri Lartigue, writing in 1914, described the enjoyment his family derived from the pianola and the music rolls then available: "Si on est abonné au 'pianola', on peut changer de rouleaux autant de fois qu'on le désire. Je viens de recevoir le nouveau paquet, avec les morceaux que j'avais choisis sur la liste: *Schéhérazade*, de Rimski-Korsakov, *les Petites suites* de Debussy. . . . Je viens de les essayer, c'est merveilleux. . . ." See his *Mémoires sans mémoire* (Paris: Robert Laffont, 1975), p. 167.
20. Apollinaire used a similar synesthetic technique in "Le Roi-lune," where a specially adapted piano reproduces the sounds of different countries. See his *Œuvres en prose*, edited by Marcel Adéma and Michel Décaudin, 2 vols., Bibliothèque de la Pléiade (Paris: Gallimard, 1977), 1: 303-19.
21. Proust fell into the same predicament because of his extreme generosity toward Agostinelli. The writer did not have any beautiful objects in his bedroom or on the walls; worse, he never got around to having the famous cork with which he had lined his room papered or covered. Louis Gautier-Vignal, who visited Proust often after Agostinelli's death, says that Proust's room was "hideous." See his *Proust connu et inconnu* (Paris: Robert Laffont, 1976), pp. 157-58.
22. We recall the restaurant scene from *Jean Santeuil*, where Bertrand de Réveillon's legs embody a past that the young hero Jean longs to possess.
23. Françoise Leriche does not believe the Narrator here. See her article "La seule femme, c'est la femme peinte," *Bulletin de la Société des Amis de Marcel Proust et de Combray* 36 (1986): 487-504. I think that while the Narrator may continue to look at Albertine as one contemplates a portrait—for its "plastic" qualities—he does reject Albertine as a *substitute* for art. Otherwise he would have remained a failed artist like Swann. The key moment in the Narrator's quest will come when he learns to convert the fragments of his various experiences—aesthetic, intellectual, and emotional—into art. For the description of this process, see the chapter entitled "The Cosmos Builder."
24. See the letter written to Robert de Montesquiou in *Correspondance*, 1880-1895, 1: 296, n. 2.
25. *Correspondance*, 1907, 7: xx. The androgynous identification of

Agostinelli first with a nun—because of his feminine-looking motoring coat and hood (see illustration on p. 55)—and then with Saint Cecilia marks a key transition point between Agostinelli and Albertine. Robert Vigneron, for his part, finds the comparison of Agostinelli to a nun and then to Saint Cecilia to be "sacrilèges métaphores." See his "Genèse de Swann," p. 103. It seems that, on the contrary, the images used by Proust in his description of car and cathedral constitute a renewal as well as a conservation of traditional Christian imagery. Images of wheels, crosses, and supernatural light link the car and the cathedral, since both are ships in time. Agostinelli-Albertine at the car-pianola work the levers that make the voyage possible—a voyage that, in Proust's article, ends with a nativity scene.

26. Mallarmé paid homage to Saint Cecilia in a poem entitled *Sainte*. She is a cosmic creature whose music, like that of the spheres, may seem to be silent: "Musicienne du silence." See his *Poésies* (Paris: Gallimard, 1945), p. 73.

27. Meditating on the beauty of Vinteuil's septet, Proust compares the composer to Michelangelo painting the Sistine Chapel: "il peignait sa grande fresque musicale, comme Michel-Ange attaché à son échelle et lançant, la tête en bas, de tumultueux coups de brosse au plafond de la chapelle Sixtine" (III, 254).

28. In Proust's symphony of street noises, musical sounds are due in part to the passage of cars: "Le ronflement d'un violon était dû parfois au passage d'une automobile . . ." (III, 137). In the next chapter, as we shall see, Proust compares Wagner's music to an airplane.

29. Even the word "chambre" in this passage anticipates his relationship with Albertine-Saint Cecilia, for it is both a bedroom and an organist's chamber.

30. Given his interest in resurrecting the past, Proust had been struck by H. G. Wells's notion of a time machine. In "Sentiments filiaux d'un parricide," he compares the eyes of a person remembering to "machines à explorer le Temps, des télescopes de l'invisible, qui deviennent à plus longue portée à mesure qu'on vieillit" (V, 152). In a letter to Mme Straus, he refers to a car as "une voiture magique avec laquelle les fées vous font explorer le passé." *Correspondance*, 1912, 11: 222. In another transposition of art from literature to architecture, reading Racine is depicted as a trip through "une ville ancienne." See Proust's "Journées de lecture" (V, 192-93).

31. The term, found here in connection with genealogy and architecture, is often used with planetary and geological imagery. This technique, which Proust developed more fully than any other writer, will be discussed in the chapter entitled "The Cosmos Builder."

32. See the photograph in *Monsieur Proust,* opposite page 385. Cf. the following description: "la femme . . . était laide . . . et peu agréable" (p. 232).

33. *Correspondance,* 1914, 13: 239. The Narrator has a similar difficulty comprehending Saint-Loup's infatuation with Rachel. The actress-cum-prostitute is not attractive when seen up close, having a face that is pockmarked (II, 175-77).

34. *Correspondance,* 1913, 12: 109, 214-15.

35. Ibid., pp. 255, 251. See also George D. Painter, *Proust: The Later Years* (Boston: Little, Brown, 1965), p. 192.

36. See Vigneron, "Genèse de Swann," p. 106.

37. Painter relates Agostinelli's passion for speed to a "disguised love of death." See *Proust: The Later Years,* p. 211.

38. Ibid., pp. 209-10.

39. *Correspondance,* 1914, 13: 228-29.

40. Proust quotes himself to this effect in a letter to Emile Straus dated June 3, 1914; see *Correspondance,* 1914, 13: 228.

41. Albaret, *Monsieur Proust,* pp. 232-33. Lartigue observed and photographed the flyers at Buc in the fall of 1913, the same period that Agostinelli was taking flying lessons. Under the entry for October 8, he writes about the exploits of one of the daredevil pilots: "A Buc, pour voir Pégoud! le fameux! dont tout le monde parle depuis quelques jours. Il paraît qu'il fait des acrobaties fantastiques, des virages encore plus penchés que ceux de Garros! des descentes à pics! Même . . . il se retourne et avance avec son aéroplane à l'envers, sur le dos! Ça y est! Il . . . part, il monte, fait de chics virages. . . ." See *Mémoires,* p. 157.

42. *Correspondance,* 1914, 13: 220.

43. Céleste believes that Anna was largely responsible for the sudden departure of the Agostinellis. According to her, Anna did not like living in Paris and was eager to return to the Riviera. See Albaret, *Monsieur Proust,* p. 233. The date of their departure was determined by Philip Kolb; see *Correspondance,* 1913, 12: 15.

44. See *Correspondance,* 1913, 12: 355-66. There are echoes of this episode throughout *La Prisonnière* and *La Fugitive.* See III, 436ff., where Saint-Loup is sent to spy on Albertine as he tries to win

her return through negotiations with her aunt Mme Bontemps. In *La Prisonnière*, there is probably a direct transposition of Proust's suspicions concerning Agostinelli's infidelities to his wife. Albertine, who had been taken to Auteuil by a chauffeur, does not dare go out for fear of being seen (III, 334–35). See also III, 216–17, where the insanely jealous Charlus has Morel tailed by a private detective agency.

45. The idea that Agostinelli drowned because "he had never learned to swim" apparently originated with Painter, who does not cite a source for this information. See *Proust: The Later Years,* p. 213. Vigneron claims that the young aviator was known to be a good swimmer. See "Genèse de Swann," p. 101. In fact, none of the earlier accounts state that Agostinelli could not swim; this assertion that Agostinelli could not swim is repeated by J. E. Rivers in *Proust and the Art of Love* (New York: Columbia University Press, 1980), p. 89.

46. For press accounts of Agostinelli's death, see Vigneron, "Genèse de Swann," p. 101; see also *Correspondance,* 1914, 13: 242, n. 3.

47. The Narrator learns of Albertine's death in a telegram sent by Mme Bontemps (III, 476); Kolb points out the similarity in *Correspondance,* 1914, 13: 230, n. 4. Much later in the novel, he receives a wire that he at first believes to be from Albertine. His reaction to this unexpected communication with the dead makes him realize that he has outlived his love for Albertine (III, 641ff.). Georges Cattaui cites Céleste Albaret as having told him that not long after Agostinelli's death, Proust received an anonymous letter from the young man. See Cattaui's article "Albertine retrouvée: Alfred Agostinelli a-t-il inspiré *La Prisonnière?*" *Adam International Review* 260 (1957): 83. If this is true, Céleste does not mention it in her memoirs.

48. Albertine owns mysterious rings that bear spread eagles and the initial A, which, when inverted, closely resembles the V symbol for velocity. See III, 63, 463.

49. *Correspondance,* 1914, 13: 238.

50. In a letter to Robert de Montesquiou written shortly after June 6, Proust confided: "J'ai renoncé à corriger les épreuves de mon second volume qui se trouve ainsi ajourné, car je suis incapable de me relire. Je n'ai que la force de rendre à la pauvre veuve le courage qui me manque." Ibid., p. 241.

51. Ibid., p. 239.

52. Ibid., p. 354.

53. See the letter to Lionel Hauser. Ibid., pp. 213, 214, n. 2.

54. Ibid., pp. 217-21. Proust's emphasis.

55. Ibid., p. 13. Cf. also Tadié: "Les autres lettres d'Albertine peuvent également être comme un monument en l'honneur d'Agostinelli." *Proust*, p. 282. Tadié remarks that Painter had guessed correctly about Proust's use of Agostinelli's letters. See Painter, *Proust: The Later Years*, p. 212.

56. See Tadié, *Proust*, p. 280, n. 3.

57. *Correspondance*, 1914, 13: 220-21 and 223, n. 25.

58. See Bonnet, *Proust*, p. 19. The arrival at Glisolles with Agostinelli is mentioned in the notebook for 1908: "Hector, Agostinelli à Glisolles." Kolb, *Carnet de 1908*, p. 52. Of course, we have no way of knowing how Proust intended to develop the episode. Ultimately, as we have seen, he transposed elements of the trip with Agostinelli to the pianola passage.

59. See Bonnet, *Proust*, p. 195.

60. For the full text of the letter, see *Correspondance*, 1914, 13: 217-21. In his introduction, Kolb quotes the Narrator's letter to Albertine and uses it to shed light on the letter that Proust must have written to Agostinelli along similar lines; see pp. xv and 222, n. 15. The corresponding passages in *la Recherche* are at III, 455-56.

61. Ibid., p. 221, n. 8.

62. Ibid., p. xvi.

63. As usual, Proust quotes from memory. For the text of Mallarmé's sonnet, see *Poésies*, pp. 123-24.

64. *Correspondance*, 1913, 12: 357.

65. Albaret, *Monsieur Proust*, pp. 231, 233. According to Proust, it was his idea that Agostinelli become his secretary. The young man had lost his job and had asked Proust to hire him as a chauffeur, but since this would be unfair to Odilon, who already had the job, Proust suggested that Agostinelli become his secretary: "Je lui avais sans confiance proposé de me faire la dactylographie de mon livre." *Correspondance*, 1914, 13: 228.

66. *Correspondance*, 1914, 13: 271ff.

67. Ibid., p. 229.

68. Ibid., pp. 228, 229, n. 3.

69. Ibid., 1907, 7: 315. Kolb points out that Agostinelli's letter may have been the basis for a similar congratulatory note that the Narrator receives in *La Fugitive*: "C'était une écriture populaire, un langage charmant" (III, 591).

70. *Correspondance*, 1914, 13: 245; see also Bonnet, *Proust,* p. 200.
71. See Gautier-Vignal, *Proust connu et inconnu,* pp. 246-47.
72. Bonnet, *Amours,* pp. 79-85.
73. Bonnet later told me that he purchased the notebook from a collector.
74. Le Cuziat's male brothel was the model for Jupien's in the novel (III, 815ff.).
75. *Correspondance*, 1914, 13: 228.
76. Gautier-Vignal, *Proust connu et inconnu,* p. 243.
77. Cf. the following passage: "il me semblait que par ma tendresse uniquement égoïste j'avais laissé mourir Albertine comme j'avais assassiné ma grand'mère" (III, 501).
78. *Correspondance*, 1914, 13: 345, 360.
79. See Vigneron, "Genèse de Swann," pp. 112-13.
80. Gautier-Vignal, *Proust connu et inconnu,* p. 246.
81. *Correspondance*, 1915, 14: 135-36.
82. Ibid., pp 76, 130.
83. See Bonnet, *Amours,* pp. 45-55.
84. *Correspondance*, 1915, 14: 281.
85. Ibid., pp. 284-85.
86. *Correspondance*, 1914, 13: 311-14; for the complete text of the letter, see *Correspondance*, 1915, 14: 357-60.
87. See *Correspondance*, 1914, 13: 351, and 352, n. 6.
88. See *Correspondance*, 1914, 13: p. xxiii, and *la Recherche*, III, 559f. Maurice Bardèche believes that *La Fugitive* was composed in the fall of 1914, before Proust wrote *A l'ombre des jeunes filles en fleurs,* which precedes *La Fugitive* by several volumes in *la Recherche*. See his *Marcel Proust: Romancier,* 2 vols. (Paris: les Sept Couleurs, 1971) 2: 72-75. The letters to Scheikévitch and Hahn support this view.
89. *Correspondance,* 1915, 14: 285.
90. Quoted by Jean Milly in his edition of *La Prisonnière* (Paris: Garnier-Flammarion, 1984), p. 530, n. 20. This text shows the Narrator's premonition of Albertine's death and his anticipated consolation. See I, 355 for the passage where Swann imagines that if Odette were dead he would free himself from his fascination for her. This passage was in the first set of proofs of *Du côté de chez Swann* and thus predated Proust's infatuation with Agostinelli.
91. Rivers, *Proust and the Art of Love,* p. 96.
92. Ibid., p. 82. Rivers mentions only one critic, James Robert Hewitt, and one biographer, Céleste Albaret, among the offenders.
93. Ibid., p. 106.

94. *Correspondance,* 1919, 18: 536.
95. Kolb, "Historique du premier roman," p. 247.
96. Bonnet, *Amours,* p. 47ff. Tadié makes the same point: "Le personnage de Maria, l'une des jeunes filles, esquissé dans le Cahier 12 en 1909, devient l'objet de l'amour du Narrateur (Cahier 29), et Proust annonce la scène du baiser dans la chambre d'hôtel. Maria deviendra Albertine: c'est dire qu'il y avait une place pour ce rôle avant la rencontre d'Agostinelli." *Proust,* pp. 269-70. See also the recent edition of *A la recherche du temps perdu,* edited by Jean-Yves Tadié, 4 vols. Bibliothèque de la Pléiade (Paris: Gallimard, 1987-89) 1: 1074, 1084.
97. Bardèche, *Proust: Romancier,* 2: 232. As Bonnet points out, Painter's keys for Albertine are useless because Painter merely lists arbitrarily as keys for her character any girl who was not considered a key for Gilberte and such young men as Albert Nahmias and Henri Rochat. See Bonnet, *Proust,* p. 196. See Painter, *Proust: The Later Years,* p. 208.
98. André Gide, *Journal, 1889-1939,* 2 vols., Bibliothèque de la Pléiade (Paris: Gallimard, 1951), 1: 694. This statement also indicates Proust's broad tolerance for a variety of sexual expression. See my article "Proust's Views on Sexuality," *Adam International Review* 413-15 (1979): 56-62.
99. Quoted by François Mauriac in *Du côté de chez Proust* (Paris: Table Ronde, 1947), pp. 21-22.
100. Douglas W. Alden, *Marcel Proust's Grasset Proofs,* North Carolina Studies in the Romance Languages and Literatures 193 (Chapel Hill: University of North Carolina Press, 1978), pp. 39, 41.
101. See Milly, *La Prisonnière,* pp. 12-13. There are other traces of " Albertine" episodes in *Le Carnet de 1908.* See Kolb's generous notes.
102. Milly, *La Prisonnière,* p. 10.
103. Painter, *Proust: The Later Years,* p. 239.
104. *Correspondance,* 1904, 4: 420-21. D'Annunzio's emphasis.
105. The metaphorical value of the airplane will be discussed in the next chapter, "The Artist and the Aviator."
106. Painter, *Proust: The Later Years,* p. 239.
107. Rivers, *Proust and the Art of Love,* p. 90.
108. All quotations from Plantevignes's memoirs are taken from *Avec Marcel Proust* (Paris: Nizet, 1966), pp. 350-53.
109. See Margaret Mein's article, "Les Ailes, le vol et l'aviation dans *la Recherche* et dans les *Cahiers* de Proust," in *Etudes proustiennes IV:*

Marcel Proust et la critique anglo-saxonne, Cahiers Marcel Proust, 11 (Paris: Gallimard, 1982), pp. 161–85. This article was later incorporated in chapters of her book *Proust et la chose envolée* (Paris: Nizet, 1986).

110. Cf. Bonnet: "dans la première version . . . [les jeunes filles] sont présentées comme des cavalières. . . ." *Proust,* p. 197.

111. The passage from Plantevignes's memoirs is referred to by Bonnet (*Proust,* p. 199, n. 41), but only in relation to Bonnet's attempts to determine the date of Albertine's first appearance in Proust's notebooks.

112. Milly also sees Albertine's death as contingent but inevitable. See his edition of *La Prisonnière,* p. 13.

113. In his reference to the text of the novel, Plantevignes is mistaken about the conclusion of the passage in *la Recherche;* the aviator does not land but instead flies off into the limitless sky, the realm of freedom.

114. See Mein, "Les Ailes, le vol, et l'aviation," pp. 166, 169.

115. Pär Bergman, *"Modernolatria" et "Simultaneità": Recherches sur deux tendances dans l'avant-garde littéraire en Italie et en France à la veille de la première guerre mondiale,* Studia Litterarum Upsaliensia, 2 (Bonniers: Svenska Bokförlaget, 1965), p. 138.

116. Lartigue, *Mémoires,* p. 78. Lartigue's emphasis and punctuation.

117. Rivers, *Proust and the Art of Love,* p. 90.

118. See Philip Kolb and Larkin B. Price, editors, *Textes retrouvés* (Urbana: University of Illinois Press, 1968), pp. 206–8.

119. Ibid., p. 196, n. 2.

120. *Correspondance,* 1909, 9: 229, 230, n. 4. See also *Correspondance,* 1912, 11: 173, n. 2.

121. Cf. the following passage for the anticipation of a voice-print: "Quand je causais avec une de mes amies, je m'apercevais que le tableau original, unique de son individualité, m'était ingénieusement dessiné, tyranniquement imposé, aussi bien par les inflexions de sa voix que par celles de son visage et que c'était deux spectacles qui traduisaient, chacun dans son plan, la même réalité singulière" (I, 908). Cf. also the following: "sa voix était comme celle que réalisera, dit-on, le photo-téléphone de l'avenir: dans le son se découpait nettement l'image visuelle" (I, 930). See also Eugène Nicole, "Les Inventions modernes dans *La Recherche du temps perdu,*" *Bulletin de la Société des Amis de Marcel Proust et de Combray* 36 (1986): 529.

122. Painter considers the pseudonym Marcel Swann to be "absurd and pathetic." See *Proust: The Later Years*, p. 212.
123. This passage is quoted in Milly's edition of *La Prisonnière*, p. 41.

7. The Artist and the Aviator

1. The first airplanes resembled automobiles and the pilots were sometimes referred to as "drivers." The planes had to "taxi" across a field to gain enough speed to rise vertically. Jacques-Henri Lartigue offers excellent descriptions of the first "cars" that became airborne. In his *Mémoires sans mémoire* (Paris: Robert Laffont, 1975), he writes that "l'aéroplane roule tout seul . . . comme une drôle d'automobile déguisée en cabane" (pp. 70-71; also p. 94).

    In a poem entitled "A mon Pégase," written in 1905, the Futurist artist Filippo Marinetti penned his own panegyric to an automobile that roars across the countryside before taking flight. This was one of Marinetti's most popular poems, and he was often asked to recite it. The line that describes the moment of lift-off reads: "Hurrah! Plus de contact avec la terre immonde!" Quoted by Pär Bergman, *"Modernolatria" et "Simultaneità": Recherches sur deux tendances dans l'avant-garde littéraire en Italie et en France à la veille de la première guerre mondiale*, Studia Litterarum Upsaliensia, 2 (Bonniers: Svenska Bokförlaget, 1965), p. 44.

2. This lesson will be repeated in the Narrator's experiences with Elstir and Albertine. At one point, the protagonist explains that Albertine was more important to his becoming an artist than was Elstir (III, 167, 907). In the final pages of the novel, where the Narrator finally understands the positive value of his suffering and its connection to Albertine, and is ready to use this knowledge in creating his great work, he is able to make a similar conversion. In the passage on Bergotte, the Narrator describes these individuals as "ceux qui ont eu le pouvoir, cessant brusquement de vivre pour eux-mêmes, de rendre leur personnalité pareil à un miroir . . ." (I, 555).

3. It will be recalled that the same image of an artist as projector of light is found on a smaller scale in another analogy that Proust frequently employed: the artist as magic lantern. Speaking of Elstir, the Narrator notes that his paintings are "comme les images lumineuses d'une lanterne magique laquelle eût été, dans

le cas présent, la tête de l'artiste" (II, 419). Vinteuil's music was a "mode sur lequel il 'entendait' et projetait hors de lui l'univers" (III, 375).

4. The image of artist as airplane was also used by Proust in an article, published posthumously, to describe the music of Reynaldo Hahn. The musical text was likened to the runway that allowed the composer to gather speed in order to achieve a better and higher flight: "C'est au contact même du texte, qu'il prend la force de s'elever plus haut que lui, comme ces aviateurs qui courent sur la terre avant de se servir de leurs ailes, mais pour mieux s'envoler et plus haut" ("Reynaldo Hahn"; V, 556). In *la Recherche,* the image is split and expanded.

5. For a discussion of the meaning of angels in Proust's writing, see Marie Miguet-Ollagnier's article "Les différents Emplois du mot 'Ange' dans *la Recherche du Temps perdu," Bulletin de la Société des Amis de Marcel Proust et de Combray* 21 (1971): 1167-77, and her book *La Mythologie de Marcel Proust* (Paris: Les Belles-Lettres, 1982), pp. 283-86. See also Margaret Mein's article "Les Ailes, le vol et l'aviation dans *la Recherche* et dans les *Cahiers* de Proust," *Etudes proustiennes IV: Marcel Proust et la critique anglo-saxonne,* Cahiers Marcel Proust 11 (Paris: Gallimard, 1982), pp. 161-85. Mein's study is concerned in particular with classical allusions related to flying.

6. The spectacle of the lethal air raids also fascinated Jacques-Henri Lartigue and Paul Valéry. Lartigue wrote in 1918: "Encore une chose à ne pas dire: j'aime les bombardements." *Mémoires,* p. 284. Valéry's reaction was much the same: "An air raid sounded and Valéry 'jumped up and rushed to the window and hung out to see the planes come over Paris, dropping bombs. . . .' The family seemed accustomed to this behavior: François [his younger son] said, 'Papa adores these raids.' Quoted by Noel Riley Fitch in *Sylvia Beach and the Lost Generation* (New York: Norton, 1983), p. 403. Cf. *la Recherche:* "je lui parlai de la beauté des avions qui montaient dans la nuit" (III, 758).

7. Stephen Kern, *The Culture of Time and Space, 1880-1918* (Cambridge, Mass: Harvard University Press, 1983), p. 242.

8. Paul Souriau, *L'Esthéthique du mouvement* (Paris: Félix Alcan, 1889), pp. 21, 22, 24.

9. Cf. Proust's admission: "Tout ce que je fais n'est pas du vrai travail, mais seulement de la documentation, de la traduction etc." *Correspondance,* 1902-1903, 3: 196.

10. In a text from the second notebook that was not used in the final version, Proust had made the association between the church of Saint-Hilaire and the airplane even more explicit. In the earlier version, an airplane is spotted in the sky near the steeple and is said to be "un insecte qui trépidait là-haut." Quoted by Henri Bonnet in *Marcel Proust de 1907 à 1914* (Paris: Nizet, 1971), p. 199, n. 41.

11. *Marcel Proust: Textes retrouvés*, edited by Philip Kolb and Larkin B. Price (Urbana: University of Illinois Press, 1968), p. 28.

12. Alison Winton, *Proust's Additions: The Making of "A la recherche du temps perdu"* 2 vols. (Cambridge: Cambridge University Press, 1977), I, p. 334.

13. Wagner's music is frequently linked to mechanics in *la Recherche*. One of these connections was first made in "Impressions de route en automobile," where the car horn reminds Proust of a scene in *Tristan und Isolde* (V, 69). This same music is used in the novel in connection with another mechanical device, the telephone: "j'entendis tout à coup, mécanique et sublime, comme dans *Tristan* l'écharpe agitée ou le chalumeau du pâtre, le bruit de toupie du téléphone" (II, 731). The war with Germany further heightened the correspondence between Wagner's music and airplanes. See III, 758-59, 777, where the German bombers are portrayed as Wagner's Walkyrie. In another passage on the fighter planes (III, 735) Proust underscores the human quality of the wartime pilots and dissociates them from the aviator he saw at Versailles on his last outing with Albertine.

14. In "A propos de Baudelaire," Proust made the same complaint about Hugo: "la fabrication . . . est visible. . . . il n'y a nulle impression de mystère" (V, 621). Here "mystère" is used in its ordinary sense, whereas in the novel Proust's analogy of the French fighter plane named *Mystère* takes on ironic overtones because the Narrator at that moment doubts the existence of such mystery, believing instead that the illusion of mystery is created by the impressive but nonetheless blatantly mechanical vehicle. Prior to this, all imagery involving airplanes had been associated with freedom and creative ability. The Narrator seems to be on the verge of adopting a form of mysticism by longing for what Proust elsewhere called "la rapidité du vol sans la matérialité des ailes." See *Textes retrouvés*, p. 255. This remark brings to mind a line of Baudelaire's from "Le Voyage" that

Proust quoted in the article "Choses d'Orient" (V, 350): "Nous voulons voyager sans vapeur et sans voile."

15. The Futurists, for their part, thought that the noises made by modern inventions should be an integral part of the new music. See Bergman, *"Modernolatria,"* p. 131.

16. Cf. the following passage: "c'est très mystérieux, l'amour, reprit la duchesse . . . avec l'intransigeante conviction d'une wagnérienne qui affirme à un homme de cercle qu'il n'y a pas que du bruit dans la *Walkyrie*" (II, 227).

17. In an earlier text, Proust used a similar analogy to show that in life things that are dreamed of often do come true, but in ways unforeseen. The lived experience then becomes an unexpected blend of dream and reality, "ressemblant à mes rêves et cependant puissamment charpentée de réalité, comme les aéroplanes dans le ciel." Quoted by Henri Bonnet in *Matinée chez la Princesse de Guermantes* (Paris: Gallimard, 1982), p. 404. Such a combination of dream and reality may serve as an accurate definition of the Proustian novel. As J. M. Cocking has pointed out, "Proust, for all his aesthetic of the separation of art and life, never takes us out of the real world, but transforms it in all its solid reality." See his chapter entitled "Proust and Painting," in *Proust: Collected Essays on the Writer and His Art* (Cambridge: Cambridge University Press, 1982), p. 161.

18. *Correspondance*, 1910-11, 10: 337; Proust's emphasis. This same remark is repeated in a letter to Maurice Barrès on October 1, 1911, op. cit., p. 353. By the time Proust wrote *La Prisonnière*, the aviator had become the dominant symbol for the artist and the aircraft spotted at Balbec represented the opposite of "lourdeur," of a heavy earthbound object. See II, 1029.

19. The train and other modes of transportation are often the impetus for reflections on the Narrator's past and moments of transition in his life. We recall his first departure for Balbec and Albertine's revelation that she was an intimate friend of Mlle Vinteuil and her friend. The climactic scene of the novel is literally "set in motion" by his experience on the train transporting him back to Paris and the car that becomes airborne on its way to the princesse de Guermantes's reception.

20. Trees and flowers often appear as mysterious signs that beckon to the Narrator in the course of his quest, urging him to begin work, but he is unable to follow their admonitions: "il me semblait recevoir d'eux [des arbres près de Balbec] le conseil de me

mettre enfin au travail, pendant que n'avait pas encore sonné l'heure du repos éternel" (II, 1013). While listening to Vinteuil's septet, he again feels the desire to write and thereby give purpose to his life. At Roussainville the Narrator expresses his frustrated creative and sexual desires when he strikes trees with his umbrella (I, 158). When the trees at Hudimesnil are connected with the first hearing of the Vinteuil septet, it is clear that they, too, had been urging him to become an artist, providing "les amorces pour la construction d'une vie véritable: l'impression éprouvée devant les clochers de Martinville, devant une rangée d'arbres près de Balbec" (III, 261). Thus, his failure to respond to this last group of trees is particularly demoralizing for him. The examples he cites are those of vertical, kinetic appeals to his will, talent, and ambition.

21. Bibliothèque Nationale, Proust manuscript 16742 NAF, p. 121. Proust had revised approximately one-third of *La Prisonnière* at the time of his death. See Jean-Yves Tadié, *Proust* (Paris: Pierre Belfond, 1983), p. 315.

22. From the first analogy, early in the novel, of Bergotte as the artist-aviator to the Narrator's ultimate "take-off" in his airborne taxi, Proust uses flight or other forms of elevation to symbolize the superiority of the artist's vision. The following is a summary of vertical imagery found in the concluding section of *la Recherche:* aviators who have the desire to fly or who take off; dreams as giant airplanes to explore the past; aviator-artists who fly from star to star; old people perched on stilts as tall as their years; numerous planetary images; trees; steeples; angels in flight; geological and archaeological strata; the sensation of supraterrestrial joy; resurrections; divers who explore unknown depths; artesian wells; past impressions stored in sealed vases and stacked vertically as high as a person's lifespan; altimeters to measure elevation; telescopes and other devices symbolizing elevated or cosmic vision; people compared to star formations; the future book as a Gothic cathedral, an edifice whose extraordinary verticality is one of its defining elements. As was noted elsewhere, the artist as aviator or flying machine is an analogy frequently employed by Proust in his writings to represent the creative powers of painters, writers, musicians, and scientists he admired; examples cited include Auguste Renoir, Richard Wagner, Proust's own fictional composer Vinteuil, Jean-Jacques-Antoine Ampère, and Antoine-Laurent Lavoisier.

23. John F. McCauley et al, "Subsurface Valleys and Geoarcheology of the Eastern Sahara Revealed by Shuttle Radar," *Science* 218 (December 1982): 1004.

24. This imagery is discussed in the concluding chapter.

25. Roger Shattuck, *Proust's Binoculars* (New York: Random House, 1963). See chapter 3 in particular.

26. Elstir's art is remarkable because, among other things, it brings to light certain laws of perspective: "l'art était le premier à les dévoiler" (I, 838). Swann has his most lucid moment when he meditates on the music of Vinteuil and sees that creative people, artists, and scientists are seeking to discover the laws of the universe. Unfortunately, he cannot sustain the vision. See I, 351.

27. Cf. the following passage: "Si j'avais compris jadis que ce n'est pas le plus spirituel, le plus instruit, le mieux relationné des hommes, mais celui qui sait devenir miroir et peut refléter ainsi sa vie, fût-elle médiocre, qui devient un Bergotte . . ." (III, 722). In another passage Bergotte's works are described as "ces miroirs de la vérité" (I, 96). Proust himself compared Monet's canvases to magic mirrors that have a "verticalizing" and creative power: "Nous sommes là, penchés sur le miroir magique, nous en éloignant, essayant de chasser toute autre pensée, tâchant de comprendre le sens de chaque couleur, chacune appelant dans notre mémoire des impressions passées qui s'associent en aussi aérienne et multicolore architecture que les couleurs sur la toile et édifient dans notre imagination un paysage . . . " ("Le Peintre. Ombres — Monet"; V, 675).

28. In a letter that Proust's mother wrote to him in 1896, she says that she does not care for those who are spiritually desiccated: "Moi qui n'aime pas les secs. . . ." *Correspondance*, 1896–1901, 2: 141. The connection between the lost paradise of Combray, trees, and the theme of spiritual aridity is stated by Proust in a note about the Narrator's final disillusionment before the revelation scene: "Avant la serviette au moment des arbres qui ne disent rien: Comme malgré la promesse faite jadis aux aubépines ma vie s'était desséchée depuis Combray." See Bonnet, *Matinée*, p. 288. It is the real presence of the grandmother, brought on after her death by an involuntary-memory experience, that saves him, if only temporarily, from aridity of the soul: "L'être qui venait à mon secours, qui me sauvait de la sécheresse de l'âme . . ." (II, 755). This scene, from a section called "Les Intermittences du cœur," prefigures (as does the

madeleine passage) the ultimate series of "moments bienheureux" when he will become an artist and thus permanently
escape spiritual aridity.

29. *Correspondance*, 1914, 13: 169-70. This remark is repeated in a
letter Proust wrote to Madame Straus: "ne donnant que des fragments j'ai préféré opposer des marines aux paysages terriens de
Combray . . ." p. 231.

30. Quoted in Cocking, *Proust: Collected Essays*, p. 147.

31. Ibid., p. 147. Roger Kempf links Elstir's vision with that of
the aviator: "Terre, mer, ciel se grignotent, s'épousent ou
s'échangent. Et comme le ciel se traduit par la mer, l'auteur du
'port de Carquethuit', Elstir, apparaît à son insu comme le peintre de l'aéronautique naissante. . . . " See Kempf, "Sur quelques
véhicules," *L'Arc* 47 (1971): 56.

32. It is significant that there are no erotic associations connected
with the airplane, whereas numerous connections are made with
the bicycle, train, and car. By achieving elevation, the airplane
rises above such mundane pursuits as social triumphs and physical
possessions. It attains an almost godlike status; Proust maintains its
symbolic purity as such throughout the novel. In an interesting
article on modern inventions in *la Recherche*, Eugène Nicole
points out that the airplane is the only invention that Proust did
not eventually banalize. This is so precisely because the airplane
symbolizes the artist. See "Les Inventions modernes dans *La
Recherche du temps perdu*," *Bulletin de la Société des Amis de Marcel
Proust et de Combray* 36 (1986): 531, 541. In the concluding line
of his article on vehicles in Proust's works, Roger Kempf also
realizes that the airplane is in a distinct category but not why this
is so: "Vers la fin de *la Recherche*, l'avion seul conserve tout son
pouvoir." See "Sur quelques véhicules," pp. 47-57. In Proust's
hierarchy, it is the creative person alone who attains demigod status, a condition whose primary attributes are the ability to transcend and create.

8. The Cosmos Builder

1. In an essay written to mark the centennial of Proust's birth,
novelist John Updike singled out the paradoxical nature of
Proust's hero and the cosmic thrust of the Proustian quest:
"In Proust's cosmos, Marcel . . . is both the most supine of
witnesses and the mightiest of Creators." See "Remembrance

of Things Past," *Horizon,* 14, no. 4 (1972): 103.

2. Chantal Robin has shown that such celestial nourishment is connected to the theme of death and resurrection in a way that recalls the fertility myths. See *L'Imaginaire du "Temps retrouvé": Hermétisme et écriture chez Proust,* Topologie de l'Imaginaire 7 (Paris: Lettres Modernes, 1977), p. 73.

3. At approximately the midpoint of the novel, Proust's narrator reminds the reader of his goal, realizing that what still lies ahead are "bien des années inutiles par lesquelles j'allais encore passer avant que se déclarât la vocation invisible dont cet ouvrage est l'histoire" (II, 397).

4. Sorrow bolsters will by forcing us to renounce vain pursuits: "Les années heureuses sont les années perdues, on attend une souffrance pour travailler" (III, 909). Cf. the following passage: "le bonheur seul est salutaire pour le corps, mais c'est le chagrin qui développe les forces de l'esprit" (III, 905-6).

5. There are in *la Recherche* a number of allusions and direct references to Ulysses' quest. Wallace Fowlie points to one that is related to Proust's use of *ardeur:* "[Ulysses'] narrative begins with his leaving Circe who had detained him a year near Gaeta. After this sensual experience, Ulysses knows that he wants more than that, and he voices a kind of confession. . . . The literal word 'ambitionù' is not in Ulysses' narrative, but there is a stronger word and one quite close to its meaning: the word *ardore.* The ardor he felt was that of gaining experience in the world and of human vice and worth." See "Epiphanies in Proust and Dante," in *The Art of the Proustian Novel Reconsidered,* edited by Lawrence D. Joiner, Winthrop Studies on Major Modern Writers 1 (Rock Hill, S.C.: Winthrop College, 1979), p. 7.

6. In an early note for *Le Temps retrouvé,* Proust wrote: "La sensibilité fournit la matière où l'intelligence porte la lumière. Elle est le combustible [mettre cela q. q. part]." See *Matinée chez la Princesse de Guermantes,* edited by Henri Bonnet in collaboration with Bernard Brun (Paris: Gallimard, 1982), p. 300. In the final version, it is pain that functions as the combustible substance.

7. Robin sees Charlus as the primary initiator of the conversion from heat to light and gives almost no weight to the Narrator's experience with Albertine. See Robin, *L'Imaginaire du "Temps retrouvé,"* pp. 33-34, 82. It is, however, this last experience that determines the hero's ultimate ability to become a creative person. He passively witnessed Charlus's experience, whereas he

actively lived the one with Albertine. She is the real crucible for the Narrator's conversion.

8. The Narrator has a dream in which he sees the two women for whose deaths he feels a perhaps unwarranted sense of guilt, Albertine and his grandmother: "Je causais avec elle [Albertine], pendant que je parlais ma grand'mère allait et venait dans le fond de la chambre. Une partie de son menton était tombée en miettes comme un marbre rongé, mais je ne trouvais à cela rien d'extraordinaire" (III, 539). The guilt he feels has its roots in the general failure of love; while the two women were alive he did not know how to cherish them enough. The love he felt for Albertine, like that of Gilberte before, disappears into the general law of oblivion (III, 644). His book will restore in a more durable form what has been destroyed by time.

9. Cf. the following passage, where Bergotte's mind has become the substance of his work: "Il était amaigri comme s'il avait été opéré [de ses livres]" (II, 328). Proust refers in his letters to his own considerable weight loss during the writing of his novel. See *Correspondance*, 1913, 12: 255, and 1915, 14: 83.

10. Cf. the following description of the mature Narrator as the optician of Combray: "En réalité, chaque lecteur est, quand il lit, le propre lecteur de soi-même. L'ouvrage de l'écrivain n'est qu'une espèce d'instrument optique qu'il offre au lecteur afin de lui permettre de discerner ce que, sans ce livre, il n'eût peut-être pas vu en soi-même" (III, 911). Proust avoids didacticism by advising the reader to discard the "optics" of the book if he finds the lens distorting (III, 1033).

11. Edmund Wilson, *Axel's Castle* (New York: Scribner's, 1931), p. 163.

12. Cf. the author of Bergotte's books: "l'Esprit éternel" (I, 557).

13. John Updike calls this discovery "a kind of Godless Golden Rule and the germinating principle of art. . . ." See "Remembrance," p. 105.

14. We recall that Proust represents social "lights" as being vain and sterile. Cf. the following: "Que tout cela fasse un astre dans la nuit!" (III, 718). The comparisons of figures of Parisian high society to planets are too numerous to list. Such comparisons are ingrained in the French language, since the word most commonly used to describe society—*le monde*—is the one whose literal meaning is "world." Such usage does not necessarily designate the planet Earth but any celestial sphere. The French use of

le monde (or *le beau monde*) for high society and *le demi-monde* (or *le bas monde*) for low society allows us to envisage these divisions as separate cosmic entities. If life as it is lived on a daily basis in society and in love is a dystopia, then what is its opposite? What is the Proustian utopia? It is clear that the latter contains two major elements: the rediscovery of the past through involuntary memory and the will to create a vision of life through the discovery of great laws in the domains of art and science.

15. See *Le Carnet de 1908,* edited by Philip Kolb (Paris: Gallimard, 1971), p. 81.

16. We recall that when the Narrator first enters Elstir's studio, he describes it as the laboratory for a new creation of the world. Cf. the following statements: "autant qu'il y a d'artistes originaux, autant nous avons des mondes à notre disposition" (III, 896). "Par l'art seulement nous pouvons sortir de nous, savoir ce que voit un autre de cet univers qui n'est pas le même que le nôtre, et dont les paysages nous seraient restés aussi inconnus que ceux qu'il peut y avoir dans la lune" (III, 895). In a letter to Antoine Bibesco Proust wrote: "Le plaisir que nous donne un artiste est de nous faire connaître un univers de plus." See *Lettres de Marcel Proust à Bibesco,* with a preface by Thierry Maulnier (Lausanne: Editions de Clairefontaine, 1949), p. 177.

17. Jean-Pierre Richard suggests that Proust himself might be the little artist: "Proust lui-même, portrait de l'artiste dans un coin de son tableau, image de l'écrivain en train de commencer son livre. . . ." See *Proust et le monde sensible* (Paris: Editions du Seuil, 1974), p. 236, n. 2.

18. Cf. the following: "Depuis que l'Olympe n'existe plus, ses habitants vivent sur la terre" (III, 167).

19. Cf. the following passage: "les vrais livres doivent être les enfants non du grand jour et de la causerie mais de l'obscurité et du silence" (III, 898). In a note contained in material to be used for *Le Temps retrouvé,* Proust likens himself to Nehemiah and says that his refusal to descend from his perch should be the motto of every writer: "Non possum descendere magnum opus facio." The creative person should no more be reproached for remaining in an ivory tower than bees for staying in their hive. See Bonnet, *Matinée,* p. 309. Cf. also the passage, quoted earlier, from *Contre Sainte-Beuve:* "un livre est le produit d'un autre moi que celui que nous manifestons dans nos habitudes, dans la société, dans nos vices" (V, 221-22).

20. According to Proust, "[Le] roman dit d'analyse . . . ne doit être nullement un roman de l'intelligence pure. . . . Il s'agit de tirer hors de l'inconscient, pour la faire entrer dans le domaine de l'intelligence, mais en tâchant de lui garder sa vie, de [ne pas] la mutiler, de lui faire subir le moins de déperdition possible, une réalité que la seule lumière de l'intelligence suffirait à détruire. . . ." See "Réponses à une enquête des annales" (V, 640-41). The subconscious was a new concept in Proust's day; the word "inconscient" only made its entry in Littré's *Dictionnaire* in 1877.

21. Proust also wrote the following in the same essay: "Ce qui semble extérieur, c'est en nous que nous le découvrons. *Cosa mentale*, dit par Léonard de Vinci de la peinture, peut s'appliquer à toute œuvre d'art" (V, 640).

22. Cf. Bonnet, *Matinée*, pp. 173-74. Cf. also the following: "Les êtres les plus bêtes . . . manifestent des lois qu'ils ne perçoivent pas . . ." (III, 901).

23. In a letter to Jacques Rivière dated September 1919, Proust wrote: "Vous dirai-je que je ne crois même pas l'intelligence *première* en nous. . . . je pose avant elle l'inconscient qu'elle est destinée à clarifier—mais qui fait la réalité, l'originalité d'une œuvre." *Marcel Proust et Jacques Rivière, Correspondance (1914-1922)*, edited by Philip Kolb (Paris: Librairie Plon, 1955), pp. 51-52. Proust's emphasis.

24. In an essay written while he was working on *Jean Santeuil*, Proust states: "A chaque homme [la nature] donne d'exprimer clairement, pendant son passage sur la terre, les mystères les plus profonds de la vie et de la mort." See "Contre l'obscurité" (V, 394). Cf. the following statement by the Narrator of his belief that each person possesses the capacity to write: "je m'apercevais que ce livre essentiel, le seul livre vrai, un grand écrivain n'a pas, dans le sens courant, à l'inventer, puisqu'il existe déjà en chacun de nous, mais à le traduire. Le devoir et la tâche d'un écrivain sont ceux d'un traducteur" (III, 890).

25. Louis Gautier-Vignal, *Proust connu et inconnu* (Paris: Robert Laffont, 1976), p. 50.

26. *Correspondance*, 1917, 16: 133. In note 5 Kolb cites the passage from Montaigne's essay *"De la solitude":* "Il se faut réserver une arrière boutique toute nostre, toute franche, en laquelle nous establissons nostre vraye liberté et principale retraicte et solitude." Proust's bedroom-workroom, lined with unadorned cork, is his

version of Montaigne's famous tower, on whose beams the essayist inscribed the classical quotes that inspired him. Montaigne's work bears many parallels with Proust's, as a number of commentators have remarked. What is especially striking about the two writers is the dynamism of their texts. Cf. Montaigne's remark, "je ne suis pas, je deviens" with Proust's statement in *Le Temps retrouvé* that "l'idée de mon œuvre était dans ma tête, toujours la même, en perpétuel devenir" (III, 1041). For Gide on Montaigne and Proust, see *Marcel Proust/Andre Gide—Autour de "La Recherche"—Lettres*, with a preface by Pierre Assouline (Paris: Editions Complexe, 1988), p. 110. (This is a new edition of the Proust-Gide letters first published in 1949 by Ides et Calendes.)

27.   The essence of seas, their salinity, and starlight both evoke Venus in the person of the girl-goddess Albertine. Racine's *Phèdre* always casts a shadow over Proust's writings about passion.

28.   Early in his quest the Narrator was aware of the riches that lay within him, but he was unable to exploit them: "c'est surtout comme à des gisements profonds de mon sol mental, comme aux terrains résistants sur lesquels je m'appuie encore, que je dois penser au côté de Méséglise et au côté de Guermantes" (I, 184).

29.   In one passage, memories are compared to bubbles of gas that rise through the different strata of the Narrator's past while keeping "leur vertu spécifique à travers les couches superposées de milieux différents qu'ils ont à franchir avant d'atteindre jusqu'à la surface" (I, 662). Saint-Loup's physical qualities are so attractive that he is compared to a vein of precious stone surrounded by baser material (I, 729). The underground "galleries" of sleep lead us to our past, which must be excavated: "le jardin où nous avons été enfant. Il n'y a pas besoin de voyager pour le revoir, il faut descendre pour le retrouver. Ce qui a couvert la terre n'est plus sur elle, mais dessous; l'excursion ne suffit pas pour visiter la ville morte, les fouilles sont nécessaires . . ." (II, 91-92). Jealousy provokes geological disturbances of the mind (II, 1078). Suffering caused by differences between lovers is situated at a deep layer of our heart (III, 88). A desired woman who makes us jealous creates a universe "tout en profondeurs que sa jalousie voudrait sonner . . ." (III, 616).

30.   See Proust's essay "A propos de Baudelaire" (V, 618).

31.   The passage quoted is from "En mémoire des églises assassinées" (V, 71-72). See also "Contre l'obscurité" (V, 394). In an earlier passage, all poets are viewed as one: "Tous les poètes me semblent

ne faire qu'un seul Poète dont les noms différents s'appliquent seulement Gérard de Nerval à ses minutes vagabondes, Baudelaire à ses réminiscences. . . ." Quoted by Bonnet, *Matinée*, pp. 184-85. In a note to himself about death, Proust reiterates his belief that the individual is an ephemeral manifestation of eternal laws. Bonnet, *Matinée*, p. 352; see also pp. 366, 401.

32.   In a letter to Antoine Bibesco, Proust wrote: "Cette substance invisible du temps, j'ai tâché de l'isoler. Mais pour cela il fallait que l'expérience pût durer." *Lettres à Bibesco*, p. 175.

33.   Quoted by Bonnet, *Matinée*, p. 299.

34.   Ibid., p. 398.

35.   *Correspondance*, 1907, 7: 139. See also note 23, where Kolb points out that the letter announces the masked ball scene in *Le Temps retrouvé* (III, 945).

36.   *Correspondance*, 1902-1903, 3: 196.

37.   See Ramon Fernandez, *Proust, ou la généalogie du roman moderne* (Paris: Grasset, 1979), p. 133. See also pp. 232-33, where Fernandez speaks of Proust's multiplication of metaphors and correspondences when describing a fountain, flowers, or the sea. Whereas a novelist might well be content with a single aspect to convey a rich impression, Proust's goal is to capture an impression in its totality.

38.   See Brian G. Rogers, *Proust's Narrative Techniques* (Geneva: Droz, 1965).

39.   For an earlier version of this text on Proust's concept of metaphor as the key element of his art, see Bonnet, *Matinée*, p. 176.

40.   Watching a play is also a complex operation. When the Narrator sees Berma as Phèdre, he does not at first comprehend the greatness of her ability because of the layering effect: the actress has superposed a masterpiece of acting on Racine's play. Once he understands this, he is able to see two superior works simultaneously: *Phèdre* and Berma's interpretation of it (II, 51-52).

41.   Robert Proust was sensitive to this aspect of his brother's novel and described the early influence of the philosophy professor Alphonse Darlu, who taught both Proust boys at the Lycée Condorcet: "Dans les cours consacrés à la critique de la réalité du monde extérieur et à sa subordination à notre pensée créatrice, Darlu avait une forme personnelle et intuitive, une manière d'exposé presque poétique qui plaisait infiniment à Marcel. . . . Mais il devait lui-même ultérieurement pénétrer bien plus profondément dans cette analyse. C'est ainsi que, non

du point de vue physique que nécessite la théorie de la relativité, mais du point de vue de l'introspection, il est arrivé à se faire une notion très personnelle d'un véritable *continuum* de temps et d'espace." See Robert Proust's reminiscence entitled "Marcel Proust Intime," in "Hommage à Marcel Proust: 1871-1922," *La Nouvelle Revue Française*, n.s., 112, vol. 20 (January 1923): 25.

42.   See III, 979-80, for the entire passage.

43.   See also I, 619.

44.   "Proust is . . . the greatest modern creator of characters. . . ." Updike on "Remembrance," p. 104.

45.   The conceptions we form of each other are necessarily limited and subjective: "notre personnalité sociale est une création de la pensée des autres" (I, 19). This passage contains another important statement about the subjective nature of vision: "Même l'acte si simple que nous appelons 'voir une personne que nous connaissons' est en partie un acte intellectuel. Nous remplissons l'apparence physique de l'être que nous voyons de toutes les notions que nous avons sur lui. . . ."

46.   In a single volume of short quotes Justin O'Brien has collected many of Proust's thoughts on the human experience. See Justin O'Brien's *Maxims of Marcel Proust* (New York: Columbia University Press, 1948). A similar volume has recently appeared in France; see Bernard de Fallois's *Marcel Proust: Maximes et Pensées dans "A la recherche du temps perdu"* (Paris: Club France de Loisirs, 1989).

47.   Edmund Wilson sees Proust's method of characterization as one of his major accomplishments: "though [his characters] appear to us in a succession of different aspects, as they are seen at different times and different places by different observers, their behavior, their personalities, have a compelling logic. Proust's method of presenting them, however, so as to show only one aspect at a time is one of his great technical discoveries. . . ." *Axel's Castle*, p. 147.

48.   See "Journées de lecture," especially V, 178.

49.   Cf. the following passage, where Proust's narrator speaks of all the threads of his past coming together: "aujourd'hui tous ces fils différents s'étaient réunis pour faire la trame . . ." (III, 972-73).

50.   Wilson, *Axel's Castle*, p. 189. *Du côté de chez Swann* was published in 1913, when Einstein's theories were coming to be widely known. They provided the first new model for the physical

universe since Newton. The articles in which Einstein expounded his theory of relativity, of which Proust had no knowledge at the time, were published between 1905 and 1916. See John D. Erickson, "The Proust-Einstein Relation: A Study in Relative Point of View," in *Marcel Proust: A Critical Panorama*, edited by Larkin B. Price (Urbana: University of Illinois Press, 1973), pp. 247-76. For an analysis of Proust's and Einstein's definitions of the creative person and the similarity of their views on religion, see my article "Proust, Einstein, et le sentiment cosmique religieux," *Bulletin de la Société des Amis de Marcel Proust et de Combray* 37 (1987): 52-62.

51. Joan Rosasco, "Le Texte et sa doublure," in *Proust et le texte producteur*, edited by John D. Erickson and Irène Pagès (Guelph, Ont.: University of Guelph Press, 1980), p. 107.

52. Robin, *L'Imaginaire du "Temps retrouvé,"* pp. 93-94.

53. See Albert Feuillerat, *Comment Marcel Proust a composé son roman* (New York: AMS Press, 1973); Gérard Genette, *Figures III* (Paris: Seuil, 1972), pp. 57-58 (quoted by Chantal Robin, *L'Imaginaire du "Temps retrouvé,"* p. 92); and J. Theodore Johnson, Jr., "Contre Saint-Proust," in *The Art of the Proustian Novel Reconsidered*, pp. 105-43.

54. Quoted by Robin, *L'Imaginaire du "Temps retrouvé,"* p. 85.

55. See Marie Miguet-Ollagnier's study *La Mythologie de Marcel Proust* (Paris: Les Belles Lettres, 1982), p. 362. Claude-Henry Joubert, speaking of Vinteuil's sonata, has this to say about the unicorn: "Swann parvient 'presque' à franchir le dernier obstacle mais sa quête n'aboutit pas, il ne comprend pas quelle fécondité lui apporte la 'blanche sonate' qui, comme la licorne dans l'iconographie gothique, est la messagère d'une [*sic*] autre monde." "La Musique dans *A la Recherche du temps perdu*," *Bulletin de la Société des Amis de Marcel Proust et de Combray* 36 (1986): 553. Albert Mingelgrün traces the idea of unity perceived through art and music to biblical symbolism and the Christian idea of paradise. See his study *Thèmes et structures bibliques dans l'œuvre de Marcel Proust* (Lausanne: Editions L'Age d'Homme, 1978), pp. 136ff.

56. Wallace Fowlie, *A Reading of Proust* (1975; rpt. Chicago: University of Chicago Press, 1985), p. 68. Robin also shows a keen appreciation of this aspect of *la Recherche*: "Chaque pas du personnage principal suscite la réintégration de tous les autres thèmes et personnages majeurs de l'œuvre. . . . Ainsi, les cellules

du récit s'emboîtent-elles les unes dans les autres et, à partir d'une cellule isolée du texte de la *Recherche,* il est possible de rejoindre la totalité de l'œuvre, représentation de la totalité du monde." Robin, *L'Imaginaire du "Temps retrouvé,"* p. 85.

57.   *Marcel Proust et Jacques Rivière,* p. 36.

58.   See, in this connection, Proust's essay "Réponses à une enquête des annales" (V, 640). In an earlier version of the passage describing the psychology of space and time, Proust does include the molecular level; see Bonnet, *Matinée,* pp. 174-75.

59.   Since he was at a distinct disadvantage because it was impossible for all the parts of his novel to be published together, Proust defended himself against such accusations in a number of letters. The following reaction to a critic dates from the publication of *Du côté de chez Swann:* "[Le critique du *Figaro* dit:] 'Vous notez tout!' Mais non, je ne note rien. . . . Pas une seule fois un de mes personnages ne ferme une fenêtre, ne se lave les mains, ne passe un pardessus, ne dit une formule de présentation. S'il y avait même quelque chose de nouveau dans ce livre, ce serait cela, et d'ailleurs nullement voulu; simplement je suis trop paresseux pour écrire des choses qui m'ennuient." *Correspondance,* 1913, 12: 394. See also the letter to Louis de Robert, p. 231.

60.   *Correspondance,* 1917, 16: 65. Proust's emphasis. Cf. the following: "Un artiste ne doit servir que la vérité et n'avoir aucun respect pour le rang." See "Un salon historique: Le salon de S. A. I. La Princesse Mathilde" (V, 451).

61.   The Narrator suffers "la cruelle inquiétude du chercheur," (I, 446).

62.   Like John Updike, Lawrence Durrell, a novelist influenced by Proust, also sees the cosmic nature of *la Recherche:* "[Proust] seems to have summed up a particular air pocket, a particular cosmology really. . . ." See the interview by Julia Mitchell and Gene Andrewski, "Lawrence Durrell, The Art of Fiction," *The Paris Review* 22 (Autumn-Winter 1960): 55. Proust is the astronomer who seeks the great laws of the universe. René Girard has pointed out that *la Recherche* is a cosmic system and the Narrator an astronomer who measures the orbits and derives the laws that govern them. See his book *Deceit, Desire, and the Novel: Self and Other in Literary Structure* (Baltimore, Md.: The Johns Hopkins University Press, 1965), p. 213.

63.   According to Updike, "Among other writers only Dante lifts us to such an altitude." "Remembrance," p. 104.

64. The buildup of infinitives is meant to indicate that the labor will be long and may never be entirely finished; like the universe of which it is a miniature version, *la Recherche* is capable of infinite expansion. Because of its ambitious nature, he realizes that his book, like the monumental Gothic cathedrals, may be beyond human capacity to finish: "Combien de grandes cathédrales restent inachevées!" (III, 1033). Proust sees the vastness of the great works of the nineteenth century as one of their most beautiful and grandiose aspects: "[Les œuvres de Wagner] participent à ce caractère d'être . . . toujours incomplètes, qui est le caractère de toutes les grandes œuvres du XIXe siècle . . . dont les plus grands écrivains ont manqué leurs livres, mais, se regardant travailler comme s'ils étaient à la fois l'ouvrier et le juge, ont tiré de cette auto-contemplation une beauté nouvelle extérieure et supérieure à l'œuvre, lui imposant rétroactivement une unité, une grandeur qu'elle n'a pas" (III, 160). The authors he has in mind are Balzac, the Hugo of *La Légende des Siècles* and *La Bible de l'Humanité,* and the Michelet of the *Histoire de France* and the *Histoire de la Révolution.*

65. Joseph Campbell reminds us that "before the separation of Eve, Adam was both male and female." See *The Masks of God: Primitive Mythology* (New York: Penguin Books, 1976), p. 104.

66. Miguet-Ollagnier, *Mythologie*, p. 266.

67. See Miguet-Ollagnier's article on hermaphroditism, in which she traces the androgynous origins of the subjects of Elstir's earlier paintings. "L'Hermaphroditisme dans l'œuvre de Proust," *Bulletin de la Société des Amis de Marcel Proust et de Combray* 32 (1982): 561-74. Joan Rosasco reminds us of the androgynous nature of Venice: "A Venise la mer et la terre s'épousent enfin comme dans les 'métaphores' d'Elstir, et on n'oublie pas que c'est la ville qui célébrait chaque année les épousailles de la mer." See "Le Texte et sa doublure," p. 133, n. 33.

68. In her article on hermaphroditism, Miguet-Ollagnier refers to drawings of hermaphrodites Proust made in the margins of his notebooks. She says they are inspired by Christian iconography, which Proust knew from his readings and translations of Ruskin's works (e.g., the hermaphroditic birth of Eve depicted in the Bible of Cologne). According to Miguet-Ollagnier, "le rêve hermaphrodite le plus profond de Proust . . . c'est le rêve d'engendrement hermaphrodite, seul capable d'aboutir à la création artistique. . . . Selon une tradition, il fallait qu'Adam eût en

lui un principe féminin pour qu'Eve naquît de lui." See "L'Hermaphroditisme dans l'œuvre de Proust," p. 569.

69. For J. E. Rivers this moment of androgynous reunification occurs in the presentation to the Narrator of Mlle de Saint-Loup, who embodies the heredity of all the Proustian characters: "The meeting of the two ways in Mlle de Saint-Loup has a deeply androgynous significance. It is the final embrace of art and eros." See *Proust and the Art of Love* (New York: Columbia University Press, 1980), p. 253.

70. Bonnet, *Matinée,* p. 300.

71. Miguet-Ollagnier, "L'Hermaphroditisme dans l'œuvre de Proust," p. 571.

72. See also, III, 1032, where the future work must be nourished like a child. Rivers quotes Leo Bersani, who sees the entire concluding sequence of *la Recherche* as suggesting the various stages of pregnancy, including "the joyful conception of the idea [for the book] at the Guermantes *matinée,* the weakness and dizziness on the staircase some time later, and a painful delivery." See Rivers, *Proust and the Art of Love,* p. 253.

73. Proust reminds us that the Narrator's models will be those other great works written by night: the *Mille et une nuits* and the *Mémoires* of Saint-Simon (III, 1043-44).

74. According to metaphysical tradition, the figure of the androgyne presides over births. See Elémire Zolla, *The Androgyne: Reconciliation of Male and Female* (New York: Crossroad, 1981), p. 66; for the metaphysical conception of cosmic man as an androgyne, see page 48.

75. Proust finds vestiges of androgyny in the world of dreams, the domain of the subconscious (II, 981).

76. Zolla, *Androgyne,* p. 70. The theme of androgyny is even found in the church of Saint-Hilaire, whose steeple is one of the principal unifying symbols of the novel. Hilaire was originally a female saint whose name, through morphological changes, became that of a man (I, 104-5).

77. See Françoise Cachin's study of androgyny in late-nineteenth-century France entitled "Monsieur Vénus et l'Ange de Sodome: l'Androgyne au temps de Gustave Moreau," *Nouvelle Revue de Psychanalyse* 7 (1973): 66. Cachin also notes that "le romantisme français a été fasciné par le travestissement et l'inversion—*Mlle de Maupin* de Gautier, *Sarrazine* et *La Fille aux yeux d'or* de Balzac. Avec *Seraphitus-Seraphita* celui-ci reprend le thème sweden-

borgien de l'androgyne comme image de l'être parfait, de l'être angélique" (p. 65).

78.   *Marcel Proust-André Gide,* p. 40. In *la Recherche,* Proust repeats the idea that Charlus's ability to appreciate poetry, music, and painting, a universe "si fermé au duc de Guermantes" is due to his sexual nature (III, 206).

79.   Robin, *L'Imaginaire du "Temps retrouvé,"* p. 90.

80.   Quoted by Mauriac in *Du côté de chez Proust* (Paris: Table Ronde, 1947), pp. 21-22.

81.   Many commentators have held that Proust, who was born in 1871, was only a social dilettante until after the deaths of both his parents, by which time the author was thirty-five. The posthumous publication of *Jean Santeuil* in 1952 showed that Proust had produced the first draft of a thousand-page novel between 1896 and 1899, providing ample proof that during his early adult years and his so-called society period he was capable of serious work. Philip Kolb has written convincingly about Proust's creative energy: "Pour achever ce qu'il a entrepris, il a fallu . . . une volonté presque surhumaine." See "Les 'Phares' de Proust," in *Entretiens sur Marcel Proust,* edited by Françoise Fabre-Luce de Gruson (Paris: Mouton, 1966), pp. 107-8.

Index

Leriche, Françoise, on Albertine, 270 n. 23
Lesbianism, see Homosexuality
Lisieux, 136, 146, 147
Lumière brothers: cinematograph, 11; *L'Arrivée du train en gare de La Ciotat,* 81

Maeterlinck, Maurice, 196
Mâle, Emile, 136, 231
Mallarmé, Stéphane, "Sonnet," 156–58
Manet, Edouard, 45
Maniai, 95
Mantegna, Andrea, 82
Marcel Swann, see Agostinelli
Marey, Etienne-Jules, 73–74, 76; chronophotography, 11, 69; photographic gun, 11
Maria, pre-Agostinelli Albertinelike figure, 171, 276 n. 96
Marinetti, Filippo, 15; "L'Ellisse e la Spirale," 180; "A mon Pégase," 278 n. 1
Marseille, 1
Martinville, 9, 14, 137, 203, 236
Mass transportation, impact on French society, 2–3, 4
Matricide, 108, 127
Maugny, Clément de, 163
Mauriac, François, 238
McCauley, John F., 200
Mein, Margaret, 177, 180
Mélusine, 48
Memory, involuntary, 207–8, 218, 224–25
Méséglise, 27, 101
Metaphor, 223–24
Metzinger, Jean, on Cubists and multiple perspective, 13
Miguet-Ollagnier, Marie, 101, 230,

236; on androgynous nature of *la Recherche,* 235
Miller, Milton, 80, 81
Milly, Jean, 63; on theme of jealousy, 174; on Albertine cycle, 174
Mirbeau, Octave, 12, 40
Modern inventions: and French society, 1–2; and awareness of speed, 8–9; and new perspectives, 15–17
Monaco, 134
Monaco, prince de, 154
Monet, Claude: water lilies, 205; model for Elstir, 242 n. 15
Montaigne, Michel Eyquem de, 217, 227, 288 n. 26
Montesquiou, Robert de, 94; *Chauves-souris,* 143
Montjouvain, 101, 111, 113, 239; importance in *la Recherche,* 172–73
Morel, 80, 174; and Mme Verdurin, 127
Moses, Swann compared to, 185
Mother, 82, 93, 98–99, 100, 115; and Albertine, 123; theme of matricide, 127
Motion: modern inventions and awareness of motion, 7; human figure in motion, 11, 249 n. 11; and eroticism, 46–53;
Motion pictures, 11–13
Multiple perspective, and Cubism, 14
Multiple selves, 227
Muybridge, Eadweard, 73–74, 76; zoopraxiscope, 11; "Occident Trotting," 11, 74; "Sallie Gardner Galloping," 74

Nabokov, Vladimir, 18, 103
Nahmias, Albert, 152; dispatched to secure Agostinelli's return, 158
Nancy, 150

About the Author

William C. Carter is Professor of French at the University of Alabama at Birmingham. A member of the editorial board of the *Bulletin Marcel Proust* and a permanent correspondent of the Proust Research Center at the Sorbonne, his current project is a documentary on Proust funded by the National Endowment for the Humanities.